WEIRD MISSOURI

WEiRD MiSSOURi

MiSSOURi

Your Travel Guide to Missouri's
Local Legends and Best Kept Secrets

by James Strait

Mark Moran and Mark Sceurman,
Executive Editors

STERLING

New York / London
www.sterlingpublishing.com

WEiRD MiSSOURi

Library of Congress Cataloging-in-Publication Data Available

10 9 8 7 6 5 4 3 2 1

Published by Sterling Publishing Co., Inc.
387 Park Avenue South, New York, NY 10016

© 2008 Mark Moran and Mark Sceurman

Distributed in Canada by Sterling Publishing
c/o Canadian Manda Group, 165 Dufferin Street
Toronto, Ontario, Canada M6K 3H6

Distributed in the United Kingdom by GMC Distribution Services
Castle Place, 166 High Street, Lewes, East Sussex, England BN7 1XU

Distributed in Australia by Capricorn Link (Australia) Pty. Ltd.
P. O. Box 704, Windsor, NSW 2756, Australia

Printed in China.

Sterling ISBN 978-1-4027-4555-3

For information about custom editions, special sales, premium and corporate purchases, please contact Sterling Special Sales Department at 800-805-5489 or specialsales@sterlingpublishing.com.

CONTENTS

DEDICATION

Dedicated to all of Missouri's weirdness. Without such, none of this would have been possible.—Jim Strait

Foreword: A Note from the Marks

Our weird journey began a long, long time ago in a far-off land called New Jersey. Once a year or so, we'd compile a homespun newsletter called *Weird N.J.*, then pass it on to our friends. The pamphlet was a collection of odd news clippings, bizarre facts, little-known historical anecdotes, and anomalous encounters from our home state. The newsletter also included the kinds of localized legends that were often whispered around a particular town but seldom heard outside the boundaries of the community where they originated.

We had started *Weird N.J.* on the simple theory that every town in the state had at least one good tale to tell. The publication soon became a full-fledged magazine, and we made the decision to actually do our own investigating to see if we could track down where all of these seemingly unbelievable stories were coming from. Was there, we wondered, any factual basis for the fantastic local legends people were telling us about? Armed with not much more than a camera and a notepad, we set off on a mystical journey of discovery. Much to our surprise and amazement, a lot of what we had initially presumed to be nothing more than urban legends turned out to be real—or at least to contain a grain of truth, which had sparked the lore to begin with.

After a dozen years of documenting the bizarre, we were asked to write a book about our adventures, and so *Weird N.J.: Your Travel Guide to New Jersey's Local Legends and Best Kept Secrets* was published in 2003. Soon people from all over the country began writing to us, telling us strange tales from their home state. As it turned out, what we had perceived to be something of very local interest was actually just a small part of a larger and more universal phenomenon.

When our publisher asked us what we wanted to do next, the answer was simple: "We'd like to do a book called *Weird U.S.*, in which we could document the local legends and strangest stories from all over the country," we replied. So for the next twelve months, we set out in search of weirdness wherever it might be found in the fifty states. And indeed, we found plenty of it!

After *Weird U.S.* was published, we came to the conclusion that this country had more great tales than could be contained in just one book. Everywhere we looked, we found unwritten folklore, creepy cemeteries, cursed locations, and outlandish roadside oddities. With this in mind, we told our publisher that we wanted to document it *all* and to do it in a series of books, each focusing on the peculiarities of a particular state.

Our plan was to work closely with local authors native to the state we were covering. This presented a bit of a problem, though, as we knew there were some great stories to be told in a number of states, but we didn't always know somebody from a particular state who'd be the right person to tell them. That was the exact dilemma we faced in the case of Missouri. We'd visited the Show Me State ourselves, investigating many of its oddities, so we knew it to be fertile ground—weirdly speaking. But it wasn't until a happy coincidence brought us together with James Strait that we realized whom we should enlist to be the author of *Weird Missouri*.

When *Weird U.S.* was published, we did literally hundreds of interviews over the phone with radio stations around the country to promote the book and spread the weird word. One radio host was very different, though—he had actually read the book, showed a genuine interest in the material, and was enthusiastic about discussing it with us. Not only that, he really seemed to get the whole weird concept! That radio host was James Strait. We talked at length with Jim on the air, sharing local legends and listening to his own strange tales of his native Missouri home. He enjoyed our conversation so much in fact that he invited us to be guests on his show a second time. After that, we knew we had found a true kindred spirit in weirdness—one with a great sense of pride in his home state and all of its peculiarities. Jim also had the gift of gab and was a born storyteller.

We could clearly see that Jim possessed what we refer to as the Weird Eye, which requires one to see the world in a different way, with a renewed sense of wonder and curiosity. And once you have it, there is no going back—you'll never see things the same way again. All of a sudden you begin to reexamine your own environs, noticing your everyday surroundings as if for the first time. And you begin to ask yourself questions like, "What the heck is *that* thing all about, anyway?" and "Doesn't anybody else think that's kind of *weird?*"

So come with us now and let Jim show you his Show

Me State—you might not believe your eyes! With all its unique mysteries and wonders, colorful characters, and unexpected sites, it's a place we like to call *Weird Missouri.*—Mark Moran and Mark Sceurman

Introduction

With over seven thousand miles traveled, visits to over 170 cities and locations, and interviews with over 250 people, I can state without reservation that Missouri is full of the subject matter needed to create a book about its weirdness: Like all of America's states, there is no shortage of weird in Missouri. *Weird Missouri* is not a history book, but it contains much history. It is also not a travel guide, per se, but it can easily be used as such to plan weekends, day trips, or even just plain mind trips. What *Weird Missouri* is, though, is informative about the strange, unique, odd, unusual, freakish, and sometimes extraordinary people, places, and things that are part of the total Show Me State experience.

There is also no shortage of beauty in the state. It was a joy to travel around it and experience the southern mountains with their amazing bluffs and steep and winding roads, and the gentle swells of the northern farm lands, the countless streams, rivers, and creeks that snake across Missouri's landscape and the bridges that span them, the inner world of Missouri's fantastic cavernous underground, and the man-made beauty in the form of art and architecture.

Missouri is also full of very nice people. I would like to thank the many generous and courteous convenience store clerks who patiently provided this sometimes harried seeker of the strange and odd with what were usually excellent driving directions. Also I want to thank the many hotel front desk personnel who collectively spent many hours sharing their knowledge of the many unusual aspects of Missouri. And I would be doing a disservice if I neglected to thank the many waitresses and waiters who listened intently as I asked if they were locals and knew of any really scary Missouri ghost stories. It is also without question that I want to express my gratitude to the countless county and city clerks, newspaper employees, historical societies, college administrative staffs, military personnel, business owners, and all others who lent a hand in guiding me to people with specific knowledge about what you will read here. Last, a very special thanks to the Global Positioning Satellite Constellation. Without your precision guidance I would still be lost in some deep Missouri hollow. I thank you one and all.

One will find frequent quotes and short accounts of the strange and unexplained offered by many of the aforementioned generous and open-minded Missourians. Had it not been for the eagerness of these kind people, my research would have been much more difficult, time-consuming, and perhaps dead-ended. For those of you who find your stories inside the pages of *Weird Missouri,* I hope that you enjoy reading them as much as I did hearing about them.

Great effort has been invested to ensure that the material contained within these pages is accurate to the best of my understanding. But much of what is written here are stories that have been handed down through literally generations of Missourians. Stories about ghosts, spook lights, spirits, UFOs, and uncaptured creatures are impossible to substantiate, but lots of fun to learn and read about.

So it is with great pleasure that I offer you these accounts of Missouri's ancient, inexplicable, extra-ordinary, unusual, and downright WEIRD.—*James Strait*

Local Legends

The Internet says, and it must therefore be true, that a legend is a narrative of human actions that are perceived both by the teller and listener to possess certain qualities that give the tale verisimilitude. We have no idea what verisimilitude means but just wanted to use it in a sentence. (Okay, looked it up in a book this time; it means "having the appearance of being true or real.")

There may be a kernel of truth to the old stories that have been told over and over through generations. But no legend is worth its salt unless it has been exaggerated five or six thousand times. Like the tale about monster catfish at Bagnell Dam. The first iteration of that saga probably discussed a large minnow, which later evolved into a monstrous human-size catfish. The finite truth is difficult to pin down when discussing legends.

Nevertheless, whether the story is accurate or grossly embellished, it takes a lot to become a legend. Legends don't come easy and, once born, will only grow in dimension. There are no shrinking legends.

All across the state are examples of the famous and the infamous, the hero and the assailant, the improbable and the almost impossible. Are they true or not? Who can say? But this we can promise: Nothing you read here has been enhanced in this retelling. What you read is the legend as we heard it.

Exorcism in St. Louis

When the movie The Exorcist *first came out,* people lined up at theaters around the country to see it. The lines may have been a bit longer in St. Louis than elsewhere in the country, however, as the real story behind the movie had connections to the area.

In 1949, a family living in a Maryland suburb near Washington, D.C., was being tortured by the aberrant behavior of their teenage son. This, coupled with strange telekinetic events that seemed to manifest around him, took the family to the edge of sanity.

After exhausting the resources of the Catholic Church in their immediate area and confounding the expertise of noted parapsychologists, the family moved to the northern suburbs of St. Louis County. Maybe they thought that they could literally relocate from the problem. But this wasn't the case, as conditions for the teenage boy and those around him grew exponentially worse.

There were many stories of shaking beds and chairs, of spontaneous words arising as welts upon the boy's body, of his speaking in tongues and in conversational Latin, and of bloodied cuts and scratches. The family and all those they approached for help were at a loss as to how to help him.

There had been one failed attempt at a church-sanctioned exorcism while in Maryland. The family approached the St. Louis Archdiocese, which agreed that a second attempt was warranted. But unlike the exorcism portrayed in the film, the real one took months. Eventually, the demon, poltergeist, satanic-force entity, or whatever it was gave up—with a little help from the archangel Michael, who apparently ordered it to leave the teenager in a most authoritative tone. The teenager, freed of his demons, went on to graduate from a Catholic high school, marry, and raise three children uneventfully.

Was he ever genuinely possessed by an evil force that caused his behavior, moved furniture, and made him channel conversational Latin as a way of intimidating those attempting to make it go away? Or did the teenager subconsciously tap into the still mysterious potential of the human mind and manifest extraordinary acts using the powers of his will and intuition? We'll never know, and so it simply goes down in the annals of *Weird Missouri* legend.

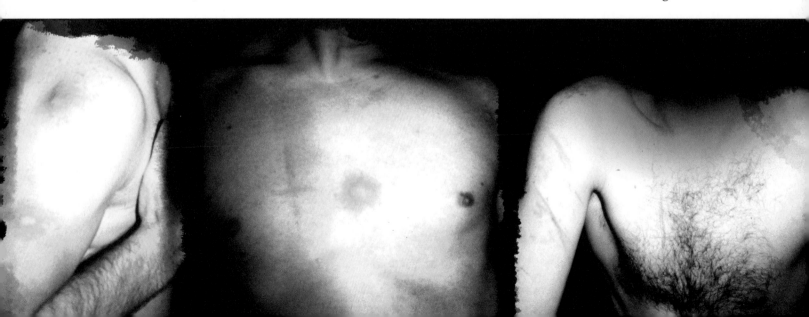

Missouri Is for Lovers'... Leaps

Missouri seems to be an unusually welcoming place for despondent lovers. With eight identifiable locations that have a historical record of being lovers' leaps, it may stand as the go-to state for geographic compatibility with the needs of the forlorn.

All the locations connect to a very similar legend of failed Native American love: A young Indian woman is promised to one brave, but she loves another. Rather than be apart, she and her true love leap from the most convenient and highest location they can find.

The lovers' leap on the south side of Hannibal is most famous, primarily because the town is the home of Samuel Clemens and because it's a promoted tourist location. Other venues for ending it all are in Camdenton, Ha Ha Tonka, Fulton, Sialom Springs, Clinton, a location in Ripley County near the Deer Leap Recreation Area, and a spot in Clark County about three miles north of Kahoka.

We have only been to the Hannibal and Ha Ha Tonka locations, but we can assure readers that stepping over the edge at either of these spots without a device to arrest their free fall would definitely seal their fate forever.

Jumping Buffalo

One hundred and fifty years ago being a successful buffalo hunter was not difficult, at least as far as making the kill—and it was necessary for settlers struggling to survive.

Bison cannot make the connection between cause and effect. They never notice the relationship between the loud muzzle report that happened just two seconds ago and the death of their fellow buffalo. The buffalo's lack of analytical thought also explains why Native Americans were successful at herding the trusting critters over the edge of cliffs—another use for a lovers' leap. Who needs gunpowder and loud explosions when you can just let gravity do the killing for you?

Buffalo jumps were common in that era. There are known locations across the country where bison routinely ended their lives by smashing their heads against the rocks at the bottom of a tall cliff. How did the Indians accomplish this brutal but efficient task? One technique was to dress an Indian decoy as a bison and have him excite the herd, then run toward the edge of a cliff with the herd following. At the last minute, the decoy escapes to some safe location on the cliff, but the bison do not notice and run off the edge, having no appreciation for the reality of free fall and sudden stops. An alternate technique was to simply stampede the herd and channel them over the cliff.

Mark Twain wrote of buffalo jumps, and when Meriwether Lewis of the Lewis and Clark expeditionary team came upon such a place in Missouri, he recorded the sight this way: "Today we passed . . . the remains of a vast many mangled carcasses of Buffalo which had been driven over a precipice of 120 feet by the Indians and perished."

Mankind has clearly labeled buffalo as expendable, so much so that they were killed off to the point of almost becoming extinct. However, there are now thriving herds in several locations in America.

Devil's Ice Box

In Rock Bridge Memorial State Park, in Columbia, lies the Devil's Ice Box. It is the seventh-longest cave in Missouri, with six miles of underground theater for exploration. It contains a unique ecosystem with a wide range of cave life, making it the sixth most biodiverse cavern in the state. And what a name! It suggests a rich history of satanic ritual or just plain bad mojo that may have taken place there over the ages. While we do not rule out such a background, we have found little evidence to support such a claim.

We did, however, speak with a student at Stephens College who is a life-long resident of Columbia and has a personal history with the icy cave. She said that while she and her friends were in high school, they would occasionally venture into the Devil's Ice Box. They would enter the cave holding hands, fearing being separated from one another. These trips into the cavern didn't go far, as the group had neither the equipment nor desire to travel deep into the cave's passages.

But the forays were daring enough that they caused trouble. Evidently, no matter how careful the group was, and no matter how tightly they held hands, upon exiting the cave they were always one person short! The young woman said she experienced this phenomenon on more than one occasion, and to this day it remains a mystery.

Getting to the Devil's Ice Box is a simple affair of following clearly marked trails. Once at the entrance, you'll immediately understand why it is so named. Temperatures drop significantly, and the contrast is remarkable on a hot August afternoon.

Pea Ridge: Passage to Hell

The world's deepest mineral mine is the Pea Ridge Mine, near Sullivan. Established in 1964, Pea Ridge is an iron ore mine, with the distinction of producing an extremely pure ore. Making the mine even more fruitful is that fact that its deposits are large. In an effort to discover the total dimensions of the underground ore body, test drillings were performed to a depth of three thousand feet, without going through the deposit. It has been estimated that the mine has at least another hundred years of production capability.

Mining is a notoriously dangerous industry, and if there is a direct relationship between the depth of a mine and the degree of danger that its workers face, then Pea Ridge is one of the world's most dangerous mines. It is reported that as many as sixteen men have died in this deep hole.

Pea Ridge was one of the most productive mines of its kind on the planet, yet production stopped in 2001. Why would this happen at a mine with a hundred-year future?

The official answer is one that is all too common—financial issues. But there is speculation that the miners discovered something at Pea Ridge that was too frightening for them to remain there. A gate or passageway to hell has been mentioned. Reports of screams and strange noises emanating from the shaft keep inquisitive minds busy second-guessing the reasons for the mine's demise. Was its closure tied to a failed business venture, a gate to hell, or possibly even an underground government facility involved in supersecret experimentation? The truth is buried in the past and in the ground. Let the next wave of speculation begin!

Hang 'em High in Galena

Galena is a small town nestled into a lovely hillside alongside the James River. Its surroundings are an excellent choice for a casual drive to check out the changing colors of the leaves in the fall. Nothing about its appearance would reveal its connection to a final deadly act in American history.

You see, as county seat of Stone County, Galena was the location of the last public execution to take place in the United States, on May 21, 1937. The man hanged was Red Jackson, who had murdered a kind and generous traveling salesman who bought the hitchhiking Jackson a meal and also paid for his lodgings the night before his own tragic demise. Jackson returned the favor by shooting the salesman twice in the back of the head and dumping him in a roadside ditch.

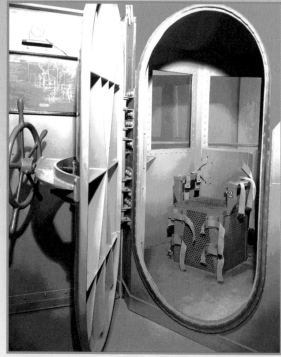

By invitation from sheriff Isaiah Coin, about four hundred people were able to get good seats or standing room to view Jackson's execution. The only privacy afforded the recipient of so much avid attention was a stockade fence that surrounded the gallows.

News spread quickly about the execution, and many people beyond those invited came to town, intending on partying. The mix of alcohol, morbid curiosity, and bad taste became a public spectacle that embarrassed the community of Galena and the entire state of Missouri.

Several months later Missouri enacted a law requiring all adjudged executions to take place in the privacy of a state penitentiary, in a gas chamber. The hanging in Galena may or may not have been the impetus for the new law mandating a more "civilized" method of ending the life of capital criminals, but eventually Missouri would send thirty-nine murderers to the hereafter with gas.

After time, the gas chamber and capital punishment in general were deemed too primal for productive social orders to endorse. Thus, in 1968, a stay of execution in the form of a nationwide moratorium was granted to all death row convicts as a result of a 5–4 ruling by the United States Supreme Court in the case of *Furman* v. *Georgia.*

After the nation's level of frustration grew as a result of watching tens of thousands of additional murders, the same United States Supreme Court ruled in July 1976 that Georgia's new reworded law was consistent with constitutional precepts, making it okay to balance the equation by taking the life of the adjudged murderer.

Presto chango: A few months later Missouri was again authorized to smoke the bad guys. The new law allowed execution by gas or lethal injection. Since then, lethal injection has been the preferred methodology. The guy still winds up dead, but at least it is done in "private."

The Monster Catfish of Bagnell Dam

Kids growing up in rural Jefferson County often heard tales of giant catfish at the base of the underwater foundation of Bagnell Dam at Lake of the Ozarks. The story was that scuba divers, while routinely inspecting the dam's underwater integrity, would see these huge whiskered monsters swimming at its base—freakishly large catfish! According to these stories, the catfish were man-size, and they were like that because of the extraordinary pressure existing at the bottom of the dam. Stories such as these are the food upon which kids' imaginations thrive. And of course kids' imaginations go further. Were the giant fish really there? And more important, were they man-eaters?

As it turns out, catfish can get big. Really big. In fact, the world record blue catfish was caught in the Osage River on July 25, 1964. It weighed 117 pounds! While even this fish does not match the size of the one in the legends, it does fall within the range of normalcy for many species of catfish. And it is certainly large enough to lend the ring of truth to the old stories.

It's not the hydrostatic pressure at the base of the dam that makes the catfish large. All that's needed is a fish-food-rich environment, because it's the food that makes them big. And even though modern bodies of water are polluted, rerouted, channeled, dammed, and conditioned, the waters of Lake of the Ozarks, large reservoirs, and the Missouri, Osage, and Mississippi rivers are still capable of producing these monster-size catfish.

We're all familiar with how fishermen exaggerate the dimensions of the fish that get away. Can you imagine the stories that would come from almost catching one of these cats?

GuberBurgers

By the time you read this, the Wheel Inn—located at the corner of Route 50 and Route 65 in Sedalia since 1947—will have been out of business for many weeks. Eminent domain has reared its sometimes ugly head, and because of highway expansion the Wheel Inn must go. But it will be fondly remembered as the home of the famous Missouri GuberBurger.

Guber what? It sounds like a Scandinavian creation, but in reality the GuberBurger was the product of good ole Sedalia ingenuity (or maybe just desperation). It was just like any other burger but with a twist. Instead of cheese as a topping, it used peanut butter.

The idea of a hamburger topped with melted peanut butter almost always wrinkles the noses of those first hearing about this odd combination. But it was unique to the Wheel Inn menu and popular beyond imagination. Over the years, tens of thousands of people traveled to Sedalia for no other purpose than to experience the GuberBurger.

Melissa Nelson, Wheel Inn manager, said millions of GuberBurgers have been sold to people ranging from actor Jack Nicholson, players on the Kansas City Chiefs, and many Route 66 aficionados. And, of course, to many longtime local GuberBurger addicts.

To those of you who have eaten a GuberBurger, you understand what is now missing from Sedalia's culture. To those of you who have not eaten a GuberBurger, all we can say is give it a shot at home. You might seriously like it.

St. Louis Brain Food

Americans will eat anything that is deep-fried. If you doubt this statement, consider fried brain sandwiches. We know for a fact that there are a few *Weird Missouri* readers who salivate over the idea of fried bovine brains sandwiched between two slices of Wonder Bread. Just how many cravers of bovine cerebellum there are we aren't certain, but given the foods eaten across all cultures, fried brains seem to fall easily within the spectrum of "normalcy."

The fried brain sandwich is said to be a St. Louis phenomenon because of the high population of Germans in the South St. Louis area. Apparently, their frugal nature during the mid-nineteenth century prompted them to waste not, want not. Hence, fried brain sandwiches (and their cousin, blood soup) evolved.

When chasing down brain sandwiches in the St. Louis area we heard one name most frequently: Dieckmeyer's. We actually attempted to get the sandwich at its South Broadway location, only to find that The Lighthouse has become the new eatery and watering hole there, and for some reason it has not continued the tradition of brain sandwiches.

We then heard that a bar and grill named Pat's, on Oakland (across from Turtle Park), served fried cow brains between two slices of bread. As it turns out, however, this was a menu item from the distant past. It seems that brain sandwiches are for only a few rare individuals and rumors of mad cow disease have diminished what was already a niche market.

But not all is lost; fried brain food has not been completely abandoned in St. Louis. If you absolutely, positively must have a brain sandwich, it remains on the menu of Ferguson's Pub, at 2925 Mount Pleasant.

Coming Down the Pike: Creation of Carny Food

St. Louis hosted the 1904 World's Fair, which brought grandeur and wonder to the gateway to the West. It was also known as the Louisiana Purchase Exposition and was designed to celebrate the centennial of this historic event. The fair was open from April 30 to December 1, and over twenty million visitors happily paid its fifty-cent admission charge. Its exuberance and down-home American appeal would inspire one of the greatest Judy Garland flicks ever: *Meet Me in St. Louis.*

Situated on over twelve hundred acres of Forest Park, an elaborate World's Fair city held buildings dedicated to the achievements and attractions of forty different states, and elaborate palaces to showcase the arts, education, machinery, mines, manufacturing, and the then rapidly evolving world of electricity. It also hosted the third modern Olympic Games, the first ever held in America. There was an expansive Festival Hall, a huge 260-foot-tall Ferris wheel (or Observation Circle as it was called then), and the marvelous St. Louis Plaza. Those interested in the new science of manned, powered flight could visit the Aeronautic Concourse. A thirty-foot-tall fence surrounded the concourse, but whether it was there to protect fairgoers from errant flights or to heighten the mystery of the contents within isn't known. The fair's main street was called the Pike. About a mile long, the Pike hosted a spectacle of carnival and science. Fairgoers wondering what new marvel might be next on the agenda soon began to ask, "What will be coming down the Pike?"

It's popular legend that the ice-cream cone, cotton candy, hot dogs, hamburgers, and iced tea were all invented at the fair. Alas, all have their roots elsewhere, but the fair certainly introduced new ways to enjoy them (hot dogs . . . with mustard!).

Most of the amazing buildings were torn down after the fair ended. All that remain are the art museum, the birdcage at the zoo, and the various improvements to Forest Park that supported the fair's needs. And maybe one very large piece of steel! Read on.

A Wheely Strange Story

One of the biggest attractions at the 1904 St. Louis World's Fair was its gigantic Ferris wheel, which had actually been created for the 1883 Columbian Exposition in Chicago and reassembled for the '04 fair.

The wheel's axle was forty-five feet long and thirty-six inches in diameter: the largest single piece of forged steel ever created at the time. The axle supported passenger cars that were so huge they were able to hold two wedding ceremonies in which the bride and groom said their vows on horseback while the wheel spun around.

When the St. Louis World's Fair ended, the giant wheel was unneeded and unwanted, even by those wishing to get married in spinning-cowboy style. It was blown up with dynamite, as there was no practical, industrial way to recycle the wheel's gargantuan center axle. The axle was buried somewhere under the grounds of Forest Park, and controversy about its whereabouts remains to this day. Readers with an interest in claiming many tons of seasoned steel (and maybe make a few bucks) might wish to break out their metal detectors and start sweeping Forest Park's 1,293 acres.

Ancient Mysteries

It takes a lot of research to try to understand what really happened on earth millions of years ago. That's why so much of ancient times remains a mystery—which is convenient for *Weird Missouri* because ancient mysteries are right up our alley.

It's documented that Europeans set foot on Show Me State soil in 1673, when Father Jacques Marquette and Louis Joliet were exploring along the Mississippi River. That's just over 330 years ago—a snap of the cosmological fingers in relative terms.

But there are stories here that predate 1673, like the account of the petroglyphs in Washington State Park or the meteor impacts that produced a string of indentations in southern Missouri, one of which has become known as the Decaturville Dome.

This chapter is full of really old stuff and things masquerading as such. We'll keep this introduction from reading like an eternity itself by ending it here, so you can now get on to the ancient mysteries in our midst.

Boney Springs and Bone Bed

You'd have to take a ride on Mr. Peabody's "Wayback" time machine to visit the reality of Missouri's mastodons. But there are some impressive displays of ancient skeletal remains mined in the Boney Springs area of Benton County.

First a home to Ice Age creatures seeking a reliable water source and now sitting beneath the vast waters of the Truman Reservoir—the largest flood control reservoir in Missouri—Boney Springs was an active and very productive archaeological excavation between 1965 and 1980. During that time, 640 bones belonging to a variety of now extinct species were recovered for ongoing study. The bones unearthed at Boney Springs were determined to be as old as 17,000 years, with the youngest being about 13,000 years of age.

About two hundred miles northeast of Boney Springs, in Jefferson County, is another location where mastodons roamed during the last Ice Age. The area of Imperial, just south of St. Louis, is home to the Kimmswick Bone Bed. It is here that man-made tools and weapons fabricated from mastodon bones were discovered; this could suggest that prehistoric man "co-existed" with the giant mastodons.

In the absence of the Wayback machine, visiting the Mastodon Historic Site in Jefferson County is an excellent alternative, as good as it gets when it comes to learning about these ancient behemoths.

To learn more about ancient Missouri mastodons, visit www.mostateparks.com/mastodon.htm.

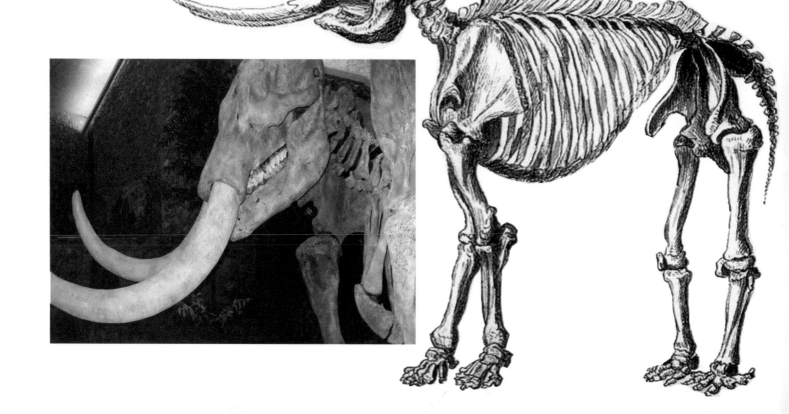

Carved in Stone in DeSoto

We have all made agreements with flexible terms and conditions. "Nothing is carved in stone," we say. But with Missouri's petroglyphs, stone is the medium, carving the method, and they are as permanent as a natural process can be.

Petroglyphs are common worldwide, existing on every continent and in every U.S. state. Ranging in age from prehistoric to as recent as the time of Columbus's discovery of the New World, petroglyphs reveal the desire of our species to indelibly record our having existed.

No one knows the true meaning of petroglyphs. Whether they are a mechanism for recording important events in Native American tribal history, stories that were used to guide or enhance rituals, an ancient open-air art gallery, or the graffiti of its era will forever remain a mystery. When the petroglyph creator dies, so dies the original intent of the message.

Washington State Park has gone to great lengths to make it easy for anyone wanting to view these old stone etchings. The park is located on State Highway 104 in DeSoto. Go there and crack the code. You'll be a legend if you do.

Pink Pachyderm Rocks

Here's a new twist on pet rocks—Elephant Rocks, part of the "go big or stay home" philosophy. Imagine a collection of rocks, and then imagine that they have names and that they are the size of small mountains or large hills. It would be a heck of a private collection.

Well, all Missourians share joint custody of such a collection in Elephant Rocks State Park, in Iron County. Part of the St. Francois Mountains, the dark pink granite rocks have been attracting hundreds of thousands of visitors by the carload for decades.

The unique setting of large granite boulders does indeed resemble a troupe of circus elephants obediently following one another's tails. The lead elephant, named Dumbo, is a massive boulder of over 680 tons of pure Missouri Red granite. This variety of granite, quarried locally until World War II, can be found in many structures in and out of Missouri.

And on the way back, if you're stopped for speeding by the Iron County gendarmes, you might not want to tell them that you've just seen some pink elephants!

Prehistoric Wood

The earth is four billion years old, give or take a few weeks. Recorded human history at its oldest appears to begin about 5,500 years ago, and Jesus Christ is said to have walked the earth just over 2,000 years ago. Why are these time frames meaningful? It turns out that Missouri rivers, lakes, and streams are all home to ancient species of wood that have been preserved since long before the beginning of recorded human time. If a tree topples into a nearby body of water and is quickly covered with sediment, it can lie preserved for many millennia, locked away from the destructive effects of oxygen. While a tree is buried in sediment, its decay slows to a relative crawl. Spruce trees that date back over 11,000 years were discovered in Medicine Creek in Putnam County, and an oak from that same body of water was dated to be as old as 13,000 years.

So the next time you're boating, skiing, or tubing down some watery Missouri real estate and see a strange-looking piece of wood, it could be that you are looking at something that had been standing erect on planet earth long before man could make that same claim.

Meteor Attacks!

Or was it a comet? Speculation continues concerning a string of geological structures in the southern part of the state. They may have been created by a disturbance resulting from multiple fragments of a meteor or comet breaking apart as it burned across the skies of North America. Lucky for us, Missouri was the terminal point of the journey.

One element of the speculation is certain. At the location of 37 degrees, 44 minutes north latitude and 92 degrees, 43 minutes west longitude, a large chunk of space junk made contact with southern Missouri topography and displaced enough of the countryside to create a curiosity significant enough to be given a name.

The Decaturville Dome sits just off Highway 5, about five miles south of Camdenton. It's estimated that the landscape-altering event occurred between 100 and 300 million years ago. Therefore, the only beings bothered by the impact were our dinosaur friends. More recently, though, modern man has become a bother to the land's current owners, and the dome is now private property and not available for access.

But if you are an aviator and want to take a peek at the dome from above, then the latitude and longitude information mentioned above will take you right to it. Otherwise, we can tell you that the area's appearance is described as a series of low hills that form a circumference for the impact crater. The center of the crater is about one mile in diameter. The impact's heat-based energy altered the molecular structure of the rock.

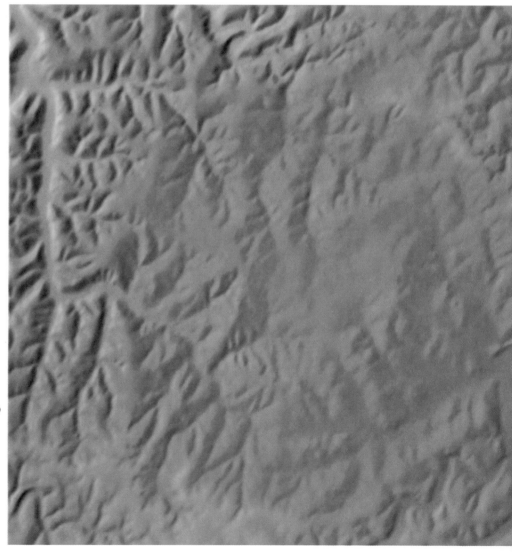

Reel 'em in

In 2007, Columbia man Eric Henley was searching for arrowheads with his two young sons along a gravel bar of the Missouri River. To their great good fortune, they stumbled across an ancient fishhook. Made of bone, the hook is estimated to be around the same age as some of the afore-mentioned ancient wood buried in Missouri rivers and streambeds.

Rolla's Modern Stonehenge

Sitting on the campus of the Missouri University of Science and Technology (Missouri S&T) in Rolla (formerly University of Missouri–Rolla) is a half-scale reproduction of the famous Stonehenge site located on the Salisbury Plain in southwestern England.

The original Stonehenge was constructed over a period of one thousand years or more. The stone was quarried far from the site, shaped with hand tools, and then transported to the site we know today. How the massive stones were raised into position and what method was used to calculate their precise locations are unknowns. But since it took a millennium to build, it seems reasonable to think that it was quite a difficult task.

The end result was an astronomical instrument that allowed an accurate prediction of seasons and cosmological phenomena. But whether it was built for religious rituals, as an aid in maximizing crop yields by determining planting schedules, or as the sole possession of an ancient David Copperfield, the original Stonehenge has fascinated people far and wide.

It is just that degree of fascination that prompted the university's Stonehenge team to build a Missouri-based model of England's real thing. However, Missouri S&T's Stonehenge was created using state-of-the-art, extreme high-pressure water jet technology. All the cuts to the Georgia granite that comprises their stone instrument took place in less time than it had taken to move an original stone its own length.

Missouri's Stonehenge has a couple of features that the original lacks. The Missouri S&T site allows a noontime visitor to determine the date of the month, and there is an aperture called a Polaris Window through which you can locate the North Star.

All in all, the 160 tons of granite that make up the Missouri Stonehenge was put to good use. Students combined ancient principles and modern technologies to plan, stonemasons made money building it, and the rest of us get to marvel.

The site is located on the northwest corner of the campus, at Fourteenth Street and Bishop Avenue.

Miami Mystery Mounds

Miami is one of those tiny burgs that drivers zip through without really noticing much, other than that they had to temporarily reduce their highway speed. But this small town in Saline County, like so many other places in Missouri, is home to an incomplete story with just enough information to be tantalizing. Miami's surroundings offer pieces of a puzzle about some out-of-the-ordinary phenomena in an area of exploration that is full of the unknown.

It all has to do with Indian mounds, those ancient cemeteries built by North America's original inhabitants. Mounds exist in several locations across Missouri, and all present their unique set of difficult-to-unravel mysteries. At least fifteen counties have had or currently have archaeological digs that have attained the status of being on the National Register of Historic Places.

The Otoe-Missouria tribe (from which Missouri gets its name) lived in the central part of the state, both north and south of the Missouri River. It was near the river that they created the burial mounds that are now located in Miami's Van Meter State Park. The mounds, or the Old Fort as the area is called (no one knows why), occupy about six acres and are literally surrounded by a mystery, in the form of a two-mile-long ditch that was dug long ago to encircle the mounds. The ditch's purpose is undetermined. Wasit used to ward off animals? Did it contain fires lit as part of elaborate rituals? Was it to be a circular mass grave?

We may never know the answer, but we can speculate our little hearts out with the opening of the Missouri American Indian Cultural Center in June 2008. The center will offer in-depth information about all nine Missouri Indian tribes, along with frequent exhibits and demonstrations from Native Americans who will share secrets of their cultures.

Amazingly, unbelievably, in a state with such a deep and rich Native American history, there is not a single "federally recognized" tribe now in Missouri.

Missouri: A Caver's Dream

With its sixty-five hundred caves, Missouri is literally an underground utopia for cavers, those individuals who love to crawl through dark, cool, wet, and sometimes impossibly confining underground passages. There are a few notable caves along the Mississippi River in the northeastern part of the state, but southern Missouri is so densely populated with caves that if you were to somehow power wash all the topsoil away from the rocky surfaces underneath, an extreme and alien-looking landscape would be revealed. It would take on the appearance of a huge, exaggerated sponge—a surreal topography of countless dangers almost impossibly difficult to negotiate by foot.

But many of Missouri's caves are navigable by foot and accessible even to those who don't display a caver's enthusiasm for exploring. Twenty-two of the state's caves are of the commercial variety and are very safe to tour, with comfortable walkways and knowledgeable guides. Most can be visited in the comfort of year-round, temperature-stable environments, as air temperatures inside a cave typically hover in the range of fifty to sixty degrees.

During our research of Missouri's caves, we explored five tourist caverns, one privately owned cave, and one of such paleontological significance as to be the new prize jewel in that arena of science.

Meramec Caverns

Possibly the best-known Missouri caves are the Meramec Caverns, located just south of Route 44 at the Stanton exit. The caverns have been used for various purposes throughout centuries: Native Americans used them as shelter; in the eighteenth century, French miner Jacques Renalt mined the caves for their vast supply of saltpeter, a required component of gunpowder; and during the Civil War they were home to a federal powder

mill that was ultimately destroyed by a group of Confederate guerrillas. One member of the raiding party was Jesse James, and he'd remember their concealing potential. It was after the war that Jesse and his gang used the caves as a hideout on several occasions.

James was one of the last people to use the caverns for this purpose, and it wasn't until the early 1930s that the caves were explored again, this time by Lester B. Dill. Dill discovered the seven upper levels of the caves, envisioned the commercial potential, and opened the Meramec Caverns to the public in 1935.

The caverns are explored on foot, using pathways that are wide and easily negotiated. Early in the tour you will be shown the Honeymoon Suite, which is an eight-by-fifteen-foot, naturally formed pocket in the wall of the caves. During the 1960s, the Art Linkletter television show held a contest offering an all-expenses-paid honeymoon to any couple who would spend a televised

honeymoon in the Honeymoon Suite. And it actually happened—a telling precursor to today's reality TV!

There is much to see beyond the Honeymoon Suite, including the natural underground seven-story mansion discovered by Dill. There is the enormous "wine table"—a massive, oddly table-shaped stalagmite—and a fifty-foot-tall natural mineral curtain that serves as the backdrop for a projected American flag as Kate Smith's version of "God Bless America" is piped into the cavernous space.

There's also a point about halfway through the tour when there is absolutely nothing to see. Your guide prepares you for an example of total darkness and then turns off the lights for you to appreciate the fact that you literally cannot see your hand in front of your face. It is the complete absence of light, and if you were to stay in that "no light" condition for six months, you would lose your eyesight due to the inactivity of the muscles in your retinas

Underworld Playground of Tom Sawyer

Mark Twain Cave, located just two miles south of Hannibal proper, is a maze cave. Most caverns seem to be single or a branched collection of tubes formed under the earth's surface either by underground rivers, lava flows, seawater erosion, or shifts in the earth's crust. But some cave interiors are more complex than meandering tubes. A maze cave is just that: a series of passageways interconnected to form an elaborate underground crosshatch. There are many four-way, sometimes five-way, and on rare occasions, six-way junctions.

Opened to the public in 1886, Mark Twain Cave was the first of Missouri's commercial caves. Mark Twain, the pen name of author Samuel Clemens, used this cave as an integral part of *The Adventures of Tom Sawyer*. Tom

and his friends and enemies had many adventures here.

The cavern was also home to real-life adventures involving local kids, and it was the perfect setting in which the regulars could pull a genuinely frightening prank on an unsuspecting newbie. This was because the cave's owner, Dr. Joseph McDowell, was a physician who had purchased it for use in medical experiments involving the preservation of the deceased human body. Sadly, Dr. McDowell's young daughter died during this time frame, and he attempted to preserve her by application of his human pickling technique. He placed her body in a container of alcohol and stored it in the cool confines of the cave.

New kids were brought to that portion of the cave where Dr. McDowell's pickled daughter rested not so peacefully and were seated unknowingly adjacent to her body. Then a regular would tell a scary ghost story, and at just the right time during the story, one of the bolder veterans would reach down into the container and lift the head of Dr. McDowell's deceased daughter, bring it into view of all present, and hold a lighted candle directly under her chin. The effect must have been intense, because many newbies were given the fright of their life in this fashion.

Mark Twain Cave has also been used as a Civil War munitions storage facility, a hideout for Jesse James (he sure liked his caves), and over the years acquired on its many walls the signatures of more than 250,000 visitors. But you won't be able to add your John Hancock to the collection: Signing the walls has not been allowed since 1972.

OZARK UNDERGROUND LABORATORY
TUMBLING CREEK CAVE

Going Batty at Tumbling Creek Cave

Given how government facilities often like to hide their purpose and activities underground, it is surprising but encouraging to learn that the very governmental-sounding Underground Lab of the Ozarks is actually a privately owned facility. Finding it required good directions and patience. It's located close to the Arkansas border in the tiny burg of Protem, and the closer you get to it the less it looks like anything of substance.

Once there, however, you learn that the Underground Lab itself is not underground, but rather a small collection of nicely maintained structures built by Tom Aley and his wife, Catherine. The lab makes assessments of trace water qualities and conditions. Tom and Catherine have been in the water-testing business for over thirty years. It is how they make the money to pay for their other passions.

It's the nature of their other ventures that makes their story unique. Tom Aley is a Berkeley-educated geologist-hydrologist who tired of the rat race in California and sought out a special kind of private world in which he could retreat to live his ideal life, the exploration of his own cave system: Tumbling Creek Cave. It is here that the underground aspect of this story takes us on a journey of vision, decades of incredibly hard work, and a commitment to preserve what cannot protect itself.

Tumbling Creek Cave sits at the bottom of a hollow that requires stamina to climb into and out of, and that's

if you're in a four-wheel-drive vehicle. It's rugged country, but Tom knows every square inch of it because he spent his first seven years here transporting over two thousand bags of cement down into the hollow by hand, then into the cave via a hand-crafted stairway. From ground level it is a thirty-foot descent into the cave. He used the cement to fashion walkways in the cave and also ran electrical feeds to provide direct and indirect lighting along the way.

The cavern is one of several Missouri caves that host a unique ecosystem, but it's also the only one that is privately owned and intensely studied and protected. It's home to more than one hundred species that reside nowhere else on earth and, as Tom says, "It's the most vibrant example of a rich, isolated ecosystem west of the Mississippi."

It was one of these unique creatures that initially attracted us to the story: the microscopically small (and federally protected) cavesnail (*Antrobia culveri*). This little guy is in rapid decline and is one of Tom's prime concerns for preservation. The snail's numbers have dwindled by ninety-nine percent, and since the population is counted only every few years, there is much suspense lingering around this critter's future.

Also at Tumbling Creek Cave are the millipedes *Chaetaspis aleyorum,* which are less than a quarter of an inch long, and the webworm *Macrocera nobilis,* with a diameter that is half that of a human hair. The Ozark Blind Salamander and the Eastern Pip Bat (*Pipistrellus subflavus)* join them. This tiny bat weighs less than a tenth of an ounce and resides in great numbers within the confines of the cave. One of the more impressive aspects of the cave is a mound of bat guano that stands about fifteen feet tall, with a diameter at its base of about fifteen feet. That portion of the cavern's ceiling must have been a very popular place to "hang" out over the centuries, because it takes a long time for tiny bats to produce such a pile of guano. Tom has carbon-dated the guano at the bottom center of the pile as being over 2,900 years old. How did he get the sample? You don't want to know.

The bat population is the impetus for the creation of the most outwardly interesting man-made adaptations to the cave's physical structure. In order to keep unwanted creatures from getting into the cavern and doing harm to the ecosystem, but still allow for the unencumbered coming and going of the bats, Tom, with the help of a federal grant, constructed a steel gate system that secures the opening of the cave. The gate is a large-mouthed chute that angles upward, allowing the bats to swoop in and out easily in a natural manner, but forcing other critters to climb at awkward angles to gain entry. Lower horizontal bars have just enough space between them to allow for pregnant bats to fly in and out easily. The early morning and late evening flights of the bat population, Tom says, are "like watching a fast-moving dark cloud" that whizzes in and out.

Visiting Tumbling Creek Cave was an extraordinary experience. The life's work of one man has added another significant notch on *Weird Missouri's* belt of impressive people, places, and things. Tom Aley had a vision for owning, maintaining, and protecting a unique ecosystem. To that end he has accomplished what most would have considered impossible.

Fabled People and Places

From the time we are children, we are attracted to stories that speak not just about real lives and places, but to the unknown possibilities that are said to exist in the world. For those seeking the weird, it is only natural that we would want to explore these possibilities and see where the limits of experience truly do begin and end.

In this chapter, we present some of the fabled people and places our state has to offer. These may or may not exist in reality—but have long had mysterious stories, legends, and tales associated with them. Some can't be found on any map but are conveyed by word of mouth—stories that have spread across the state and endured for generations. So come with us as we explore some of the people and places that challenge us to test the limits of what we know or what we think we know.

McDonnell Laboratory versus Project Alpha

Washington University in St. Louis is a highly regarded institution. The school is thought of as equal in so many ways to Ivy League institutions. It's evident that academic respect and integrity are highly valued here.

From 1979 through 1985, though, Washington University was quietly the home of a strange experimental and ultimately disgraced laboratory that is still talked about. Known as the McDonnell Laboratory for Psychical Research, it was dedicated to exploring the field known as para-psychology. In an academic setting, the topics of ESP, clairvoyance, spiritualism, and psychic powers were analyzed and examined.

The lab was the brainchild of James S. McDonnell, a businessman who donated $630,000 to Washington University in 1979 for the establishment of the laboratory. McDonnell had an intense interest in the supernatural, but perhaps should have watched more carefully how his money was being spent. The short history of the McDonnell Laboratory saw the institution become embroiled in a strange affair known as Project Alpha, which pitted the scientists and paranormalists of the lab against the oldest rivals of psychics everywhere—magicians.

Spiritualism became a national craze in 1848, when two young girls, Margaret and Kate Fox—later joined by their sister Leah—of Hydesville, New York, claimed they could communicate with the dead. They took their talent on tour and became the centerpiece of a new movement, a pseudo-religion called spiritualism, which was based on psychic abilities. Most often, members of the movement would charge visitors money for communicating messages between deceased relatives and living customers, and it became a multimillion-dollar industry.

Many people took notice, and among the wary was another group who professionally tricked people—magicians. Leading the charge was Harry Houdini, who became interested in spiritualism after the death of his mother. He quickly learned that a number of tricks, both sleight of hand and psychological, were being used in the movement's ceremonies, and he dedicated the last thirteen years of his life to exposing spiritualists as frauds. Houdini's battle turned into an out-and-out war between magicians and psychics. Even after Houdini's death, magicians—who use deception and illusion as a form of entertainment—continued the effort to debunk those who used theatrics to prey on the vulnerable. It was in the spirit of this epic battle that Project Alpha was born.

James Randi, known on stage as the magician *The Amazing Randi*, makes his living through magic on display and has become one of the world's leading

skeptics of spiritualism. Randi's educational foundation, in fact, has put out a "million-dollar challenge," which offers a cool million bucks to anyone who can demonstrate paranormal, supernatural, or occult incidents that can be held up to scrutiny by the scientific method. Randi started the fund in 1964, and so far no one has managed to take the prize.

When Washington University established the McDonnell Laboratory for Psychical Research, it's fair to say that Randi was outraged. As a result, he organized Project Alpha and perpetrated one of the most famous debunkings in the history of magic.

Randi trained two teenage magicians, Steve Shaw and Mike Edwards, on techniques they could use to replicate psychic abilities. When they were sufficiently sly enough to demonstrate their newfound skills, Shaw and Edwards joined three hundred others and applied to be a part of the McDonnell Laboratory's research. Out of all the applicants, Edwards and Shaw were the only two picked as subjects for the studies. Randi sent them in to prove one of his main theories—that those researching psychic phenomena are willing to set aside scientific methods in order to validate their pro-psychic beliefs.

Project Alpha succeeded beyond any of the participants' wildest dreams. For four years, from 1979 to 1983, Shaw and Edwards were experimented upon. The bulk of their abilities put on display involved such feats as bending metal spoons with their minds. The scientists at the laboratory were amazed at the results they were getting.

Simultaneous with the experiments, James Randi began contacting the institution. He suggested protocols the researchers could follow to ensure that their test subjects weren't tricking them. He was rejected

Above, Washington University; right, the Fox sisters; from left to right Margaret, Kate, and Leah

numerous times, but when even pro-parapsychology types began pointing out the flaws of the "studies," the researchers decided to implement some of the protocols Randi had suggested. As soon as they did, the boys were unable to produce evidence of their psychic abilities.

It was then that James Randi swept in and revealed the details of Project Alpha to the world. It garnered tons of mainstream attention and proved a death blow to the McDonnell Laboratory for Psychical Research, which closed its doors a few years later.

Thousands still make their living by claiming they have true psychic abilities. And magicians continue the fight to disprove them as exploitative, profiteering tricksters. The war wages on, despite the battle won by the magicians in St. Louis many years ago.

The Lost Tribe

The story of the Northern Cherokee is a complicated affair. Currently unrecognized by the federal government, the tribe is scattered largely around Missouri, Arkansas, and parts of Louisiana. According to their oral history, tribal members were forced to live as whites, with their true culture kept secret to avoid harsh and racist laws meant to deport any and all Native Americans living in Missouri to reservations out west. This has led to an unclear history that has proved hard to sort out in a manner sufficient to meet the standards for approval as a Native American tribe by the federal Department of the Interior.

The origins of the Northern Cherokee may be hard to decipher, but certain members of the tribe have one theory about their beginnings that goes against the common mythology of the Native American. If in any way true, the theory would change the way every American thinks about the settling of America. While most anthropologists believe that Native Americans came to North America by walking over an icy land bridge that spanned the Bering Strait, many alternate theories have been bandied about in recent years. They involve European settlers, Viking explorers, and even mysterious early

Cherokee Syllabary

Chinese explorers, offering new ideas of how this land came to be settled.

The Northern Cherokee have an alternate version of this tale. In 2003, some tribal leaders went on record with their belief that the Northern Cherokee actually have their roots in a group of Jewish refugees who escaped from the famous fortresses at Masada during a Roman siege.

The story of Masada is one of extremism and violence. Forts were built there by King Herod but were taken over in the first century by an extremist wing of Jews known as the Sicarii. The Sicarii had been expelled from Jerusalem and used the forts at Masada to stage raids against both the Romans and other sects of Jewish settlers.

After years of these raids, the Romans sent a legion to Masada to lay siege to the fort. Roman soldiers used Jewish slaves to build a large wall and rampart to aid in their efforts, knowing the Sicarii would feel morally unable to kill the builders. Once the rampart was built, the Romans were able to enter the fort rather easily—but what they encountered was completely unexpected.

Rather than be enslaved or killed at Roman hands, the Sicarii had torched the bulk of the fort and killed themselves. Due to Jewish laws that prohibit suicide, they instead had lined up and killed each other one by one. They left their food-storage rooms untouched amid the burning wreckage, to show the Romans that they could have survived a longer siege and had taken their own lives to spite their invaders.

Beverly Baker Northup is a Northern Cherokee leader who went on record to explain the theories that the Cherokee were descendants of the Sicarii. According to her, there are a number of similarities between the Cherokee and Hebrew languages. Further, the Jewish defenders at Masada were said to sport braided hair. Northup theorizes that this is the root of the Cherokee

FABLED PEOPLE AND PLACES 47

penchant for that same hairstyle. The Jewish scholar Josephus wrote a history of the Masada attacks that accounts for survivors among the extremist Jewish sect. It is Northup's theory that these survivors found their way to the sea and eventually across it to America, where they settled and grew into the tribe we know as the Northern Cherokee.

Further evidence of Jewish influence on the early North American continent does exist. The Bat Creek Stone that was discovered in Tennessee in 1889 appears to be engraved with ancient Hebrew writing and has been carbon-dated to be old enough so as to not be a hoax. The stone was found in an Indian burial mound outside Knoxville and is today stored at the Smithsonian Institution.

The Bat Creek Stone's origins and meaning have been hotly debated since its discovery. Some still claim it is a hoax; others say that the writing isn't Judaic at all, but an ancient form of Cherokee. Scholars from Brigham Young University have researched the stone in hopes of proving its authenticity, which would support the Mormon belief that the Jews settled America earlier than Europeans.

It's not hard to imagine that with enough distance and time, the word *Sicarii* could transform into Cherokee—especially when you take into account that the Cherokee themselves pronounce their tribal name as *tsa-la-gi*, and Cherokee is actually a Western misinterpretation. Sicarii and Tsalagi are linguistically similar enough that the theory may have some credence.

Outside of intense research and genetic testing, it's hard to say whether these theories are simply fanciful legends or if they do in fact hold some water. Are the Northern Cherokee not just a tribe, but members of the Lost Tribe? The answer, if it is ever figured out, could change our perception of American history from day one.

Equadome

Some buildings are alive, bustling with activity and purpose. Others seem dead, deteriorating and empty. But the Equadome was a zombie—a living dead building that stood vacant for fifty years while devilish deeds stirred within its decaying walls.

If St. Charles County had a "bad place," it was the concrete husk that stood off Highway 94 on what is now a sheriff's department firing range. Its name, when it was alive, was Water Treatment Plant No. 2. The main structures included an office building, two lime storage towers, and a water tower. The federal government began building the plant in 1941 to purify water used to make TNT at the Weldon Spring Ordnance Works. Throughout World War II, the plant pumped between twenty million and thirty-eight million gallons of water per day. It "died" when the government shut it down in 1946.

But it didn't stay dead. The building became a legendary hangout for young people. Rumors spread that satanic cults performed occult rituals and animal sacrifices within its cavernous chambers. The lure of mystery and danger attracted more thrill-seeking teens year after year. Some dubbed the plant the Echo Dome. Others called it the Aqua Dome. In time, the nicknames merged into one: the Equadome.

Novelist and photographer Jason Pettus grew up in St. Charles and remembers that when in high school he heard stories that were circulating in the county about satanic cults. "One of these persistent urban legends was that there was a satanic cult that met at the Equadome on weekends and would cut off the heads of live chickens on the top floor of the biggest tower," Pettus said. "The stories originated in the way they always do in high school—excited whispers among classmates, a supposed 'Yeah, dude, I was there and saw the whole thing,' even though details could never be provided." Pettus's peers spoke of the "weird things you could find at the Equadome," including burnt candles, pentagrams, and strange splashes of dark red on the floors. "No one was quite sure if it was blood or not."

The kids were not exaggerating. There really were strange events, even deaths, in the cavernous old building. One teen fell through a manhole and was impaled on a steel spike. There were numerous dark crawl spaces and missing sewer lids where an inexperienced explorer could run into trouble.

Not everything that took place there was accidental. According to Lieutenant Craig McGuire of the St. Charles County Sheriff's Department, police arrested about twenty people each year for trespassing, but occasionally found people engaged in more serious crimes. "We had assaults, sexual assaults, even a case where a sniper in its tower shot a pastor's wife as she was riding on Highway 94," McGuire said.

Pettus visited the Equadome for his first and only time when he was twenty-two years old. "It was announced that the government would finally be bulldozing the compound," he remembers. "So I thought it was important to go out there and see it at least once before it was gone. It was a much more complex structure than I was expecting—multiple buildings with multiple floors, many subbasements, all of them miraculously standing even after all these years. The most immediate feeling I got was simply a remembrance of how hard it is to find places to call your own when you're a teen, of how young people have been seeking out places like this since the beginning of time."

Pettus has constructed a Web page about his Equadome visit, which can be found at www.jasonpettus.com/photos/equa.htm.

One of the strangest things about the old plant is what happened when the U.S. Army Corps of Engineers decided to destroy it. Retired Army Corps engineer Karl Daubel was on hand in 1998 when a hired contractor attempted to demolish the water plant.

"They put a load of explosives in the towers and set them off, but the towers did not fall," Daubel remembers. "They just moved over about a foot and set back down." Like a movie monster, the undead structure absorbed hit after explosive hit, withstanding blasts that would have toppled any normal building. According to news reports, one tower stood even after its bottom was blown out. Finally, the Equadome's remaining structure fell over and died. In its place, the St. Charles County Sheriff's Department built its Law Enforcement Training Center.

But the sinister water plant still lingers in the minds of who explored its dark corridors or grew up with the even darker urban mythology surrounding it. "It was quite a strange building, not like anything else you're used to seeing," McGuire said. "We are glad that place is gone."—*Ray Castile*

Visit to the Legendary Equadome

I visited the Equadome many times in my youth. In high school, you basically had to go see it at least once, or you would be branded as a yellow-bellied coward of the highest caliber.

Every story I ever heard about the Equadome was more terrifying than the last. Obviously, the most common tales were of the group of Satan worshippers who claimed the Equadome as their own territory. These people would be there every weekend night, on the top floor of the Equadome's tallest tower. Just showing up, I was told, you would be able to hear them chanting in tongues from high above. On some occasions, you could see flashes of light produced by the evil spells they were known to cast. They often sacrificed animals, and smeared the blood from these sacrifices all over the walls of the Equadome to warn trespassers to mind their own business.

Long abandoned, the Equadome was structurally unsound. Every one of us heard tales of poor kids who were on stairways that collapsed, sending them plummeting hundreds of feet to their doom. Just stepping on a nail in that place would kill you, as everything was covered in asbestos, diseases, and grime.

By my junior year in high school, almost all of my friends had paid a visit to the Equadome, and they were all laying it on thick that I hadn't. One November weekend, a few of my friends planned a trip. The whole week prior, they had been taunting me over never having gone to the Equadome. I had had enough, and told them I was going.

Saturday night came and it was finally time. I wore all black. My friends picked me up, and we made our way out to Highway 94. Everyone was joking and messing with me the whole time, but I just stayed quiet. I knew that this would be the night I would finally conquer my fears and stop being scared of everything. Eventually the guys got the message and stopped ribbing me. By the time we got there, everyone was pretty quiet.

Driving up to the Equadome was completely terrifying. In the dark of the night, the old tower looked like it had been born in hell, and just kept growing until it cracked the surface of the earth. There was something truly evil about its appearance. It probably didn't help that the building itself and the walkway leading up to it were covered in graffiti: some was 666 and Satan stuff, and some were words like "Help," "Don't go," and other such evidence of people who came here previously and had bad nights.

We tiptoed up to the building, watching for any sign of other people. But we found none—no movement, no sound, no nothing. So we had no reason to run, and could only inch our way further into that dark, crumbling tower from hell.

Inside, the building looked exactly like what it was—an abandoned monstrosity that had been left to sit and rot for five decades while destructive kids and lunatics took it over. Garbage and old machinery littered the floors. And the smell was of mildew, rot, and rain. It was like walking into one of my own nightmares. We made our way through the building and everyone was completely quiet.

The quiet made it all the more shocking when someone above us dropped a metal object down. It clanged against walls and pipes before hitting the floor around us. Every single one of my friends scattered. Some screamed. They were all out of the place in record time.

But for some reason, I froze: just for a moment. I was scared, but more so, I was calm. When everyone freaked out, I had ducked behind a hunk of machinery that was rusting away. And before leaving, I walked out from behind it, looked up, and laughed out loud.

I don't know exactly what came over me, but I think I was just completely happy to have overcome my fear after all that time. I turned and jogged back out to the car. When I got there, everyone was there waiting for me, wide eyed. They thought Satanists had caught me, and that I was already dead and being turned over a fire on a spit while my blood was drained into some sort of bejeweled chalice.

All I could do was laugh. These guys who had teased me had newfound respect, and I had a newfound courage.

I returned to the Equadome many times after that, and had many crazy experiences. But that first visit will always stand out as the time I stopped being scared of life's dark edges and found a way to embrace them instead.—*Mark Abser*

The Albino Farm

Near Springfield's Greenlawn Cemetery is a weathered iron gate, beyond which stands the crumbling remains of a farm. That farm has, for decades, been the subject of stories and rumors. The former residents of this evil place, it is said, were secretive, violent, and guarded against outsiders. Needless to say, this is no ordinary farm. Welcome to the Albino Farm.

According to legend, the farm was once the home of a family of albinos. Due to their affected pigmentation, this clan was subject to much ridicule and derision from mainstream society. So they retreated from it. They bought their own farm, where they stayed, away from prying curious eyes, eking out a living. It was a hard life, but one where they were allowed to exist without the mockery of judgmental outside eyes.

Sometimes, though, intruders poked into the lives of the inhabitants of the Albino Farm. Stories spread about the what happened to outsiders who tried to enter the property to get a look at the strange people who lived there. It was said that these intruders were met with violence, and there were terrifying instances when people were said to be held against their will and tortured.

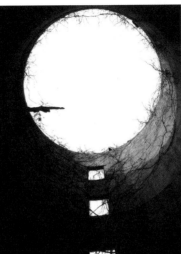

Whichever version of the legend you've heard, and wherever the truth really lies, there's one thing that cannot be argued—the Albino Farm is one of the most enduring and intriguing legends in Missouri.

The farm where this family once lived has long been abandoned and now stands crumbling in the woods of Springfield. Yet, the stories remain. People come from all corners of the state to seek out this evil site, and many still tell stories of lone albinos who lurk in the woods and protect their former stomping grounds. A tiny burial ground nearby is said to be the final resting place of many members of the albino clan.

Other variations of the story exist. In some, there was only one albino who called the farm home. He was the caretaker of the property, hired by a sect of secretive nuns who lived within the woods. He was fiercely protective of the sisters and often chased out intruders at gunpoint. Yet another tale is darker: A renegade doctor set up a secret medical facility in the woods, where he tested a number of experimental procedures on unwilling albinos. After breaking free from his control, they lurked in the area of the farm, never able to trust society enough to rejoin it.

Whichever version of the legend you've heard, and wherever the truth really lies, there's one thing that cannot be argued—the Albino Farm is one of the most enduring and intriguing legends in Missouri.

Visiting the Farm

I have been to the Albino Farm many times. It was easily the most talked about place at my high school. We had heard the family was gone, but their youngest son still hung out at the farm to protect their home and property. If you messed with the Albino Farm, he would not hesitate to get you out of there, often times employing his infamous shotgun.

I never saw any albinos in all of the times I had driven through there. This made me think the stories were fakes, just meant to scare kids and give bored people something to do on weekend nights. The last time I went there, though, it changed my perspective forever.

I had just gotten my first car: a beat up 1982 Monte Carlo. It was nothing special, but it was mine. It had a certain amount of charm and I took great care of it.

One night, my friends and I found our way out to the Albino Farm. By this point, it wasn't even someplace we took seriously; it was just a good, out-of-the-way place to have a few beers without anyone bothering us. I was driving the night in question, so I wasn't drinking, but my buddies had a few cold ones to get rid of, so I drove them out there and we were hanging out, leaning against the car.

After about half an hour, we heard a deafening blast from very close by. Without saying it, we knew what we had heard—a gun. We scrambled to get inside the car. Looking back now, seeing my friends falling over each other makes me laugh—but back then, the fear was so intense there was nothing to laugh at.

As we drove away, we heard another blast, and I got out as fast as that beat-up old-man car could go. We were screaming until we got back out to civilization. All of us were terrified, and not in any condition to be alone, so we decided to get some food and try to relax.

We went to an all-night diner and calmed down. We convinced ourselves that there was some logical explanation, that it wasn't gunshots. We reminded each other that the stories were just stories, and by the end of our meal, we were laughing about how scared we had been. Before the check came, we had reverted

back to being the goofy gang of wanna-be tough guys we were before the incident ever happened.

But all of that bravado, gusto, and machismo went right down the drain when we made our way back to the car. I had parked under a light, and as we got up to the car, my friend Craig gasped in shock. Then he pointed. And all of our attention was drawn straight to where his finger was pointing.

Buckshot: unmistakable buckshot. It left holes and dents in a burst along the back edge of the car. How the tire hadn't blown out or none of us got hit I will never know. But someone had fired at me from somewhere hidden within the Albino Farm.

We drove home in silence, and I dropped my friends off one by one. After that night, we never visited Albino Farm again, and to be honest, we never even talked about it. We just stopped going there, found new drinking spots, and moved on to other teenage activities—like desperately chasing girls and whatnot.

Just a few years ago, I was back in the old neighborhood. I moved out shortly after high school and only make it back once every few years. Because of this, I hadn't seen Craig in close to a decade. I ran into him on a homecoming trip, and we laughed about a lot of the people we remembered. In the course of the conversation, I jokingly asked him if he remembered our experience at Albino Farm. Within a heartbeat, he got deadly serious.

"I don't want to talk about it," he snapped at me, changing in about a second's time from an old friend reminiscing to a scared, scared man. I apologized and he calmed down.

"Look," he said, staring me dead in the eye, "you moved far away from here. That's fine. But I still live in the neighborhood. And it still scares the hell out of me that a place that messed up is so close to my home."

I nodded and told him that I understood. We continued talking about other, lighter topics. But in a way, it made me glad to see that my old friend was still scared. Deep down, I was too. And I always will be when I think about Albino Farm.
—*Dave Bassham*

Molly Crenshaw

The witch was chopped to pieces, her butchered body parts buried in separate graves scattered through the wooded countryside. But beneath the shallow soil, the pieces are moving. Year by year, inch by inch, they draw closer together—crawling, wriggling, and struggling to reassemble into the living corpse of Molly Crenshaw.

From one generation to the next, teenagers throughout St. Charles County have passed down this homegrown urban legend about a supposed witch who died a century ago but still haunts the local forests. The tale varies, depending on the storyteller. According to most versions, Molly Crenshaw was a freed Jamaican slave who lived in western St. Charles County during the late nineteenth century. A voodoo practitioner, Molly was often called upon to dispense spells and potions for local townsfolk.

One year an unusually harsh winter decimated local crops. Villagers blamed Molly and her evil witchcraft. Pitchforks raised, they descended on her modest home. Molly defiantly confronted them, placing a curse on anyone who touched her. Unflinching, the mob attacked and killed her. Some say they cut her in half. Others say she was drawn and quartered. But every version of the tale ends with the townspeople burying the dismembered portions in separate graves.

"I heard she was hanged or burned," said Ryan Scherr, a seventeen-year-old senior at Francis Howell North High School. Scherr is the opinions editor of the school newspaper, *North Star,* which ran a story on Molly one Halloween.

"I first started hearing about her in my freshman year," he said. "As my friends got their driver's licenses, they started driving out to where they thought her grave was. They said they went to the site and felt something

eerie, and then hightailed it out of there. Maybe it was just their mind tricking them."

Is there any truth to the Molly Crenshaw legend? As is often the case with mythology, the answer is a fuzzy blend of "yes" and "no."

According to a February 26, 1913, newspaper story in the *St. Charles Cosmos-Monitor*, the real-life Molly Crenshaw committed suicide at ten-twenty a.m. February 22 of that year in the home of Harry Towers near Cottleville.

Crenshaw, whose first name was actually spelled Mollie, had been staying at the Towers home for a week when she was discovered in her room, unconscious and frothing at the mouth. An inquest determined she had swallowed carbolic acid.

According to the story, Crenshaw was related to several prominent St. Charles families. She was educated at the now defunct St. Charles College and taught school until she lost her hearing. For a time, she worked in St. Louis, but her deafness made her so despondent that she finally took her life. Interment was made in the family burying grounds, the story states.

Her death record lists her as Miss Mollie J. Crenshaw, a fifty-two-year-old single white female born in St. Louis. The 1910 census also lists her as white, dispelling the myth that she was a freed Jamaican slave. Genealogical records indicate that Mollie Crenshaw was the niece by marriage of Marianne Towers. A marriage index lists the 1849 union of Robert A. W. Crenshaw and Ann Eliza Towers. The pair may have been Mollie Crenshaw's parents, but this has not been verified.

Ann King, local history and genealogy librarian at the Kathryn Linnemann Library in St. Charles, compiled much of this genealogical information. "Every year around Halloween, we get so many high school kids

coming in here asking questions about Mollie," King said. "I got tired of not having anything on file, so in the last couple years, a couple of staff members and I went through cemetery and census records and old newspapers to find information."

King said she found nothing connecting Crenshaw to voodoo or witchcraft. It seemed the only unusual thing about Crenshaw was the fact that she committed suicide, King stated.

"I always thought the subject was kind of sad," she said. "When I found out she killed herself, I thought it was kind of tragic. We contacted some people who were related to Mollie, but they didn't want to talk about it. I can understand why a family wouldn't want to be reminded of something like that."

Crenshaw's only surviving relatives are the Towers family. Because of repeated vandalism over the years, the family has removed Crenshaw's tombstone from its place in their small private cemetery in southern St. Charles County to an undisclosed location.

"From what I understand, the tombstone was removed by the family in the 1970s because kids were partying there," said Doug Glenn, a 1978 graduate of Francis Howell High School. "We used to drive around looking for her grave," he said. "We heard that people who tried to take away her tombstone met dire consequences."

Glenn is president and executive director of Renaissance St. Louis, a nonprofit organization that stages living-history performances, including the Greater St. Louis Renaissance Faire every spring in Rotary Park in Wentzville. The organization has also staged a different kind of attraction in the park; Molly Crenshaw's Haunted Forest is an outdoor, walk-through "haunted house" loosely based on the urban legend. "We had been wanting to do some kind of haunted attraction at the park for a long time," Glenn said. "Our other projects were geared around living history, so we wanted something with a historical basis."

Jill Hampton, the organization's spokesperson, said they have been careful to separate the real-life Mollie Crenshaw from the fictional Molly. "The only connection between the legend and the real person seems to be the name," Hampton said. "We contacted her relatives, and they did not mind what we were doing. They didn't even realize they were related to her."

Hampton said her group is fascinated with how the Crenshaw mythology seemingly developed out of nothing. "Every group that perpetuated it has put a different twist on it," she said. "That's how urban legends are created."—*Raymond Castile*

Visiting Molly Crenshaw

I'm sure you've heard the stories of Molly Crenshaw. My friends and I have attempted to find her grave many, many times. It always seems like some sort of bad luck happens to us on these trips.

Once, after visiting the forest and joking around about Molly, we found that my friend's car would not start when we got back to it. It had been working 100% fine when we made our way there. We had to get it towed and he had to put hundreds of dollars into fixing it.

Another time, we got lost for over four hours in the woods. This is strange, when you consider we've been there hundreds of times and know it like the back of our hands. It was almost like we got stuck in some kind of time warp. It sounds silly, but I guarantee, it was completely horrible.

I've brought friends here who come down with headaches or get stomach problems as soon as they enter the woods. I've always attributed these things to the curse of Molly Crenshaw.

We joke around about it, but I always warn my friends not to be disrespectful. The ghost of Molly doesn't take disrespect lying down.—*Ann Hockins*

Unity Village

Unity Village, in Jackson County, is about as small and quiet as a town can be. Like many small western Missouri towns, it's a place that not many pass through in their lifetimes. With only one hundred and forty residents spread over just two square miles, the town seems to the uninitiated to be, at best, a blip on the map one might pass by on the way to larger destinations.

And yet, Unity is the base of a powerful organization that boasts over two million members. This tiny town is the home of the Unity School of Christianity, also known as the Unity Church or just Unity. It is a New Age-y type church, founded in the past one hundred and fifty years, and many say it's one of the most influential religious cults in American history.

Charles and Myrtle Fillmore founded Unity Church in Kansas City in 1889. While, in its official name, the church promotes itself as being affiliated with Christianity, there are many differences in the beliefs of the two. For one, the Unity Church believes that Jesus was a man who attained spiritual perfection but is not necessarily the literal Son of God or was resurrected from the dead. And whereas Christianity is taught largely based on the New Testament of the Bible, Unity uses the Bible, its self-published *Unity* magazine, the *Metaphysical Bible Dictionary*, and texts from a number of other religions as the foundation for its teachings. Instead of being purely Christian, Unity teachings veer more toward combining a belief in God with the power of positive thinking.

The Fillmores founded Unity after Myrtle was stricken with tuberculosis. In an effort to find a cure, the couple began seeking spiritual methods of healing. They fell in with Christian Scientists shortly before Myrtle was cured. The couple began researching spirituality's effect on Myrtle's miraculous recovery. Charles later used similar thought processes to heal a hobbled leg that had bothered him for the majority of his life.

To spread news of their experiences and their new beliefs, the Fillmores began publishing *Modern Thought* magazine. They also founded the Society of Silent Help. Over time, these organizations converged into what is now known as the Unity Church. Unity became its own distinct religion—the Fillmores kept ties with the Christian Science movement but branched out into a new sect that incorporated spiritualism, Hinduism, and a number of other religious beliefs. In time, Charles Fillmore set himself up as the figurehead of the entire movement. Before his death, he was fond of preaching to followers that he was the reincarnation of the Apostle Paul.

Charles Fillmore passed away in 1948, but the church has stayed in the family; the current leader is Connie Fillmore Bazzy, the great-granddaughter of Charles and Myrtle.

Unity's literature is all marked with its logo—a globe with wings. This symbol is in many ways a sign of the incorporation of occult imagery into their beliefs and, in Egyptian times, represented the sun god Ra fleeing across the sky. To those who believe in the Unity Church, the wings represent the earth itself being lifted to a new consciousness.

Whether or not Unity is a cult or a legitimate church is a hot-button issue, with passionate debaters on each side. The organization does exhibit some classical cult tendencies—for one, merging a number of religions' most inviting practices and beliefs into one mega-religion. The church also encourages members to continue worship in their prior churches, be they Methodist, Catholic, Presbyterian, and so forth. In this way, members can embed themselves into other religious groups and subtly spread the teachings of Unity among those who are already spiritually motivated. It is strange, and some say sinister, that this group teaches elements of non-Christian beliefs and yet retains the word Christianity in its own name and encourages members to infiltrate Christian churches.

The Unity Church today has celebrity followers— among them "Golden Girl" Betty White—and is active in fifteen countries. It is a part of the International New Thought Alliance and the New Thought Movement, an umbrella organization of fringe religious groups that all preach a New Age, metaphysical message. Because of this, Unity is closely associated with Divine Science and Religious Science, two other groups within the New Thought Movement that preach similar although not identical values.

The Unity Church is an influential organization with a large, die-hard group of followers and is based out of tiny, sleepy Unity Village, at the western edge of Missouri.

Need Some Used False Teeth?

Kohler City is still around, but not in its original form. And the character of that original form is a challenge to communicate in writing.

The Kohler City of the early 1950s, located in Barnhart, was a general store in the literal sense of the name. Within its confines you could expect to find virtually anything under God's warm sun to be on display and for sale. Items such as prosthetic limbs hung from the ceilings next to used saddles. In other words, if you were thrown from your spirited steed, got your leg caught up in a stirrup, and were dragged until said limb was lost, you knew you could just visit good ole Kohler City to get an inexpensive replacement.

Or if artificial limbs were not your need, how about some almost good-as-new dentures? When taking purchases to the front register, you could choose from barrels full of previously owned false teeth and eyeglasses.

And if you anticipated that death was in your near future, you might save your grieving relatives some time by making a selection from the new AND used coffins that were on display along the top of the shelves holding staple foodstuffs. You could even buy used Bibles and hymnals for the funeral service. We're just amazed that they didn't sell the contents of the spittoons.

Sadly, the old Kohler City was destroyed in a fire and not reproduced in the same fashion as the original. But Kohler City is famous all around the Jefferson County area and beyond.

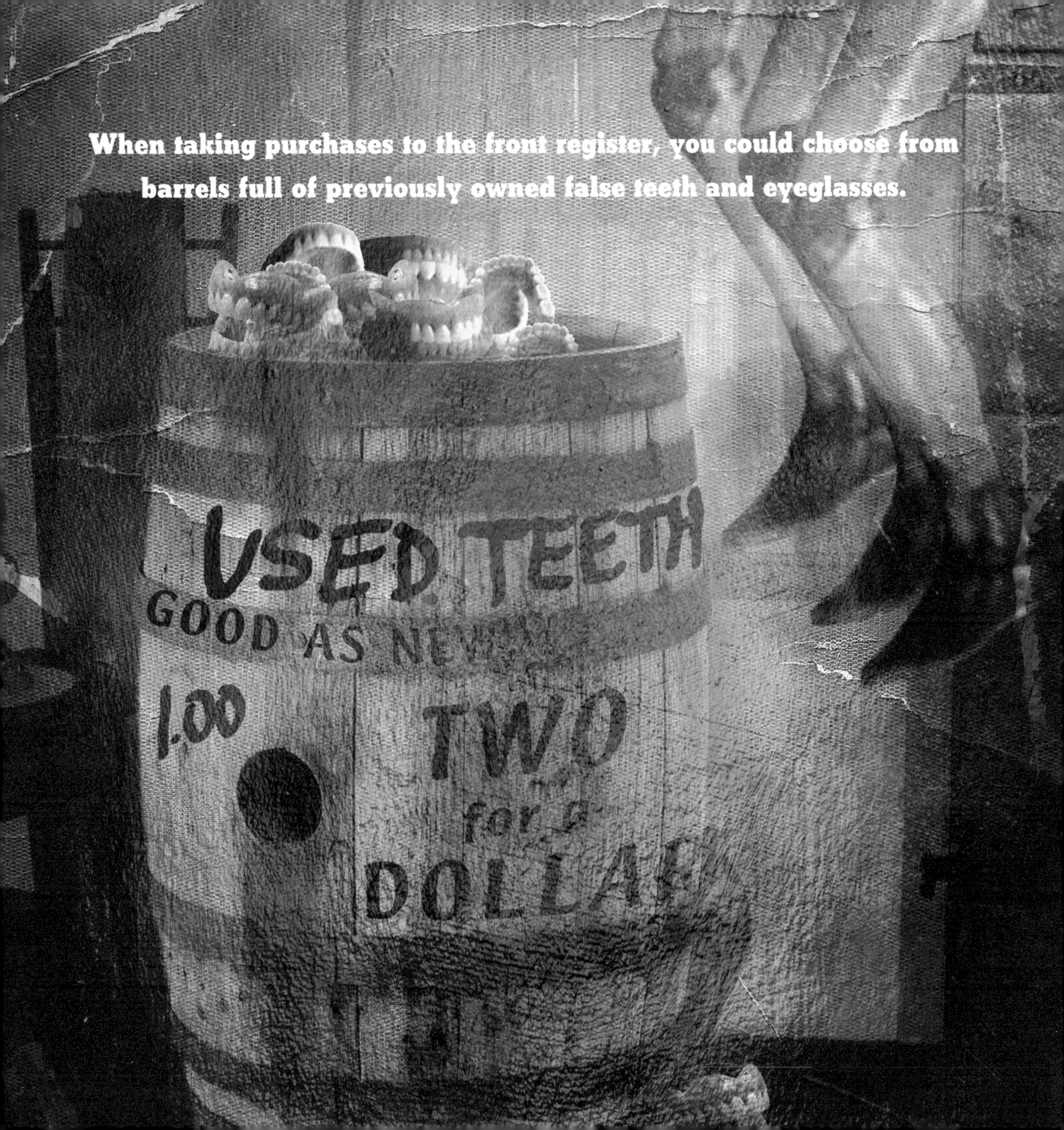

When taking purchases to the front register, you could choose from barrels full of previously owned false teeth and eyeglasses.

USED TEETH
GOOD AS NEW

1.00

TWO
for a
DOLLAR

Unexplained Phenomena

Did you know that *Liar's Lake* is home to a herd of Fainting Goats? Or that Maysville was the birthplace of a fifty-six-pound mushroom? While these oddities may seem strange, they are, of course, naturally occurring phenomena and can be easily explained. But what about the flying cow in Elsberry or the infamous spook light near Joplin?—not to mention the 1941 UFO incident in Cape Girardeau (The REAL first encounter of the third kind, a full six years prior to Roswell!).

While this chapter provides explanations for some of these seemingly unexplainable events, it will also unapologetically offer speculations and hearsay. Why? Because we believe that the only way to find answers to things we do not understand is to open our minds to possibilities. Every corner of our unique state has been the scene or source of some story that can only be described as bizarre and inexplicable. Here now are just a few of Missouri's many mysteries for you to ponder.

Of Spook Lights and Missouri

There is no shortage of the phenomenon called spook lights in this country, including in Missouri. These strange lights are so plentiful that it almost diminishes their unique quality. What do they all have in common? If we could find the common denominator among all spook lights, we'd win the paranormal equivalent of the Emmy.

Virtually all spook lights are in isolated areas, which makes sense, as a dark location makes the lights stand out. They are frequently associated with railroad tracks, which explains how someone could mistake a distant locomotive's headlamp for something supernatural. They are also usually roundish in shape, but how brightly they shine or how long they last seems to vary. And the stories of their origins are typically old. We wish this all revealed something meaningful, but we must surrender to the reality that spook lights are just that: spook lights. Anyway, what fun is it to understand everything?

Missouri's most famous spook light is the Joplin Spook Light, also known as the Hornet Spook Light and the Seneca Light. *Weird Missouri* has not seen the Joplin light for ourselves, but enough credible people have seen SOMETHING there and are convinced that it's real. Therefore, we can't simply dismiss the stories as urban legend.

The Joplin Spook Light has perplexed people for years and has even drawn the curiosity and analytical scrutiny of the U.S. Army Corps of Engineers. Their conclusion was that it was "a mysterious light of unknown origin." In other words, "Beats us!" Countless other investigations have arrived at the same destination: Speculationville.

And while we're speculating, what is the difference between a spook light and a UFO sighting? How often are spook lights incorrectly identified as UFOs and vice versa? Having never seen a UFO or a spook light, it makes us wonder if the lights reveal their presence only to people with intuitive or psychic capabilities. If so, there must be many Missourians with that capability, for we've received several stories about the curious light southwest of Joplin. Read, enjoy, and draw your own conclusions.

Fifty Years of Spook Lights

You would have to look long and hard to find another person with as much experience with the Joplin Spook Light as JoAnne Scarpellini. She and her husband, Richard, have been regular visitors to the spook light since 1957—a half century of spook lights.

JoAnne spent thirty-five years as a neurochemist, and it is her nature to observe, record, analyze, and make connections between cause and effect. Being a scientist and analytical thinker, she is not likely to mistake distant automobile lights (as is frequently done) as the Joplin Spook Light. She and her husband have witnessed the light hundreds of times, during all four seasons and under all kinds of weather conditions. JoAnne can relate in articulate detail the characteristics that make the Joplin Spook Light unique and also why it is probably the most impressive phenomenon of its kind anywhere in the country.

Over the years, she has taken a multitude of technological sensing and measuring devices to the spook light site. While all the equipment produced measurable results, none of the data brought her any closer to a scientific explanation for the light's luminous characteristics or its behavior.

Is there more than physics involved with the spook light? Much of what JoAnne has witnessed defies present-day understanding of the physical universe. She once encountered another spook light near West Plains, which was similar in size to the Joplin light and of an equally unknown origin, but the bright ball of white light cast no light and made no shadow. White light radiates, so such a condition is counter to logic. At times, the Joplin Spook Light radiates like a streetlight.

Frustratingly, JoAnne's attempts at knowing the light's source take her no closer to the answer now than when she first saw the light. She says, "It is unlike any other spook light that I have seen anywhere else in the country."

While she remains uncertain about the source of the Joplin Spook Light, JoAnne is more confident in her observation that it is slowly fading away. In her early years of visiting the light, it was an almost guaranteed event. But now the light is hit or miss. She has observed that the Joplin light is behaving the way a similar phenomenon in Farrenburg acted during periods of agricultural ground preparation: plowing, tilling, and disking the topsoil. She theorizes that the reshaping and sculpting of the earth's crust plays a role in the disappearance of the lights and that the same thing is happening at Joplin. Until three years ago, the road was gravel, but it is now asphalt and the area's population is growing. The days of the Joplin Spook Light may be numbered.

But no matter how or why, the spook light of Joplin has enriched the lives of one Missouri couple by being a consistently fascinating and inexplicable friend.

Show Me Some Missouri UFOs!

On June 24, 1947, a former World War II fighter pilot named Kenneth Arnold witnessed a cluster of disk- or saucer-shaped objects flying at high speed along the Cascade Mountains in Washington State. Arnold's sighting was the beginning of the UFO phenomenon. His descriptions of the objects led to the term "flying saucers," and after his report, people started seeing UFOs all around the world.

Missouri was not to be left out of the UFO excitement. In fact, the skies of the Show Me State could well be a hub of UFO activity. According to the J. Allen Hynek Center for UFO Studies, two cities in Missouri are listed as "semi-hot re-occurring cities" for UFO activity: Springfield and St. Louis. The center's "Hotspot" map of the United States shows that Missouri is clearly the busiest state in the eastern half of the country.

UFO reports come from all over. During the early 1970s, people ranging from the Boy Scouts to the chief of police reported hundreds of sightings at Clearwater Lake in Piedmont. Lights were seen skimming across the lake, leading to suspicions that there was an underwater UFO base there. Reynolds and Iron counties are also locations where it is common to witness UFO activity. Reports of vessels shaped like blimps, rocket ships, or saucers are common from that region. There are even stories of an underground UFO base in Pevely, but the folk at city hall have no knowledge of such a facility.

One of the best pictures of a UFO was taken over Cassville above the Roaring River in 1966. Three hunters returned to their campsite to find their tent and other belongings on fire. Rising into the sky not far away was a UFO, which they were able to capture on film.

While the Hynek Center map shows a large pocket of activity in the northeastern part of the state and smaller pockets west and central, it's southern Missouri that has the most sightings. In the mountainous Ozarks, with all of its hollows and caves, UFOs could land and remain unknown long enough for their occupants to catch a cab to Branson and take in a couple of shows. In fact, I am nearly certain that I sat next to one such visitor at the Shoji Tabuchi show.

Left, Roaring River Camp; right, J. Allen Hynek, (left) with his colleague Jacques Vallee

Mystery Farmer Speaks

We recently met a middle-aged man whose four-hundred-acre farm in Oregon County—close to the Arkansas border—has for almost two decades been host to what might be UFOs. This gentleman talked with us for three hours one afternoon about the strange lights in the night skies that he, his family, many friends and relatives, UFO experts, and others have seen for eighteen years. The sightings occur so frequently, the family actually holds cookouts with groups who watch and attempt to deduce what the strange phenomenon may be.

To protect the man's identity, we will refer to him as the Mystery Farmer. It is important to note that he does not believe in aliens, at least not those from other worlds. But since he cannot explain the origin and nature of the weird lights that appear over his property, and because he sees them consistently, he feels that he must place them in the UFO category. He takes the sightings very seriously and has kept meticulous diaries of each occurrence, with photos of most.

The Mystery Farmer's photographs are usually of good quality but offer little evidence as to the origin of the strange lights. Some look as if they are quite distant from the observer, while others look much closer. One photograph shows a brightly glowing light source behind a stand of trees that almost appears to be out of a Spielberg movie.

If nothing else, the lights are pleasant to look at. And they are not threatening; the Mystery Farmer says that he has never felt uneasy when seeing them. This seems to be parallel to what people who have seen the Joplin Spook Light often say about the experience: It's fascinating and leaves them wanting to see more.

After several years of documenting sightings, the Mystery Farmer decided to seek out people who had knowledge of this kind of phenomenon, including world-renowned UFO investigator Ted Phillips. Ted is the director of the Center for Physical Trace Research, an organization that seeks physical proof to develop explanations about what UFOs might be and from where they might originate. Ted has visited the Mystery Farmer's rural property on several occasions and has witnessed and photographed the lights. He remains as unsure of their nature and origins as any other observer.

What IS known by all observers is that when the glowing lights begin deploying smaller balls of light that streak off horizontally to all points of the compass, it is not long before the roar of military aircraft can be heard overhead; they frequently give chase to the small streaking lights. One thing is certain: There is a lot of action in the night skies over southern Missouri.

Mystery Farmer's Crop Circle

Lights aren't the only unexplained phenomena on the Mystery Farmer's property. A crop circle appeared there in the summer of 1999. The Mystery Farmer discovered a nine-foot-diameter crop circle while walking through his fields; it was near a fence line, with no hoofprints nearby. It is a precise circular pattern, with blades of tall field grass all lying down in the same clockwise direction. What created the circle is a mystery.

JoAnne Scarpellini is a friend of our Mystery Farmer and lifelong investigator of the unexplained. Her work has exposed her to a multitude of crop circle reports, both domestically and internationally, and she has spent more time looking into the mysterious Oregon County lights and possibly related crop circle than any other investigator.

She says, "It takes only a few minutes to determine if a crop circle is man-made." With bogus circles there is always evidence of man's encroachment, but in genuine circles, there are no such lingering telltales. All that exists within a genuine crop circle is the continuing conundrum of how, who, why, and when. Her best guess as to how crop circles are formed is "manipulated energy," which is what she says created the Mystery Farmer's circle and thus makes it genuine. But who did it and why is still a mystery to her, also.

UFO Hub in the Capital City?

If you hop on down a state or so to Memphis, Tennessee, you'll find out it's the overnight hub to which all FedEx parcels are sent, then dispatched to their final destinations. This has proved to be an efficient routing mechanism for getting packages delivered in good time. Is Jefferson City now a central hub for alien spacecraft? Inquiring terrestrial minds want to know.

There are those who think alien craft are using Jeff City just as FedEx does Memphis. The common thought is that aliens use the capital city as a command-and-control facility at which they arrive and are then dispatched to their nightly abduction missions. The sightings people have made of alien "shuttle craft," "cruisers," and "freighters" suggest that a serious threat could exist just a stone's throw (in cosmological terms) from Missouri's state capital.

Why have only a handful of individuals seen these craft, which evidently frequently fly in clusters as large as twenty ships? And why do they see only ancillary craft and no "mother ship"? The explanation offered is that the mother ships are cloaked by a technology that hides their outline within the infrared spectrum. But if this were true, they would be hiding only from the civilian population: All but the most antiquated of our air force interceptors would see the craft. Does this suggest that the government is aware of their existence? And if so, has the state government been infiltrated by extraterrestrial entities? Are we powerless against UFOs and those who dispatch them? Or are WE the power behind them?

Jefferson City: When aliens absolutely, positively have to accomplish their abductions overnight.

The three were clearly not human and
unlike anything he had seen before. They
were about four feet tall, with large round
eyes and minimal noses and mouths.

Cape Girardeau's 1941 UFO Incident

It's assumed that Roswell, New Mexico, is home to the United States's most famous close encounter of the third kind. This incident, which occurred in 1947, may also be the first time the U.S. government carefully documented a UFO event and then did a so-so job of hiding the facts from the public. In early 1941, however, a series of events took place in Cape Girardeau that might give Roswell a run for the title of "first government cover-up of an encounter with extraterrestrials."

The story comes from the deathbed confession of the wife of the Reverend William Huffman, who told of an experience her husband had in early 1941. Authorities summoned Huffman to an aircraft crash site a few miles outside Cape Girardeau. They wanted him to approach the downed craft and pray over it and the deceased occupants.

Upon arriving at the crash site, Huffman could see there were already military personnel, firemen, police, the FBI, and photographers present. When he was directed to approach the area, he noticed that this wasn't a typical airplane. The craft in front of him was an unconventional saucer shape.

Then Huffman saw the creatures he was about to pray over, beings he was not sure even possessed souls. The three were clearly not human and unlike anything he had seen before. They were about four feet tall, with large round eyes and minimal noses and mouths. Each had very long, thin arms and hands that ended in three long fingers. The beings wore strange suits or uniforms, along with headgear that looked like crinkled aluminum.

The Reverend Mr. Huffman could also see that the interior of the saucer was full of dials, gauges, and instruments that he had not seen before. Most impressive to him was the abundance of what he thought resembled Egyptian hieroglyphics.

After Huffman performed last rites over the deceased beings, the military swore him to secrecy. Had the authorities had their way, the story would have ended there. But Huffman went straight home and told his wife and family about the encounter.

Cases like this lead people to question what is really happening in the skies over the earth. Learning the truth is difficult, and world governments use myriad methods to introduce disinformation and diversions from the facts. Often, however, just enough documented information is leaked to keep the curious engaged in the search for accurate knowledge. Such might be the situation with the Cape Girardeau case. There are rumors of references to it in Project Bluebook—the U.S. government's official UFO investigation program—and even the may-or-may-not-exist Project Majestic 12—the purported secret committee investigating the phenomenon. But for now, the story is only as solid as its sole source: the deathbed recollections of the Reverend William Huffman's wife.

Missouri's Museum of the Unexplained

In 1985, while driving to Las Vegas from Denver, Colorado, Bob White and a friend witnessed what they believe to be an unidentified flying object. By their estimation, the sighting brought them to within one hundred yards of the craft. Soon, for reasons known only to the occupants of the UFO, it streaked off across the Colorado night sky. As it did, an orange, glowing light fell away. White carefully watched the falling object and was able to locate and recover it. And the rest is now controversial history.

The object recovered by White looks like a meteor or space debris composed of an almost pure metallic compound. As it streaked through the atmosphere, it seems its surface altered as the heated metal began to flow or blow back, forming overlapping layers that reduce to a teardrop point. In photographs, it appears to be petrified aluminum, which is a meaningless concept, but it helps describe its otherworldly facade.

To his credit, White authorized an independent scientific analysis of the object. The National Institute for Discovery Science sectioned a small portion and sent it to the New Mexico Institute of Mining and Technology for metallurgical study. Thus far, all independent tests have found that the object has qualities consistent with earthbound alloys. It is most similar to a terrestrial material with the trade name Alloy 360. Thus, the consensus is that the artifact is not extraterrestrial in origin.

But Bob White has evidence of an encounter, and the nature of the encounter is up for debate by all but him. In White's words, "What I saw was not of this world." Bob's version of the sighting involves a huge ship with many lights that joined up with a mother ship; then both streaked into the heavens. White is so convinced that his close encounter is real, he devoted the last two decades of his life to generating interest in his discovery. His Museum of the Unexplained was located in Reed Springs about fifteen miles north of Branson but has now gone mobile with a rolling museum contained in a large tour bus.

At times, White has been the brunt of criticism and ridicule, yet through it all he has maintained that the object is more than just a curiosity that fatefully fell into his lap. White's passion about sharing the artifact and its significance with the rest of the world has not diminished. To him this teardrop-shaped piece of aluminum is mankind's Rosetta Stone, the key to understanding alien visitations.

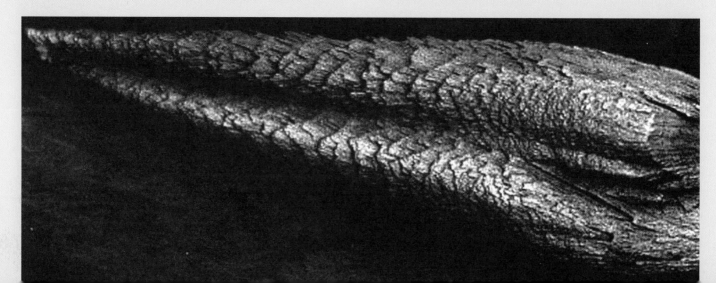

When Cows Flew in Elsberry

Elsberry is a quiet hamlet lying along Route 79 about an hour north of St. Louis and a good stone's throw from the Mississippi River. It is a town that minds its own business. Yet in 1978 lots of strange business of the inexplicable kind was happening here. For approximately two months, residents experienced all kinds of weird things: unidentified lights in the sky, many kinds of strange creatures, cattle abductions and mutilations. All those are curious events, indeed, but there's one even more curious.

Elsberry had several bovine events within a short period of time in 1978. Typically, the cows were found drained of blood with their sexual organs surgically removed. The wounds associated with the removal of the body parts seemed to suggest that who or whatever performed the criminal acts had done so with a good knowledge of surgical processes, using high tech equipment.

In one particularly strange incident, a mature, mutilated, dead cow was found under a tree in the middle of a field. This in itself is not unusual: Cows will seek shade under trees, and ones that are ill or at the end of life might die under them too. But in this case the cow was found positioned in a way that suggested she had fallen from the top of the large tree, clearing the branches of the tree—from top to bottom—as she fell.

Despite nursery rhymes that feature moon-jumping bovines, no cow would ever attempt to jump over a sixty-foot tree, at least under its own steam. The improbability forces an investigator to think in unconventional terms about causes. Did an airplane or helicopter fly across the field with this cow and drop it on top of the tree? Was a crane brought in to lift and then drop the cow? Was it a tornado with fateful aim? Perhaps a trebuchet was used to catapult the unfortunate animal to the top of the tree. Who would do such a thing? And having done it, why remove poor Bossy's sexual organs?

There was another odd thing about the mutilations. The local bluebottle flies would have little to do with the cows, mainly because the flies were dead too. Thousands of dead flies lay under the surrounding trees. They died strange deaths, many fused to the twigs upon which they had been resting. And their bodies were plasticized, as if exposed to high heat. Missouri summers get hot, but not that hot.

Just as suddenly as they had come, the strange occurrences in Elsberry stopped and never started again. Whoever or whatever was causing the strange cow and fly deaths evidently had its fill of the mayhem and never came back. There are many questions that will continue to be asked about these bizarre cattle mutilations. Questions with answers that are going to remain contested, at least until the cows come home.

White Squirrels of Marionville

Many townships and cities across the country lay claim to being the capital of some form of manufacturing, natural phenomenon, sports team, or extraordinary person. Detroit has autos, Pittsburgh has steel, and Dallas has America's Team. But none can beat Marionville, in Lawrence County, which is where the white squirrel reigns.

Several towns across America have white squirrels, but only two others vie for the title of White Squirrel Capital: Olney, Illinois, and Kenton, Tennessee. Which of the three has the largest white squirrel population is unknown; performing a census would be difficult and the outcome suspect. Since most reference material has Marionville claiming the largest estimated population of three hundred to six hundred squirrels, we are going to lean toward Marionville. This is *Weird Missouri*, after all!

Your author, in fact, has first-hand knowledge of these ghostly creatures. Two white squirrels now claim the backyard of my home, to the delight of my entire family. While our white squirrels do not blend in with the landscaping, they certainly mix in well with the other squirrels on our property. Their color does not seem to make them outcasts.

Are white squirrels albinos or a unique species? Albinos are white because their systems fail to produce melanin, a pigment that would provide color to the coat. Albinos also have pink eyes. Many white squirrels fit that description, and so seem to be just an aberration of an existing species. Whatever they are, their rarity makes them a joy to watch.

Marionville is very protective of its population of white rodents. It is against the law to kill a white squirrel in that township, and there is a $1,000 fine associated with violating the ordinance. The stable white squirrel population is one of the reasons people feel confident to travel from abroad to see the rare rodent.

Fainting Goats of Liar's Lake

The name Liar's Lake sounds like a fishing hole where tall tales are born about the one that got away. There are four man-made lakes on the Liar's Lake property in Sparta, and one of them is called Liar's Lake. But you aren't going to do any fishing there. Instead, it is home to an exotic animal business run by Cindi Darling, an extraordinary woman who speaks as fluently about African plains animals as she does about her Fainting Goats, which were what caught our eye when we first visited her Web site, www.liarslake.com.

Cindi informed us that the Fainting Goats (also known as scare goats, stiff-legged goats, and nervous goats) get their name because they fall over when startled. It's due to a genetic brain anomaly called *Myotonia congenita*, which causes mixed brain signals to be dispatched to the goats' hind legs, producing temporary paralysis. The goats then stumble and fall over, or "faint."

Each goat's fainting episode is different, the degree of paralysis being typically a function of how startled the goat is and the goat's age. Fainting events are short-lived and cause no additional harm to the goats; it is just an affliction with which the breed has to live.

Unless, of course, the Fainting Goat is being used as a "sacrificial goat." Whether myth or truth, stories are told about shepherds and ranchers who would mix Fainting Goats into herds of sheep so that when the herd was attacked by a predator, the goat would be startled, experience temporary paralysis, and remain the lone prey for the predator. Talk about taking one for the team!

Fainting Goats are only one of over fifty species of rare and exotic animals living on the two thousand acres of Cindi's ranch, which is enclosed by an eight-foot-high fence. The inventory includes her fast-selling mini donkeys and horses, zebras, watusi, elands, camels, pot-bellied pigs, buffalo, emus, ostriches, and our favorite: the double-wattled cassowary. But none of them swoon quite as well as the Fainting Goats.

Massive Mushroom

When you think of Maysville, you don't typically think of world records. But a world record holder it is. In the fall of 2005, Kansas City resident Ty Whitmore was cutting firewood. The nineteen-year-old woodsman noticed an abnormally large mushroom growing around the base of a maple tree. It was bigger than anything he had ever seen.

Thinking that he might have stumbled upon a rare growth, Whitmore took his saw and cut the giant mushroom away from the tree. Unfortunately, in the process almost half of what turned out to be a sulfur shelf mushroom fell into a nearby creek and could not be recovered. But what was left turned out to be enough. At fifty-six pounds, it beat the existing record held by a giant puffball by seven and a half pounds.

Amazingly, it was calculated that the giant had grown to its massive size in just two weeks! Which possibly makes sulfur shelf mushrooms the only living organisms that gain weight faster than this author on an ice-cream binge.

Missouri as National Bellwether?

When predicting the outcome of presidential elections, the smart money looks at the Missouri outcome. Every presidential election since 1904 (less 1956) has aligned itself with Missouri's outcome. And since 1960, the popular vote in Missouri has fallen within one and one-half percent of the national popular vote ratio.

Even in years when the popular vote was too close to call—1948, 1960, 1976, and 2000—the Show Me State has picked the winner. As the vote goes in Missouri, so goes the presidency.

Missouri is often used as a measure by which America's voting performance in total is estimated and even anticipated. Bellwether status is also awarded to Missouri in areas such as stem cell research, school vouchers, same sex marriage, abortion, and even as an economic indicator for unemployment rates and potential trends in consumer performance.

But why Missouri? Why not a large population base like New York City or Los Angeles or Chicago? Maybe it is because Missouri is in the middle, literally. It seems to genuinely reflect the mean condition across the entire country on a very broad spectrum of topics.

Another curious aspect to this mean condition is that Missouri was the twenty-fourth state to be granted statehood. Which placed it dead center when there were forty-eight states and keeps it close enough to center to conform to its interesting status as a national predictor.

Bizarre Beasts

Whether it's a seven-foot-tall Bigfoot at Ft. Leonard Wood, booger dogs, or the Ozark Howler, monstrous beasts seem to be lurking in every nook and cranny of Missouri. Here in the Show Me State, these creatures are usually all grouped under an umbrella classification of MoMo. MoMo, the Missouri Monster. And some of the reports of these mysterious creatures are scary to the point of making a fellow not want to go out at night.

There is also that category of beasts that, while truly bizarre, are really just a part of the natural scheme of things. Primitive alligator fish, feral hogs, and giant centipedes are all off-putting in their appearance, but probably hold no hostile intent toward us humans—unless provoked.

We can take some relief in knowing that most Missouri Monsters are the product of overactive imaginations. However, some of them have been reported by very reliable sources.

So proceed with caution the next time you venture into the woods. Warning, bizarre beasts ahead.

The Many Faces of MoMo . . .

Missouri's main monster is clearly MoMo, the Missouri Monster. MoMo takes on many shapes and forms, but typically remains something close to a bipedal humanoid that lacks social interaction skills, is impossibly sneaky, and clearly has personal hygiene issues—sort of like a neighbor, but not around as much. It all began about thirty-six years ago.

Creature of Marzolf Hill

On July 11, 1972, two young boys, Terry and Walley Harrison, ages eight and five respectively, were playing close to their home near Marzolf Hill in Louisiana, Missouri. Louisiana is located about thirty miles south of Hannibal and about ten miles east of Bowling Green.

The two children sighted a creature that matches all the countless later descriptions of MoMo. Did they set the standard by which MoMo was to be described? A man-shaped biped that stood between six to seven feet tall and was covered head to toe in long hair. They, along with their sister Doris, who witnessed the sighting through a window from their house, said that "it stood like a man, but it didn't look like one to me." They both also said it seemed to have no neck, and held what looked like a bloody dead dog under its arm.

Of course this story spread like wildfire within the press and had a profound psychological impact on the community. The Louisiana chief of police organized a twenty-man team, who searched Marzolf Hill from top to bottom and along its entire length. Paranormal and UFO investigators converged on the scene to offer their unique take on the origins and purposes of this disturbing addition to the countryside's population.

But yes, you guessed it. All the efforts to sight the creature on the investigators' terms went for naught. One thing is for sure, MoMo must be far smarter than those folks trying to track, photograph, and capture his likeness. Because to this day, the Creature of Marzolf Hill remains free to roam the countryside, often wandering into our neck of the woods.

Hump-Shouldered Ape Man of Festus

A sighting in 1999 took place near Festus, in Jefferson County. In the early morning, with excellent light, a man driving east on Hillsboro Hematite Road witnessed a large hump-shouldered creature walking across the road headed north. It appeared to be about six feet in height, with slightly elongated arms and a walking gait similar to that of an ape. Even though the apelike creature was large and stoop-shouldered, it moved with swiftness and stealth, and was not heard to make a sound as it disappeared into the heavily wooded thickets. Later the witness reported that the creature was heavily muscled and covered in dark black hair from head to toe.

MoMo Witness Admits to Being a "Little Drunk"

At least this witness was honest. His report stems from a 1985 sighting of a Bigfoot after the witness had had a "couple" of beers at a local tavern and began to walk home.

As he walked, he heard a loud animal-like roar, causing him to look just in time to see a large shape run into the woods. His fear factor now elevated, his walk took on a brisk pace, and he was purposely not looking into the woods, hoping that, by ignoring whatever it was, it would not exist. However, soon he sensed something directly in front of him.

Fearing the worst, he looked slowly in the direction of his fear and found a thing standing in the middle of the road just a few yards ahead. A stare-down lasted for a few seconds until the witness finally found his legs and made a run for home. He did have the presence of mind to look back to see if the thing had given chase, only to see it walking back into the woods.

The next day he returned to the site of the encounter and found huge footprints; he also discovered that corn had been taken from his field and that someone had broken into his chicken coop.

MoMo Sighting at "Fort Lost in the Woods"

MoMos seem to be evenly distributed across the entire state of Missouri. And they either have no fear of military firepower or lack the ability to distinguish the difference between an unarmed civilian and an M-16–wielding army recruit.

On a beautiful spring day in 1982, a U.S. Army recruit was taking basic training at Ft. Leonard Wood. On this particular morning the recruit had been assigned to guard a bridge crossing where combat engineers routinely trained. He was armed with an M-16 and three rounds of live ammunition. While being transported to this remotely located bridge crossing, his two-and-one-half-ton transport truck stopped at a T intersection. It was during this brief stop that the MoMo sighting took place.

The MoMo was standing in the middle of the joining road where no one except the reporting soldier could see it. It had a height of about six to seven feet and hair that was light brown. The creature seemed unconcerned at the sight of the truck and casually walked into the woods. While the guard duty was actually a training event, the soldier was glad to have been issued live ammunition.

This soldier went on to spend fifteen years as an army intelligence officer and worked as a civilian employee for the U.S. Coast Guard as an intelligence specialist. He maintains that he is a most credible witness.

Jugging Leads to MoMo Sighting

Over thirty years ago, a man and his wife were jugging for catfish while floating in their boat just north of the St. Louis Water Department facility on the Missouri River. They had just set the jugs when they both noticed a Sasquatch-looking creature on the river's bank getting a drink of water. The beast was very relaxed and at first seemed oblivious to their presence. However, once aware that he had been seen, he calmly walked back into the woods.

They actually got very close to this Sasquatch, as they described its appearance in detail, telling of its black body hair, about six inches in length. They were even near enough to smell it, saying it had a musky odor like a wet dog. The husband stated that he had been deer hunting in the same area several other times and had heard trees being knocked down—a sound such as they had heard the day of the sighting. It appears that this six-foot-tall long-armed Sasquatch is hell on trees.

On the other hand, if the stinking, hairy beast left a trail of uprooted and mangled trees, wouldn't it be relatively easy to track him? But then, if you find MoMo, you have to deal with him. Maybe the wise choice is merely to relate the story to those who will listen.

Let Sleeping MoMos Lie

As recently as 1997 a MoMo was sighted near the St. Louis Water Works. This account comes from a man who was bow hunting all day long and had climbed down from his tree stand to "stalk" along the parallel Missouri River bank.

As he walked the trail, he caught movement out of the corner of his eye and immediately spun around. His skilled hunter's eye recognized that the shape was not that of a deer—it was more like a man. He immediately released the tension on the bow. But what he saw was not a man.

It was a large-torsoed being that by his estimate would have reached seven feet in height had it stood erect. The creature seemed to be either relaxing or sleeping on the ground. Sleeping, that is, until it noticed the bowman's presence. It made direct eye contact with the hunter, and from there on the story simply reveals that the hunter's first and foremost urge was to go somewhere else. He stated that he was not frightened, but that his need to leave the area was intense—also known as "scared, er, silly."

Booger Dogs of the Show Me State

Booger dogs is a term that was clearly developed during less delicate times. Modern man has become thick-skinned when it comes to enduring the madness of the world, but bring up the topic of a booger dog at the local pretentious coffee shop and you will instantly become *persona non grata*.

Folklorist Vance Randolf wrote, "Some night hunter swore they saw an enormous black dog, fully eight feet long, without any head. They came close to the creature, and one man threw his ax at it, but the ax passed right through the body of the booger dog and stuck fast in a tree." This would certainly imply that the booger dog is of supernatural origins and is either cursed or blessed with abilities that defy logical explanation.

Ozark Howler

Of all the beasts we have heard of, either biological reality or fabricated hoax, the Ozark Howler is the one that we would love to be real. Its name suggests a creature that has endured generations of humans, impressed them all with its vocalizations, and has thus become legendary.

Depending on which article you read, the writer is either convinced that the creature is real and truly roams the wilds of the Ozarks or convinced that it is purely the result of human imagination. It may be a little of both.

Most accounts suggest that the Howler is an overgrown wildcat, a species of large cat that hides effectively by being nocturnal and uses the silence of the night to impose its vocal influence upon any within earshot. It is not difficult to imagine the howl of a wildcat reverberating through the hills and hollows of the Ozarks. Amplified by the night and the listener's imagination, the Howler's potential would seem large.

It seems that the Ozark Howler is going to remain a legendary mystery. Though many individuals have heard his scream, none have seen him. Maybe it was only the wail of a wounded animal that touched some primitive aspect of the human brain. Or maybe it's just the sound of one bad motor scooter.

Raw Head and the Bloody Bones

This story takes place in the Ozarks, way back in the woods in a deep hollow—the perfect setting for moonshiners, hog boilers, and magical practices long since forgotten.

It is said that an ancient-looking mountain woman named Betty lived alone in this dark hollow, alone, that is, except for her closet companion, a razorback hog. This hog had been given the name of Raw Head. Raw Head loved to root through the trash and thrived on the goodies found there. He rooted so much and so eagerly that he had rubbed his forehead completely raw. Thus, his simple name. By Betty's measure, Raw Head was a loyal and unassuming friend.

As an aged mountain woman, Betty was a skilled practitioner of mountain magic. Her skills and knowledge were passed on to her by generations of spellbinders and brewers of potions both good and evil. Her potions required many components, and when a magical recipe was complete Betty would discard the unneeded excess into the trash. The residuals from the potions discarded in the trash began to also work their magic on Raw Head. He changed both physically and mentally. He was reported to walk upright and speak the mountain tongue.

Sometimes the two would take the long walk into town, where the razorback hog would relish the extra goodies saved for him by the town's butcher. Everyone in town was fond of Betty and her socially compatible hog—except one malicious hog hunter who lived in the next hollow to Betty.

Betty was accustomed to the live and let live lifestyle of her Ozark homestead. She rarely practiced any kind of sorcery other than white magic. There was no need, because everyone respected the other's ways. But this one mean as a snake hog-hunting loner would soon force Betty to draw from the dark side of her skills.

One day Raw Head came up missing. Betty was concerned and made the trip into town to see if anyone had seen him. No one had seen the unique razorback since the last time he and Betty had been to town together. She knew what she had to do.

As soon as Betty returned to the hollow, she used an old potion-seasoned kettle to whip up a magical brew that provided a window to the truth. The truth was shown in the form of the trapper capturing Raw Head, killing him, and boiling, skinning, and butchering Betty's closest friend. It was now time for her to dig deeper into her black magic potential.

Hunting through her collection of books on spells, potions, and brews, she quickly chose one that contained a very powerful spell. Soon a plate filled with swirling liquids produced a bolt of energy that shot toward the trapper's place in the next hollow. The bolt shot directly into the severed head of the razorback hog. Immediately, Raw Head was back among the living—or at least the animated. The newly brought-to-life head of the murdered hog began to seek its other body parts, which by this time were scattered far and wide. But the severed head eventually found all its skeletal remains, and soon the bones, though bloodied, were magically reassembling into an upright form that was topped by the gruesome-looking skull. Raw Head had been brought back to turn the tables on the hunter.

The now very mobile Raw Head made a direct path to the shack of the backwoods hog hunter. With the patience of the dead, he lay waiting in the barn

for his killer's return. When the hog-murdering hunter returned, Raw Head began to tortuously toy with the miscreant. The hog purposefully made a noise that he knew would force the hunter to see what was in his barn. When the hunter entered the barn, he was greeted with red glowing eyes that slowly moved forward to reveal hideous-looking claws attached to bloody white bones . . . and the voice that came from the tortured mouth revealed to the hunter that the equation was about to be balanced. Raw Head moved into the light and took only a brief moment to relish the look of horror on the face of the disbelieving hog hunter. The end was quick.

No one in town was too surprised not to see the hog hunter again. And no one was completely surprised to find that Betty no longer anguished over the death of her closest friend. She was back to her normal self. In fact, Betty seemed quite content while shopping in town humming a mountain tune and gently singing lyrics about Raw Head and the Bloody Bones.

Local Heroes and Villains

Heroes and villains are many times differentiated by little more than perception: One man's terrorist is another man's freedom fighter. Jesse James was a notorious outlaw who participated in border raids, robbed banks and trains, and used his gun with little restraint. Yet suppose you talked to the woman to whom he donated a portion of his ill-gotten gains so she could pay off her foreclosed mortgage? She'd tell you that he was a true hero, a regular Robin Hood.

Defending the actions of psychotic sociopaths is not our intent. But sometimes the events surrounding a historical character would need to have been only slightly different and they would have gone from hero to zero in a New York minute. Timing and blind luck can be pivotal elements in a person's life. This hero and villains stuff is in many ways a coin toss kind of thing. Take the characters in this chapter, for example. Some were genuine heroes and others were purely villains. And some might have been both.

Calamity Jane

Princeton is home to one of Missouri's famous characters from the Old West: a gal with the working handle of Calamity Jane.

Had she lived in our modern era, the public relations folk could have had a glorious time marketing her persona. Just imagine the endorsements for the Calamity Signature Series Winchester rifle or the designer riding chaps or maybe the au naturel colognes. But Martha Jane Cannary lived in a day when being a ropin', shoot'n', cowboy-rescuing female was an oddity to the extreme.

And extreme she was, on all fronts. Her life started harsh and remained such until her death from pneumonia in 1903, when she was fifty-one years old. But she stuffed a lot of life into those years. She was the oldest of six siblings, and by age thirteen she found herself the lone provider for the family. With no formal education, she gravitated to what came natural to her, which was mixing in with the male sex in a way that few frontier women would dream of doing.

Calamity Jane, Gen. Crook's Scout.
Copyrighted by H. R. Locke, 1895.

Evidently, she early on acquired the manner of speech of the common cowboy and could cuss with the best of them. She could also shoot proficiently and had horse skills second to none. That, along with her preferred manner of dress, in trouser-wearing, chaps-clad cowboy-style, made her seem to fit in naturally with the opposite sex—so well that they openly accepted her, and she found herself performing male duties virtually all of her life.

She gained the nickname Calamity Jane, one story goes, by riding in to rescue a wounded cavalry officer in the course of a fierce battle with Native Americans. During his recovery, the man told the tale and supposedly assigned her the name Calamity. However, another version goes that she would often warn men that to mess with her would be to "flirt with calamity." We like the latter version.

Some historians treat her memory more kindly than others, but what is consistent is that she did have a close connection to a man whom she admired, Wild Bill Hickok. She claimed to have had the closest kind of relationship with Hickok that a man and woman can share, and she gave birth to a child who was later documented by testimonials as being a Hickok product. If her reaction to his murder—she went after Hickok's accused killer with a meat cleaver, but never found him—was an indicator of how she felt about Wild Bill, then they may indeed have been an item. If not in life, certainly in death, as she is buried next to Wild Bill in the Black Hills Pioneer Cemetery.

Just as with most legends from the Old West, or any era, the reality was probably less than the embellished tales of derring-do, but there so many documented exploits by this unique Missourian that there is little doubt she was deserving of the name Calamity Jane.

William "Bloody Bill" Anderson

It never pays to murder a young man's father, then follow up with killing one sister and maiming another. A feller can take right unkindly to that kind of treatment.

Such was the case with one William Anderson, born in Randolph County in 1839. Bill's rage came from the killing and dishonoring of his family members. His father was killed in 1862 by a neighbor whom Anderson later killed. As if his rage wasn't already reaching new heights, the Union army imprisoned two of his sisters for assisting the Confederate cause. The prison they were being held in collapsed, killing one sister and crippling another for life. It was this that led Bloody Bill to become a Confederate guerrilla warrior, battling the Union army at every turn.

William "Bloody Bill" Anderson had not yet reached our modern legal drinking age before he became a member of William Quantrill's raiders. Quantrill was also a wild child guerrilla fighter, but one who was able to slay monsters without becoming one himself. Bloody Bill, on the other hand, crossed over to the dark side during the process of what he believed to be balancing the equation on behalf of his father and sisters.

Anderson was at first

content to run with Quantrill, but he found the raiders just a little too conservative in their prosecution of federal troops. Soon Anderson separated from Quantrill to go off on his own and begin a series of encounters with Northern troops that had only one outcome. It was an era of no quarter asked, no quarter given. Thus a run-in with Bill and his gang of ruffians was always fatal.

His anger was legendary. Wild-eyed and frothing at the mouth during battle was his style. Clearly, if the accounts are accurate, emotion had superseded intellect, and Bloody Bill had devolved into a merciless mayhem-spreading mass murderer. One eyewitness story has him lining up over twenty Union troops and executing them singlehandedly, all while the ranking noncommissioned Union officer stood by to watch. He was the eyewitness for the report, his life no doubt spared only so he could tell his story and help grow the intimidation factor surrounding Anderson.

But he who lives exclusively by the sword should not be surprised to perish by the same, and so it was with Bloody Bill. As with so many others of history's famous and infamous personalities, true accounts of his demise are nebulous at best, but the most common story surrounding Anderson's death is that he had the bushwhacking tables turned on him by a troop of federal soldiers. Caught flat-footed near the town of Albany, he was met with a hail of accurately directed gunfire, and his bullet-riddled body did not even fall from his horse. His body was then put on display as a trophy, telling his potential victims and enemies that he was to be feared no more.

Today, Bloody Bill lies at rest surrounded by the beautifully manicured lawns and trees of the Pioneer Cemetery in Richmond. If you didn't know his history, you would read his tombstone and think him to be just another ordinary Civil War fatality. But there was nothing ordinary about our Bill.

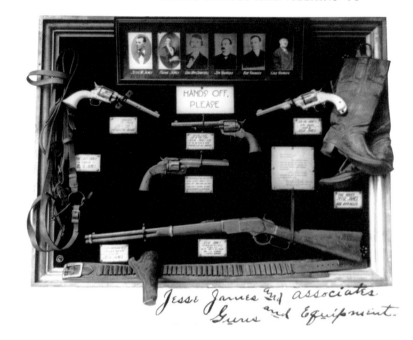

Jesse James and associates Guns and Equipment.

Jesse James as Robin Hood

As the story goes, Jesse James and his merry men were riding boldly across Missouri and getting hungry as they went. It was then the tradition for homeowners to provide weary travelers a meal—even if it was an entire band of outlaws. Luckily for James and company, they came across a farmhouse.

It turns out that a woman lived alone in the house with three small children. But she shared what food she had, and while eating it became apparent to Jesse that the woman was troubled. Her story involved the death of her husband and the need to make the mortgage payment or lose her home. Jesse asked how much money was needed to pay off the mortgage, to which she replied, $1,500. He promptly opened his bag of ill-gotten gains and counted out that amount. He then advised the woman to get a receipt for the money when paying the banker, who was on his way to the house at that moment, intending to collect the mortgage or evict the woman and her children.

The story ends in true poetic Robin Hood fashion. Jesse and his gang rode off into the woods and waited for the arrival of the banker and the transaction between him and the woman. As the banker rode back to town with the $1,500 mortgage payment in hand, Jesse and his merry men relieved the mean man of his money.

Ma Barker

Everyone comes from somewhere, and unfortunately for the citizens of Aurora, in Lawrence County, that quiet hamlet was home to a family of sociopaths that went by the name of Barker. The matriarch, Arizona "Ma" Barker, is widely believed to have been the mastermind behind the prolific criminal exploits of the Karpis-Barker gang, but some people argue that nothing could be further from the truth.

Ma Barker was an early victim of spousal abandonment. She and her drunkard husband produced four sons, Arthur, Fred, Herman, and Lloyd. Probably because of the challenges associated with having to work to feed the four boys on her own and the resulting lack of consistent parental supervision, the boys devolved into juvenile delinquents. And the rest, as they say, is history—a notorious history.

Some believe that the admittedly less than attractive Ms. Barker was very much aware of her sons' criminal involvement and that she would appoint herself with extravagant clothing and jewelry courtesy of their ill-gotten cash. Others say she did no more than remain loyal to her boys during those turbulent years. And it was indeed many years of hell-raising that the Karpis-Barker gang managed to inflict upon the Midwest.

Their heydays were during the "public enemy" years, and some say that the famous, allegedly transvestite lawman J. Edgar Hoover ramped up her bad reputation to justify the FBI's crime-busting campaign. Ultimately, it was the FBI that ended the tortured life of Ma Barker by killing her and her son Fred, in a shoot-out in Weir, FL. But the FBI had been provoked, there is no doubt about that. Between 1910 and Ma Barker's death in 1935, the Karpis-Barker gang was responsible for a crime wave that took many a life during their armed robberies and countless other crimes.

But one man's crime spree is another's job security. The press loved the exploits of the gangsters, and Ma Barker's clan contributed mightily to the sales of many a newspaper and to the growth of an agency known as the FBI.

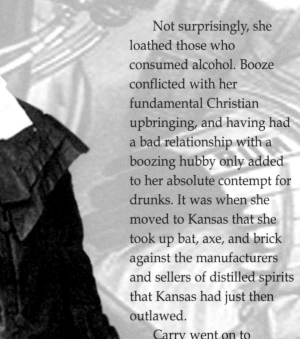

The Ginerator

Carry Amelia Nation aggressively promoted the abolition of alcohol thirty years prior to Prohibition. Had she been around during Al Capone's time, Eliot Ness and his boys would have had far less work on their hands. (Either that, or they would have found her dead in a ditch, courtesy of Scarface.)

Nation was a Missouri resident during her early years and received a teaching certificate while living in Belton. She married a local physician who displayed the bad behavior of being a perpetual drunk and soon died, leaving her alone to fend for their mentally challenged daughter.

Not surprisingly, she loathed those who consumed alcohol. Booze conflicted with her fundamental Christian upbringing, and having had a bad relationship with a boozing hubby only added to her absolute contempt for drunks. It was when she moved to Kansas that she took up bat, axe, and brick against the manufacturers and sellers of distilled spirits that Kansas had just then outlawed.

Carry went on to brazenly crash into gin joints and literally break the place up in a fashion that would make the Terminator proud.

Lamar, Starting Point of Wyatt Earp's Legend

All legends have a starting point. One of history's most famous lawmen, Wyatt Earp, began his career as a constable in Lamar, Barton County, on November 17, 1869. There were not many volunteers for such work, and Wyatt chose it at the age of twenty-one—quite a burden of responsibility for a man that young, especially when his career began with controversy.

Given Earp's notorious reputation as a skull-cracking, pistol-wielding sheriff, it is a little surprising to learn that the difficulties faced by the young Earp revolved around public finances. He was actually sued by Barton County for suspected mis-appropriation of funds during his tenure as sheriff. However, the case was never resolved because Wyatt had by that time left the state of Missouri, so could not be prosecuted.

He went on to have the most celebrated career (and handlebar mustache) in western law-enforcement history, working in Dodge City, Kansas, and Tombstone, Arizona, culminating in the infamous shoot-out at the OK Corral. He survived it all to live a long life, dying in 1929 in Los Angeles, of natural causes at the age of eighty.

Bob's Bizarre Bazaar

Bob Berdella owned one of those stores where you hope your kids never go to shop. Bob's Bizarre Bazaar was a "novelty" shop that sold items like human skulls, lava lamps, incense, rolling papers, oddities from around the world, and all the ancillary needs to support the behaviors of occultists and satanists. All in all, it was a shop for the tastes of people living at the margins.

But the store was a front. Bob was not your normal business owner. He was not normal in any sense of the word. Bob was a sexually motivated serial murderer and insane.

A lifelong Kansas City resident, during the 1980s Bob would lure young men to his home, sometimes after meeting them at his retail store, other times picking up male prostitutes. He would then take them captive and use them for experiments that would have made the nastiest Nazi psycho go to sleep with a warm fuzzy feeling. Bob's version of his torture practices was that he was merely living out his dark fantasies. His victims must have certainly considered his fantasies their unholy nightmare.

His mode of operation was to use these unfortunates until they lacked the strength to provide him with the feedback that gave him the thrill. Once they became less than fun, he would kill them outright by lethal injection of household cleaners or suffocation. He would then dismember them in his bathtub and place their parts at the curb, mixed into his everyday trash.

His downfall came when one of his victims escaped and gained the attention of a neighbor. What followed was a story that shook the Kansas City area and held the attention of the nation. Investigations revealed that Bob had killed at least six men. To the frustration of the loved

POLICE DEPT.
KANSAS CITY, MISSOURI

1 1 6 9 2 1 0 2 0 8 85

ones of his victims and the nation as a whole, he was granted a plea agreement that provided him with a life sentence. This despite his having kept a detailed log of his torture activities as well as Polaroid pictures of his victims.

The murderous shopkeeper died of a "heart attack" only four years into his sentence. Rumors abound about the true cause of his death, with many suggesting that the prison officials simply didn't give Bob his heart medication. We will never know for sure; we're just surprised he even had a heart.

The NWA Champion of the (Little) World

Shigeru Akabane was born and raised in Japan and now lives in St. Joseph. His life in between those destinations saw him travel the world, entertain millions, and reach the pinnacle of his profession. For Akabane is better known as Little Tokyo, the three-time midget class wrestling champion of the world under the banner of the National Wrestling Alliance.

Little Tokyo worked the entire nation, as well as Canada and Japan, performing in front of crowds that reached well into the tens of thousands. Besides the NWA, he wrestled throughout the 1970s and '80s in the larger promotions of the time, including the UWF, AWA, and WWF. This means that he crossed over into every separately run wrestling territory and performed in most of the largest arenas spread across the country, including Madison Square Garden in New York City. As one of the best little-person grapplers, Little Tokyo was almost always guaranteed constant work. Wrestling promoters liked midget wrestlers, as their presence consistently drew a larger audience than a card without them. Little Tokyo last wrestled in 2001, but according to the champ himself, the door is not closed on future appearances. He is still considered only semiretired.

Little Tokyo's most notable feud involved his numerous battles with Cowboy Lang. Throughout the 1980s, they wrestled in a memorable series of matches during which they traded the midget championship back and forth a handful of times. Wrestling purists maintain that while many matches between midgets were nothing more than exploitive freak shows meant to appeal to the lowest common denominator, Little Tokyo and Cowboy Lang broke the mold. They truly gained the respect of others in the sport for their wrestling abilities, and they refused to settle for being regarded simply as a sideshow act to the big boys. Their matches stand the test of time and are still considered classics today.

The pinnacle of Tokyo's success and fame came when he wrestled in the famous Wrestlemania III. He battled with the average-sized Hillbilly Jim and fellow little people Little Beaver and the Haiti Kid while teaming with the larger-than-average-sized King Kong Bundy, as well as fellow diminutive wrestler Lord Littlebrook. Over 93,000 people attended this event, making it the largest indoor sporting event in United States history to date.

Although he is not currently wrestling on a routine basis, Little Tokyo is keeping busy. Akabane still works part-time in St. Joseph, making leather hats. Keep your eyes peeled for another wrestling appearance in the future. It's hard to keep a good little man down.

Edwin Powell Hubble—Stargazer

Man still believed right up into the 1920s that the universe didn't extend beyond our own Milky Way galaxy. Astronomers had already spotted other galaxies, but these were generally determined to be nebulae—clouds of dust and gas—and were presumed to lie within the Milky Way along with everything else.

In 1925, that view changed, and in a big way. After spending countless hours peering through an eyepiece atop California's Mount Wilson, a little-known astronomer named Edwin Powell Hubble publicly concluded that the universe was far more vast than previously accepted. Those supposed nebulae, he determined, were entire galaxies unto themselves, some more massive than our own, and were very, very far away. Hubble had realized that the cosmos was not just big, it was really, really big. Bigger, perhaps, than the mind could grasp.

He also determined that Einstein's equations of general relativity for a homogeneous, isotropic expanding universe held true. In other words, space was not only big, it was getting bigger. By measuring wavelengths of light from celestial bodies he was able to show that galaxies were spreading outward in a way that supported the then nascent big bang theory. Thanks to Hubble, our understanding of creation made enormous leaps.

Yet, despite Hubble's accomplishments, your average Joe hadn't heard of the man until around 1990, when the much anticipated Hubble Space Telescope was launched into orbit, promising new and extraordinary views into deep space. Unfortunately, the name Hubble quickly became synonymous with colossal failure when the most celebrated astronomical instrument in history and the poster child for NASA was discovered to work about as well as a cell phone camera. Thankfully, however, technicians were able to fix it, and the HST's unprecedented imagery eventually made the scope a fitting tribute to Edwin Hubble.

Nevertheless, anyone who might wish to pay homage to the great astronomer for himself had no terrestrial focal point for his admiration. A satellite, a moon crater, and an asteroid were all named after him, but earth itself was devoid of Hubble shrines. In fact, when he died in 1953 not only was there no funeral, but his wife refused to reveal what was done with his body, so there's not even a grave site to visit.

As a result, the folks in Hubble's hometown of Marshfield took it upon themselves to correct the situation. They would build their own shrine, a suitable memorial that could stand in the center of town and properly honor their local hero. Rather than create a plaque or some type of cenotaph, though, officials chose to go in another direction. In 1994, they erected on the local courthouse lawn a one-fourth-scale replica of the eponymous satellite in stainless steel. Sort of a tribute to a tribute, like a memorial once removed.

Sure, they could have gone with a statue of Hubble himself, but we think it's safe to say they went with the safer, more recognizable option. Makes for a better postcard, too.
—*Wesley Treat*

Jim the Wonder Dog

In 1925, an unassuming dog was born in a Louisiana, Missouri, kennel. He wasn't bred in any special fashion, and his parents were ordinary in every way. But when he was sent to Sam Van Arsdale of Marshall, this dog, Jim, displayed some very peculiar qualities. His amazing feats have led to his being remembered today, many years after his 1937 passing, as Jim the Wonder Dog. He is regarded by those who know of his life and his deeds as the smartest dog to ever walk the earth.

From the very start, Jim seemed to be far more intelligent than the average canine. One early indicator was that, despite the fact that dogs are color blind, Jim was able to identify the colors people were wearing. Mr. Van Arsdale found that he could write down answers on sheets of paper, ask Jim questions, and the dog would proceed to indicate the slips of paper that held the correct answer. For example, for an astonishing seven years in a row, Jim predicted the winner of the Kentucky Derby. He could match car owners with their cars, and identify who owned what car simply by being shown a license plate number. Jim could respond to commands in English, Spanish, Italian, French, and even Greek. Amazingly, he predicted President Roosevelt's reelection in the months before a presidential election. Jim wasn't some dog taught simple parlor tricks. He seemed to possess both a human level of intelligence as well as indicators of downright psychic abilities.

Jim's most famous and mystifying ability was identifying the sex of unborn infants. Pregnant women would visit Jim, who would indicate a paper marking the sex he believed the child to be. Legend states that Jim was correct one hundred percent of the time.

After Jim's passing, Van Arsdale had him buried in a cemetery in Marshall. At the time, it was not permissible to bury a dog within the cemetery, so he was placed outside its property line. But in the years since, the cemetery has expanded, and now Jim rests well within its borders.

In 1999, the city of Marshall also unveiled the Jim the Wonder Dog Memorial Park and Garden.

JIM THE WONDER DOG
1925 — 1937

4. UNEXPLAINABLE FEATS

Jim could go into a crowd and select a certain person, such as "an out-of-town hardware salesman", or "the man who had the most change in his pocket". Jim could pick out a "man with a red tie" or a "girl in a blue dress" (dogs are supposed to be color-blind). It was a common request that Jim go out and find an automobile with a certain license number, a car from out of state, or a particular kind of automobile. He would do this even if the car was quite a distance away. Mr. VanArsdale could write a request on a piece of paper, show it to Jim and say "Do whatever it says".

Skeptics thought that Mr. VanArsdale was somehow signaling Jim, but some people would write requests in foreign languages or shorthand, neither of which Sam understood. Perhaps the most astounding thing Jim could do was predict the sex of a baby before it was born or select winners of elections, games, or races yet to be held. He chose the winner of the Kentucky Derby for 7 straight years. This was conducted by writing possible choices on slips of paper and Jim would touch the paper of his choice. No one was allowed to look at it, but it would be marked and put in a safe until after the event. Jim never failed to select the right one. Another time he showed extrasensory power was when he was taken to Dr. J.C. Flynn, a Kansas City Veterinarian, and left for some time for treatment. When the phone would ring, Jim would usually pay no attention, but sometimes he would go immediately and stand by the phone. Dr. Flynn said that even before he answered, he knew the call would be from Mr. VanArsdale, calling to inquire about Jim.

This park features a full-sized statue of Jim, as well as a series of stone tablets embedded in the ground that tell of the creature's many adventures and exploits.

In fond and flowery language, one tablet tells of the scientific testing done on the dog to determine the truth and source of his abilities. It claims that scientists found Jim to have a wider skull than most dogs, indicating that he had a larger brain. The next tablet details some of Jim's best-known feats, as well as some lesser ones, including his ability to look at a crowd of people and determine which person had the most change in his pocket. Another stone tells of Jim's fame, chronicling the many newspapers, magazines, and television shows that featured the pup. This stone also tells a frightening story. Apparently, while on tour with Jim the Van Arsdales entrusted a bellhop from their hotel to walk him. He used the dog's ability to correctly guess the future winners of a number of horse races. Word went around town, and the Van Arsdales were warned that some very unhappy parties were seeking to hurt Jim in response to his gambling know-how. They quickly got out of town, with Jim safely in tow. Another stone details Jim's relationship with Pearl, Sam Van Arsdale's wife. Apparently Jim hated domestic strife. Pearl would routinely get angry at Sam for throwing pillows on the floor when he went to bed at night. One morning, to her astonishment, Pearl found Jim placing the pillows on the couple's bed before she could discover them.

The last tablet tells the sad story of Jim the Wonder Dog's demise. This touching stone details not just the incident itself but the massive worldwide remorse and remembrance that arose after the dog's death. Jim's burial attracted thousands of people, and the beloved superhero of the dog world was interred in a specially built casket fitted to his canine body.

Although Jim is gone, he is absolutely not forgotten. Videos of Jim in action are available for those who missed out on the opportunity to see what the—powered pooch was able to accomplish throughout his lifetime. More information can be found at www.jimthewonderdog.com.

The Automatic Writing of Pearl Curran

Benjamin Franklin may have created one of the most famous pseudonyms in American history in his Silence Dogood alter ego. However, he was not the only person of note who has utilized an alternative persona as a way of communicating his thoughts and opinions. Sometimes it was prudent to remain hidden from all the king's men, or whatever minions might object to your ideas. It is therefore not without precedent that one unusual and extraordinary Missourian used an alter ego to convey volumes of thought.

Pearl Lenore Curran (1883–1937) was a St. Louis resident who gained much attention both nationally and internationally. Her acclaim came from her unique ability to channel the thoughts of a seventeenth-century spinster named Patience Worth. Curran was a woman of little formal education and seemed to have little to no curiosity about poetry or literature, thus she was not especially well read. However, her prose was often com-pared to that of Chaucer and Shakespeare.

This extraordinary ability drew the attention of that era's most famous and infamous mediums, skeptics, and critics. But no one could catch her cheating. She had no tricks, no techniques, no diversions or sleight of hand, but did have a demeanor that suggested complete sincerity. She would simply sit down with pen and paper, and then allow the words to flow through her, from the essence of Patience. As she once abruptly replied when asked if Patience and Pearl were the same person, "She be, but she and I be me."

The team of Pearl and Patience produced massive amounts of material. In one seven- year period, Pearl wrote over two million words dictated through her from Patience and onto paper via a process called automatic writing. This process is described as a separation from the conscious self that produces a harmonious fluid relationship between the writer and the source. Automatic writing can take place anywhere, even in a dark room. The writer merely places pen to paper, allows the arm to remain relaxed, and then waits for the flow of information from the source to take its natural course and pace—which can be at blistering speed.

During her twenty-four years of channeling, Pearl put over four million words to paper in the form of seven books, and countless poems, short stories, and plays. In one sitting, she produced five thousand handwritten words that withstood the test of the most discriminating skeptic. She once wrote fifteen poems of world-class quality in one hour and fifteen minutes. It was said that "words poured forth at a speed to be envied by even Tennyson or Browning." Often the Old English was so obscure that many of the words offered little meaning until looked up in dialect dictionaries.

Amazingly, her works were always dialectically precise. In what is frequently regarded as her most important work, "The Sorry Tale," an account of the last days of Jesus, the prose is that of seventeenth-century English. The Old English produced by Pearl is without error, accurate to the era, and without expected contradictions. Her skill and understanding of a dead dialect have confounded even the most dubious doubters.

During her twenty-four years of channeling, Pearl put over four million words to paper in the form of seven books, and countless poems, short stories, and plays.

Professor of literature W. T. Allison of the University of Manitoba offered this observation about the Curran-Worth team: "They must be regarded as the outstanding phenomenon of our age, and I cannot help thinking of all time."

When asked opinions about events or subjects of the day, Curran would often reply in a one-of-a-kind hybrid language using different dialects from various times. When asked about the nature of life, her reply was, "Life is a gay trickster. Yea, life poureth about the atoms o' man wines of cunning, and equally is he filled up of Him. Thereby is man given freely and his lightening unto life leaveth him for his choosing. Aye, and the giving be wry-fallen atimes, for flesh to tarry long and dance with life, fearing the greater thing athin it."

Published far and wide, Pearl Lenore Curran is one of this country's most controversial yet respected writers. Given her unique and abundant history, it is surprising in the extreme that she is anything but a household name. Had she kept the nature and source of her writing to herself, she may have sat alone as America's finest author. However, when you give credit to an alter ego from two centuries prior, your history can never be truly your own.

Was Pearl Curran speaking her own conscious thoughts and using Patience Worth as a mechanism to give her own observations and opinions more weight and value? Or was she actually a conduit connecting an intellectual energy from the past to the early twentieth century? Maybe some day a modern man or woman may channel the intellect of Curran, and then we will know. Or would that be another version of déjà vu all over again?

Arch Weird

The Arch, on the western bank of the Mississippi River in St. Louis, ranks with skyline features like the Statue of Liberty, the Washington Monument, and the Eiffel Tower. It is the fourth most visited tourist attraction on earth.

In addition to being the eighth wonder of the world, the Arch is also a magnet for thrill seekers attempting to make it their personal playground. It is illegal to use the Arch for anything other than inspiration and a study of history, but this is not a deterrent to many.

Such was the case on June 23, 1966, when a small aircraft flew through the legs of the Arch from an east to west direction. This prompted the Park Service to install surveillance cameras to deter future barnstormers. Despite the cameras, it happened again on April 17, 1971, when another cowboy pilot swooped between the legs of the Arch. Misguided pilots have flown five aircraft between its legs. But pilots are not the only wild men drawn to the legendary attraction.

On November 22, 1980, a skydiver jumped from an airplane and guided his parachute toward the top of the Arch. He intended to land dead center on top, then discard his primary chute and complete the stunt by using his reserve chute to jump to the ground. But his attempt to land on top went awry. He was fatally injured as he slid down the leg of the Arch.

Then came suction-cup man. On September 14, 1992, John Vincent scaled the Arch using suction cups. He made it to the top, and then leaped off to perform a BASE jump. BASE is an acronym for Buildings, Antenna, Spans, and Earth. Maybe he mistakenly thought the A stood for Arch? Mr. Vincent survived, only to be arrested, prosecuted, fined, and put on a ninety-day probation. Not surprisingly, he violated the probation. During Mr. Vincent's revocation hearing, the U.S. district attorney stated, "Mr. Vincent has a serious attitude problem." Ya think?!

Don't let stories of wild men using the Arch as their personal playground prevent you from making the trip to visit this spectacular creation. If you have not been there, put it on your high priority list of things to do.

See How Joel Stacks Up

Most parents have to tell their kids half a dozen times to put away the dishes. However, in the Brown household, when Mom or Dad asks their son Joel to put the cups away, it happens so fast that even the Flash would have to blink twice to see the movements.

You see, Joel Brown, age twelve, is a national and world record holder in the little-known sport of cup stacking. The basics of the sport are simple. While standing at a flat surfaced table of normal height, the object is to see how quickly you can stack and unstack combinations of cups in a specific fashion.

Not just any cups will do. The cups used by the World Sport Stacking Association are sanctioned by that same body and produced to exacting standards by a Colorado-based company, Speed Stacks. In the world of Sport Stacking, all cups must be created equal.

There are three fundamental categories in which to compete. Joel holds national records in his age group in the 3-3-3 (2.27 seconds) and 3-6-3 (2.81 seconds) categories, and a world record in a category called the Cycle, which involves over forty separate motions to complete. Joel completed it in 7.53 seconds. If you want to see animations and detailed instructions of the categories, check out speedstacks.com.

With over twelve thousand schools nationwide having stacking programs as part of their curriculum, it appears the sport may be here to stay, giving future generations hand–eye coordination that would make today's finest sleight of hand artist feel inadequate. At the 2007 World Speed Stacking Association Championships held at the Coliseum in Denver, CO, the 1,153 contestants ranged in age from four to over sixty. So if you thought your athletic career ended three decades ago, this is your opportunity to get back into the game.

Price of Fame

"Holy mother of feathered foul Batman, it's Egghead!" The television series *Batman* was a campy production that enjoyed more popularity in reruns than during its active period in the 1960s. Famous for its over-the-top staged fight scenes along with cartoonish phonetic overlays describing the sounds of a fight, Kapow!, Bonk!, Slaam!, the series was also famous for its villains. Characters like The Riddler, The Penguin, Cat Woman, and the unusually intelligent villain, Egghead. The brainiac Egghead was played by none other than St. Louis's own Vincent Leonard Price.

Price was a perfect choice for the overly smart villain with the exaggerated skull, because if Price was nothing else, he looked smart. If you knew nothing of the man and were to see his photograph, a probable guess as to his occupation would be that he was a distinguished university professor. That would be a good guess, because prior to taking up acting he had obtained degrees in English and art history from Yale University and taught school briefly. Then he attended school in London, where he caught the acting bug.

Price's love and knowledge of Shakespeare boded well for his attaining leading-man dramatic roles, and the additional good fortune of having the facial structure of a nobleman helped significantly. Ironically, his speaking voice was nasal, which might have diminished his potential had it not been that the London-based productions he applied to needed American accents. And so he won leading-man roles, although he had relatively little acting experience. That same nasal quality in his voice lent itself perfectly to the genre of film that for lack of a better term is called horror. While Price did many serious dramatic portrayals, he is best known for his horror gigs.

Anyone who was around in the 1950s and '60s remembers movies such as *The House of Wax, House on Haunted Hill,* and *House of Usher.* If a movie was coming out with the word "house" in its title, you pretty much knew that Vincent Price was going to be the star. With classics like the original *The Fly, The Raven,* and *Tales of Terror,* he had a track record of films that performed solidly.

Vincent's horror movie characters gave him room for a subtle playfulness that seemed to reveal that he was just acting and not really capable of encapsulating your entire body within a shroud of hot wax. After his career as a master of horror had waned, Price remained busy doing television—from *Batman* and *Hollywood Squares* to Michael Jackson's music video for *Thriller* and countless guest spots on programs of the era. He also remained active in theater, and deeply involved in the world of art appreciation and preservation. Vincent Leonard Price died on October 25, 1993, at the age of eighty-two.

Good Ole Father Time

St. Louis has its own Father Time, in the person of eighty-four-year-old Paul Pagano. A resident of Overland, Pagano has for the last twenty-seven years endeared himself to St. Louisans by sharing his special form of unquestioning joy and goodwill at area sporting events, parades, pageants, and holiday festivals.

He is like the Wal-Mart greeter, only genuine. No doubt many people reading this story have seen Paul at some event around the greater St. Louis area. Paul says, "I am known as the St. Louis Patriot, the St. Louis Icon. My nickname is Father Time; I got this name from a Halloween party, dressed like an old man with a beard and called myself Father Time."

Though an unassuming sort, Paul is never shy about having his picture taken with a pretty pageant queen, local celebrity, or just your average Jack and Jill. If his smile is not the element that attracts your attention, it may then be the almost overwhelming amount of red, white, and blue with which he routinely surrounds himself. To say that Paul is patriotic is a monumental understatement. A veteran of the Normandy invasion during World War II, he has earned the right to display his patriotic fervor in any fashion that he chooses.

Paul has been patiently yet eagerly awaiting the time when an advertiser picks him up for use in television and print ads. We say there is no time like the present for Father Time. We'd like to see that beaming smile on local billboards or as part of an endlessly looping television promotion. We think it is time for Father Time to sell cars, homes, entertainment, and St. Louis atmosphere. What do you think?

Personalized Properties

For some people, their house, apartment, or yard is just a place to rest between bouts of work or play. For them, white walls, simple furniture, and irregularly mowed lawns are adequate and anonymous enough, and are all they want to present to their community about themselves. It's as true in Missouri as anywhere else.

But just the same, in Missouri there are plenty of people whose property is out of the ordinary and eye-catching to those of us on the lookout for weirdness. Some of these places take on their unusual appearance out of pure utility, such as the trailers and homes on stilts lining the banks of many Missouri rivers. Then there are other places, created with a passion—some might say an obsession—to show the world their uniqueness. These places can turn into lifetimes of artistic work, perhaps not recognized in the big-time gallery world, but art nevertheless, for their art is in the eye of the beholder.

It's places like these that cause passersby to do double takes, make U-turns, and reach for their cameras. The rich variety encountered in Missouri almost calls for revising its nickname from the Show Me State to the Look at Me State!

Can't See the Forest for the Cars

If someone told you about a place where there were cars stuck in the trees, what would be your best guess as to how they got there? Maybe they washed up in a flood, or maybe they were tossed into a tree by one of Tornado Alley's violent twisters. But that's not the case in Steelville. How these particular cars became arboreal has nothing to do with what you might expect.

Sitting in a deep hollow a few miles west of Steelville is the property of John Marsh. It took quite a bit of effort to find Mr. Marsh's place, as even the local residents (including lifelong residents of the town) had not heard of the "cars in the trees." We were told, however, that John Marsh was easygoing and the salt of the earth, and that virtually anyone in need could drive onto his property, search his vast collection of odds and ends, and then feel welcome to take whatever was needed, free of charge. Mr. Marsh is eighty-two and lives the life of a hermit, with no indoor plumbing or telephone.

Our journey to Mr. Marsh's tarpaper shack began with a turn onto his driveway, which was clearly marked by multicolor plastic soda bottles hanging from the trees. These ornamental efforts are seen sporadically all over his more than five-hundred-acre homestead. When we were on the steeply descending dirt driveway, we were greeted by hundreds upon hundreds of bicycles lining the entire quarter-mile length of the rapidly dropping path that ultimately leads to this monument to clutter.

Marsh's property is part of Missouri's most beautiful landscape overall; however, his years of "collecting" have given it a new appearance. At the bottom of the drive sat a dozen old, dilapidated mobile home trailers. They were all in bad shape, with few having doors or windows. Whatever had been stored in them at some time in the past now decorates the outside surrounds and adds to the mounting debris around his ramshackle living space.

It is when you reach his living quarters that the true experience of John Marsh begins. Surrounding his twenty-by-fifteen-foot shack is a collection of junk that can best be described as a monumental justification for tetanus shots. There are more rusting relics of machines, toys, contraptions, furniture, tires, auto parts, and half-finished projects than is humanly possible to catalogue. A narrow pathway leads to the front door of his tarpaper abode, the facade of which is adorned with the skulls of countless long-dead four-legged beasts (and the remnants of a few that slithered).

In another life, John Marsh was a machinist by trade. He would drive from his hollow-based home on a daily basis on a journey that took him from Steelville through the town of Cuba and then on into work near St. Louis. Along the way, he would pick up collectibles, and this is how John slowly built his empire of trash — er — collectibles.

When *Weird Missouri* told him that we were there because we'd heard about the cars in the trees, John didn't seem surprised. To him the treed cars serve a very practical purpose: They function as deer stands that protect him from the weather while hunting. We had to agree that it was a clever use of what would otherwise be just another rusting hulk in his vast collection of rusting hulks.

But how did this elderly man hoist cars forty feet into the air and into the trees? When asked, John said he would simply climb the chosen tree, dragging along a block and tackle. He would then hoist the cab of a car or truck up the tree and secure it with chains and a substructure of wood. A come-along completed the job of getting the entire car up the tree.

John does not limit himself to merely placing cars aboveground. Prior to building his tarpaper shack, John lived in a thirty-foot school bus that leans into the trees, chained in place and supported by a foundation of stone and used car wheels. It seems that John can put anything in the trees that his heart desires. Luckily, he does not see any obstacles to making it happen.

To say the least, John Marsh is a unique and independent person. He is also innovative and hard-working. And, as confirmed by the many people we spoke to both before and after meeting him, he is indeed a very nice guy who happens to be a little eccentric. Which, here at *Weird Missouri*, is our favorite kind of person.

Steel Wheels

Over time, tires have been made of many different materials. Steel and iron tires were wrapped around wooden wagon wheels. Stagecoaches and hay wagons were commonly found with metal tires, and both heavy excavation equipment and railroad locomotives sported steel tires.

Steel-wheeled farm machines represent a time when American agribusiness was burgeoning. But steel-tired tractors were notorious for their unforgiving harsh ride. In 1931, tractor technology made a leap forward in capability when the Allis-Chalmers Company developed the rubber pneumatic tractor tire. This new tire greatly increased safety and longevity for both the tractor and its operator.

Pneumatic tires spelled the end of an era, but not an end to those who appreciate the steel-wheel generation of farm machines. One such admirer has amassed an amazing collection of relics from yesteryear, most in surprisingly good condition. It includes countless tractors, combines, harrows, discs, baling machines, rakes, plows, ride-behind seats, and many other items that *Weird Missouri* can't figure out. He keeps them proudly displayed on his front yard for all to see as they travel that harrowing road, Route 160 near West Plains.

Bob Smithy, the Trucker Artist

Bob Smithy never set out to be a folk artist. In fact, from the 1950s onward he has spent his life as a trucker. After many decades out on the road, Smithy realized he knew how to fix trucks pretty well, so he opened a shop in Plevna. It was there, and with those tools, that he entered the world of outsider art.

Sometimes great artists learn their craft in art school. Some immerse themselves into big-city art scenes to soak up as much culture and craft as they can from fellow talent. Bob Smithy never had these luxuries. Instead, his work was born out of what was lying around him and a desire to get people on the road to stop at his shop.

To advertise the shop, Smithy took a few leftover junked metal items and welded them into the shapes of male and female figures. From there, something of an obsession grew. He continues to make human figures and even throws in an animal from time to time. All his sculptures continue to be made of found materials. He generally has about twenty figures standing outside his shop, which actually outnumbers the total living residents of the town.

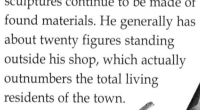

BoatHenge

The Katy Trail, at 225 miles long, is a Missouri state park recognized as the longest Rails-to-Trails path in the United States. Visitors know it as a fantastic place to jog and bike. Others regard its sections along the Missouri River as a great place to launch a canoe for a lazy afternoon of paddling in quiet bliss.

Since 2003, the Katy Trail has become known for something far different from any of these recreational uses. It was during that year that BoatHenge was born. In the few years since, BoatHenge has grown into a personalized property of the highest caliber.

A semicircular ring of boats buried standing upright halfway into the ground, BoatHenge may seem to the bewildered joggers passing by to be the worshiping grounds of some strange cult dedicated to seafaring. In reality, it is the brainchild of one Scott Melton, a Boone County resident who has lived along the Missouri River since 1978.

Throughout those three decades, Melton, who is better known by his nickname, Catfish, has spent a lot of time boating up and down the river. And in the course of doing so, he has wound up with a lot of boats that became so worn out they were eventually retired. He placed them outside the small cabin he rents on a farm owned by Carl and Anne Orazio, located along the trail between Rocheport and Jefferson City. Simply put, Catfish had a lot of sentimental memories attached to each boat and couldn't bear the thought of putting any of them out to pasture for good.

As the number of boats grew, the Orazios began expressing concerns. They had young children who enjoyed roaming the grounds of the farm and spent a lot of their time down at the riverfront. The couple were afraid that the junked boats would be too tempting for the kids and that they might climb up on them, fall, and get hurt.

It's easy to see that few are as devoted as Scott "Catfish" Melton, and his affection for [the Missouri River] shines through in his upright creation, BoatHenge.

While the Orazios are conscientious parents, they're also not dictators bent on imposing their will on those around them. They had known Catfish for years and asked him not to junk the boats, but to find a creative way to make them safe. When an acquaintance was working on property in the area with a backhoe, Catfish saw his chance. He asked his friend to bring the equipment up by his cabin, where they then spent the day drinking and digging holes. They placed the boats in the formation in which they currently stand.

BoatHenge is fascinating, but it is hard to come across casually. Its location along the Katy Trail means that only bikers, joggers, and boaters who make their way deep into the Boone County woods get a chance to see it up close with their own eyes. For those who are unable to make this trek, www.boathenge.net has been created. This tongue-in-cheek Web site treats BoatHenge as if it were as ancient and mysterious as its inspiration, Stonehenge in England. The site weaves fantastical tales about BoatHenge's history, claiming it simply fell from the sky, as well as making grandiose claims in regard to its magical properties. It captures not just images of BoatHenge but the irreverent, creative attitudes that led to its creation.

Many who spend time along this desolate section of the Missouri River find themselves fiercely devoted to it. It's easy to see that few are as devoted as Scott "Catfish" Melton, and his affection for this place shines through in his upright creation, BoatHenge.

Cathedral of the Prince of Peace

Bishop Karl Pruter was already a very accomplished man by the time he moved to Highlandville in the early 1980s. He was a leader in Christ Catholic Church, and in that position he had been regarded as one of the more influential members of the Old Catholic movement—a group that split from the Roman Catholic Church in the nineteenth century. Bishop Pruter's move to the quiet Ozark town was an intentional effort to find a place where things moved a little more slowly and where things were a little bit smaller.

Things certainly were smaller here than they were in Pruter's previous stomping grounds of Philadelphia and Boston—and not just metaphorically but literally as well. Pruter made sure of this personally by building the Cathedral of the Prince of Peace. Upon arriving in his new home, Pruter noticed that an old, broken-down shed stood on his property. He immediately renovated the space and turned it into an elaborate, beautiful, yet tiny cathedral, which, at fourteen by eighteen feet, can seat only about a dozen people. It has been certified by no less an authority than *Guinness World Records* as the smallest cathedral in the world.

Pruter immediately went to work in his cathedral, delivering sermons on a regular basis. He held daily Mass there, and services were taken as seriously as they would be in any average-sized church. While other tiny churches throughout America serve more as tourist attractions or novelties, Pruter's was a fully functioning worship site. Pruter preached out of the Cathedral of the Prince of Peace from the time of its building until his retirement in 2007. Now Bishop Brian E. Brown leads services there on a weekly basis.

Despite its diminutive nature, the cathedral has many of the accoutrements one would expect to find in any church. Catholic iconography adorns the tiny altar. And while the building is so small that there is room for only one small square window on each side, those windows are stained glass, as one might expect to find at any Catholic church.

Father Pruter was known for having the energy of a much younger man. His retirement was a sign to many who knew him that the years were finally catching up to him. This proved to be true. In November 2007, the good bishop passed away.

Pruter's memorial service was going to be held at the Cathedral of the Prince of Peace, but the number of people who came out to show their affection for the bishop was far beyond the capacity of the World's Smallest Cathedral. A Mass was held that morning at the cathedral, and then a larger service was held nearby, at a location where people could fit comfortably.

Fittingly, Karl Pruter's remains are interred at the Cathedral of the Prince of Peace. Not only was the cathedral a large part of Pruter's life work, but it is the ultimate reflection of how he wanted to spend that life—in a peaceful, quiet place.

The Hammer Man

It is said that true love knows no limits. And Glenn Albrecht of Norborne loves hammers. In 1978, when he was already over the age of sixty, Glenn bought himself an antique hammer. This led to an outright obsession with the tools. Glenn set out to track down and purchase rare, antique hammers from around the world. His collection grew large, to well over three thousand hammers. Eventually, he opened up a museum dedicated to putting his massive collection on display.

Glenn's museum is a completely overwhelming place. The walls are nearly three stories high and are, along with the rafters and a series of freestanding walls Glenn has erected throughout the space, covered with hammers and other tools. There is not an inch of the building that isn't devoted to hammers or tools closely related to them.

Albrecht is also famous for personally taking people on tours of his museum. His boundless enthusiasm will convert even the most unconvinced to believe that seeing thousands of hammers is a worthy endeavor.

Voltaire once said that "love is a canvas furnished by nature and embroidered by imagination." In the case of Glenn Albrecht, known more commonly as the Hammer Man, it would probably be more accurate to say that "love is a canvas furnished by hammers and embroidered by one man's complete dedication to them."

Bobs and Bobras

When traveling down Aspen Road in Highlandville, be careful. Some of the residents love to stare you down. This isn't a *Deliverance* type situation, where untrusting locals try to intimidate you with their menacing looks. In fact, it isn't even the people that stare out at you—it's the statues.

The statues in question, known as Bobs and Bobras, are the handiwork of sculptor John Tygart. They are large stone heads, some male and some female, that he has placed all over his property. Some stick out of the ground, others are stuck to walls, others are hidden in hard-to-find places, but they're everywhere. Besides the multitude of large stone heads, Tygart has also placed ceramic animals and people all over his property. The man, simply put, is driven to set his own personal world in stone.

Tygart runs a pottery studio to pay the bills. But his profession clearly doesn't stay in the office. One look at his yard shows that John Tygart always has sculpting on his mind!

MO Castles

Castles are a statement primarily associated with European landscapes. However, castles in some form can be found in most cultures across the globe, including the United States. Many Americans found the robust and secure architectural style of the castle sufficiently compelling to invest time and money to create their own structures.

Across the country are several castles that were purchased in Europe, dismantled, transported to the States and reassembled to provide a genuine experience for the owners. To our knowledge, no such building exists in Missouri. But the state is home to about twenty castlelike structures, and there are four in particular that leave no doubt that the intent was to build something with the feel of a European original.

Stuart Castle is located on the Meramec River in St. Louis County. Its style is similar to those of early European residences that were surrounded by a defensive wall. With its handsome facade it evokes the sense that titled lords and ladies must live inside. Adding to the aura of nobility is the boldly emblazoned, ten-foot-tall S that is displayed at the front entrance. The structure was apparently built over an existing turn-of-the-nineteenth-century home and has endured periods of neglect; however, it has recently been given a facelift by new owners.

In the Pendleton Heights area of Kansas City there is Tiffany Castle. Built in 1908 for $35,000, it boasts a huge rooftop garden, a basement gymnasium, and floors imported from Great Britain. The castle's original owner was Dr. Flavel B. Tiffany, an optometrist who founded the University Medical College in 1889. He was a mover and shaker of his time, and his castle is reflective of his desire to flash his cash.

The City Work House castle is also located in the Kansas City area, on Vine Street. Constructed in 1897, it served as a city prison. The building's substantial appearance must have diminished any thoughts of escape entertained by the desperate men arriving there.

Old Cross Castle looks as if it has been transplanted from Disney World onto a Lake of the Ozarks hillside. It is an imposing building of concrete-block construction and one of Missouri's newest efforts at living the castle lifestyle. This edifice is the handiwork of one man and his highly supportive and energetic spouse. Work began in 1988 and is expected to be finished when the last detail is complete; meaning it is a labor of love that will go on for as long as it goes on.

Across the country are several castles that were purchased in Europe, dismantled, transported to the States and reassembled to provide a genuine experience for the owners.

left, Tiffany Castle

David Smith's Whirligigs from Beyond

Those traveling down Kirkham Avenue in Webster Groves may be under the mistaken perception that they're under attack from alien invaders. In actuality, they're experiencing the strange work of artist David Smith.

Whirligigs are objects that spin in the wind. Smith creates the metallic pieces, then adds his own personal twist—his show-off imagery of green aliens. He takes metal objects from junkyards and refashions them into funky, spinning, bright green, literally out of this world art.

Smith didn't establish an alien theme in his art due to a longstanding fascination with visitors from beyond. Instead, he just liked bright green because of his poor eyesight. This limitation has created a truly unique piece of property where spinning aliens have taken to the skies.

It is a private residence, and we know nothing of its owner other than that he or she could survive during any era of the human time line.

Maysville's Dirt Igloo

Maysville, the seat of Dekalb County, is an isolated burg in northeast Missouri. With a population of just over twelve hundred people, it is one of those farm communities where you expect to experience good old American consistency, including in the kinds of houses that are built there.

But Maysville is also home to what is believed to be Missouri's only earthen igloo. It is a private residence, and we know nothing of its owner other than that he or she could survive during any era of the human time line. This is your dirt-basic domicile.

It's easy to miss. From the road it looks like a large pile of dirt, maybe an excavation in progress. It is about forty feet in diameter and about fifteen feet high. It is wrapped in what looks like roofing tarpaper that is supported by tall stakes driven into the ground to support the vertical rise of the pile of dirt and what pass for the exterior walls. It resembles a bunker as much as it does an igloo and is not the most attractive place to live.

But then we've not seen the interior. How the owner heats the inner space is unknown. Possibly it has the climate of a cave, with stable annual temperatures. One thing is clear: While Maysville may indeed be the county seat, zoning standards there are minimal.

The Eagle Has Nested

Reeds Spring is a small hamlet just northwest of Branson. Past home to Bob White's Museum of the Unexplained (see "Unexplained Phenomena"), it is also the longtime site of what could be called the Eagle's Nest: Stone Experience. At least, that's what we call it.

Running for about the length of a football field on East Main Street (Route 265), Eagle's Nest is a remarkable, if questionable, creation. It looks like it simply evolved from moment to moment, as if a formal plan was never considered.

But it does have many extraordinary features and creatures. A *Tyrannosaurus rex* sits center stage, along with a huge soaring eagle. Expertly constructed stone terraces abound, and there are water features with jumping fish, turtles, giant mushrooms, and an alligator. There are also two gigantic satellite dishes that either suck in television signals or maintain contact with the home planet.

A long, eight-foot-tall iron fence protects the entire creation. The home next to it is a sprawling arrangement of contemporary-looking buildings that probably total several thousand square feet of living space. At the time of our visit, the property was for sale. It will be a difficult place to market if the owner's asking price reflects the emotional investment made in what is obviously a work of passion.

So if you happen to drive through Reeds Spring (don't blink; it isn't big) be sure to try to take in all that Eagle's Nest is trying to communicate. The exact message is difficult to decipher, but no matter what one thinks of the odd collection of yard ornaments, it is an impressive creation in total.

Centralia: Land of the Lost

Many millions of years ago, dinosaurs roamed the earth. But the rumors that they have gone extinct are in fact incorrect. Many metal versions of the monsters still stand on the property of Larry Vennard, a unique artist who lives in Centralia.

Vennard first constructed a *Tyrannosaurus rex* on his property because he lives on the T Highway. Fearing that the monstrous metallic rendition of the lizard looked lonely out there, he followed this up with a series of other dinosaurs, then sculpted an accompanying band of prehistoric men set in poses to show they were fighting off those beasts, ignoring scientific history. From there, Vennard's imagination spiraled out of control and his productivity shot through the roof. This has led to a lawn packed with many creatures, both real and fantastical, which make it look more like a vision from the prehistoric Land of the Lost than a modern Centralia yard.

While the land and the statues on it are private property, Vennard does welcome visitors. Please be respectful and come at a reasonable hour, but beyond that, feel free to experience and enjoy these incredible creations up close and personal.

Mobile Homes on Stilts

We were unlucky in our quest to see the phantom steamboat reported to appear at the confluence of the Osage and Missouri rivers near Bonnots Mill, but in the process of trying to do so we found something equally odd: mobile homes on stilts.

The flood of '93 prompted a lot of river folk to adapt or leave. When in Bonnots Mill proper, use the post office as a point of orientation and then walk toward the river. The trailers on stilts will be a couple of hundred feet in front of you.

Mobile homes on stilts: What clever and stubborn Missouri River folk do to keep the view that they love.

Lanning Garden Lawn Museum

"I knew right off that you was from out of town, because locals just whiz by," said the diminutive Ralph Lanning as we walked up to the massive collection of concrete statues in his yard. He was dressed in a layered look reminiscent of Katharine Hepburn in the *African Queen*, and his wavering speech patterns and high energy have a Hepburn-like quality to them. He is the kind of person that you like immediately, with the energy of a far more youthful person. Ralph must be in his late eighties, but he appears much younger.

Finding the Lanning Garden Lawn Museum was quite easy. It's located about ten miles south of Springfield and is almost impossible to miss if you are driving north on Route 60. Adorned with almost one hundred Lanning-made concrete lawn statues, the homestead's nicely manicured lawn is indeed an eye-catcher. Travelers will often pull off to ogle the handiwork, and frequently their children will run through the yard and climb on the statues as if it were a public playground. Lanning said, "I do not mind children climbing on the statues, but I do take exception to the parents placing their kids on statues to take pictures."

Lanning has answered countless tactless questions from visitors, including the all-encompassing, "Why?" He almost immediately volunteered, "People think I'm crazy, but I don't care." Ralph Lanning is anything but crazy. He is actually a person that you soon feel protective of, a gentle soul with a unique vision.

The amount of work involved in creating the lawn museum is substantial. Lanning started in 1963, when he found his mission in creating statuary-based messages for anyone who will pay attention. Some of his work has its roots in mythology, including a formidable-looking, two-headed dragon-type beast, and mermaids. Other pieces have a religious influence: a small, white chapel with a sweeping staircase that leads to a see-through entrance, a crucifixion, angels, and praying hands. There is also a sculpture that looks like a giant wedding ring and another of a huge heart with the inscription IF HEAVEN IS HALF AS BEAUTIFUL AS HERE ON EARTH I DON'T WANT TO MISS IT.

Lanning's creative efforts are ongoing. He has already strung extension cords to power an electric jackhammer, intending to undo some of his earlier work and make changes that are more to his liking. It seems that as long as Ralph Lanning has the physical wherewithal, he will be out in the sunshine creating statues that make people stop and take notice.

Jesse "Outlaw" Howard, the Sign Man of Missouri

When Jesse "Outlaw" Howard died in 1983, it marked the passing of one of America's most prolific folk artists. Passionate not necessarily about art but about his message, Howard's persistence in spreading his words led him to become an artist nonetheless.

Howard lived in Fulton, and it's fair to say that he was mad. He was mad about politics, he was mad about taxation, and he was mad that his neighbors were always trying to have the police come and take him away. So to vent his frustrations he went grassroots and began posting handmade signs detailing his various views on all of his various causes. At any given point there would be literally thousands of signs on his property.

They eventually came to cover not just his entire yard but also his entire house. He then began to mix religious-themed signs in with the political ones. As his signs grew in number, Outlaw's home went from being a soapbox for his political opinions to becoming a huge collage.

At one point, some residents of Fulton got together and tried to have Jesse committed to an institution. The effort failed because, by this time, most people in the town had come to embrace Mr. Howard and his strange signs. In fact, Howard eventually stopped making signs because people kept taking them. When everyone wanted Howard to stop, he kept going. When people started expressing interest in the signs and even outright taking them for their own, he stopped.

Though the home where his signs were originally displayed was bulldozed in 1989, some of Jesse Howard's work still survives and occasionally comes up for auction. It has been put on display in the Kansas City Art Institute and New York City's Museum of American Folk Art.

Who Could It Yurt?

The town of Branson is home to a large collection of Americana-based attractions (many of which barely cling to normal architectural margins themselves), but it's not where one would expect to find something as exotic as a Mongolian yurt.

Yet there it is, large and permanently nestled into the roadside trees. It's easy to miss if you're not looking for a yurt, but whether you find it on your first attempt or have to make a U-turn, once you're in the small parking lot you'll be able to take in the odd roofline covering this roughly fifty-foot-diameter structure.

While Branson's yurt holds true to the general shape of the genuine Mongolian variety, its permanence negates its authenticity. True Mongolian yurts are collapsible tents that can be quickly assembled or disassembled for easy transport, similar to Native American tepees. They are typically composed of a simple wooden frame and covered with wool.

Tom Hess and Lory Brown chose far more substantial materials, as they wanted to create a commercial space to produce and market their artistic wares to the tourists drawn to the Branson area every year. They chose large-dimension timbers as the supporting structure and then found a deal on six thousand board feet of southern yellow pine in Hot Springs, Arizona. With the help of friends this pine became the rigid ceiling that defines the yurt's roof outline. The side walls are also wooden and contain large, open-air windows that allow summer breezes to cool the inside. The floor is crushed stone, and Tom and Lory display their wares on tables around the yurt's inner circumference.

The center portion of the yurt is the working space. On one winter visit this space was surrounded by hanging canvases in order to keep it a comfortable temperature for Tom, a lifelong potter. Lory is an experienced basket weaver. Tom and Lory have over fifty-five years of artistic experience between them. If you'd like to meet these creative Missourians and see their unusual roadside structure, then a trip to the Branson area on Route 413 is in order.

Chinaman's Castle

On Alswel Road, in the Sunset Hills section of St. Louis, stands a large mansion known officially as Alswel. Originally built by William Lemp of the Lemp Brewing Company, the building is known more commonly by the politically incorrect moniker of Chinaman's Castle.

For this to make sense, it must be mentioned that the area around Alswel did not always look the way it does now. Decades ago, Alswel sat atop a hill, surrounded only by a series of small, outlying buildings built in the same style as the mansion. This was private property, and visitors could only get close enough to see the mansion from the bottom of the hill. If they were daring, they would walk up the hill, hoping not to get caught. This was a very popular rite of passage for many a youth who grew up in the St. Louis area.

According to one rumor, the reason the estate was referred to as Chinaman's Castle is that between the different buildings were statues of Chinese men. This ornamentation seemed odd to those who were sneaking up the long gravel driveway to the ominous house on the hill. Others say that the elaborate architecture was so out of place in mid-century St. Louis that it was given a nickname that reflected the perception that it was an exotic building. Either way, the name stuck, and still sticks, to the building.

All the outlying buildings surrounding Alswel were destroyed in the 1980s. The main building was almost lost as well. Thankfully, its place on the National Register ultimately saved it. These days its legend is not as widespread, although many still whisper about the lore surrounding the intriguing Chinaman's Castle.

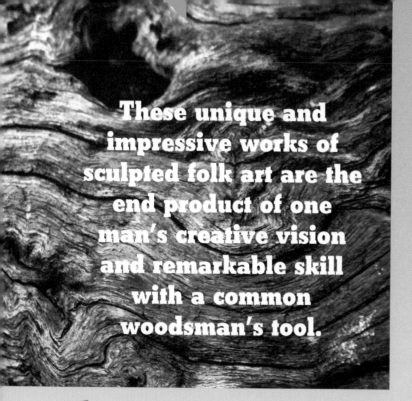

These unique and impressive works of sculpted folk art are the end product of one man's creative vision and remarkable skill with a common woodsman's tool.

Champion with a Chain Saw

Located just a half mile south of Interstate 44 at the Stanton exit is a small, log-cabin–style building. You can't miss it on your way to Meramec Caverns, as it has many eye-catching sculptures sitting on its front porch, adorning the exterior walls, and placed proudly around the building's exterior. There's also a full-sized caboose that sits adjacent to the log structure.

That the building is made of logs is only appropriate, since all the art being displayed in and around the store began as a tree. These unique and impressive works of sculpted folk art are the end product of one man's creative vision and remarkable skill with a common woodsman's tool. The man with the vision? Gary Patterson. The sculpting tool? The chain saw.

A retired railroad conductor, Gary began sculpting with chain saws in 1986 and went on to help pioneer this style of art. His artistic flair and innovative techniques allowed him to win five grand national championships and two world titles. Unfortunately, he died in 2003 at the age of fifty-two.

Gary's sculptures are typically based upon nature and the American West. From his work it is obvious that he admired both Native Americans and the American eagle, and the majority of his pieces revolve around the close relationship that exists between America's original inhabitants and Mother Nature.

His ability to convey the majesty of the American eagle is seen in his amazing duplication of the dimensions of the bird's wingspan and the shape of the wing. The revealing expressions he carved on the faces of Indians he portrayed further demonstrate his ability with what most people think of as a coarse sculpting instrument.

One of Gary's special gifts was his ability to work fast. Many of his fantastic pieces were created in competitions where artists have only eight hours to complete their sculptures. His last competitive piece—ironically titled *That Final Cut*—was created in six hours. He would often complete his sculpture during a competition and then walk among his fellow artists, offering encouragement as they struggled to complete their work within the allotted time.

Hundreds of tourists on their way to tour Jesse James's reputed hideout, Meramec Caverns, would stop at Gary's store. They frequently commissioned custom pieces of chain saw art, which Gary would complete during their two-hour tour of the caverns.

Gary Patterson's work is unusual and impressive because of the tools of his trade, and his art has virtually tripled in value since his death. So if you are in the market for a unique form of true Missouri folk art that's also an investment, take the Stanton exit off Interstate 44.

Leila's Hair Museum

Located in what used to be a Wendy's restaurant, the Hair Museum sits on the busy commercial interchange of South Noland Road in Independence, Jackson County. When you enter the museum, a docent greets you and cheerfully takes you on a guided tour. It definitely helps to have some background on this unique form of folk art as you view the hundred-plus hair wreaths and over two thousand examples of human hair-based jewelry in the museum.

Charlotte Plamer, a longtime friend of museum founder Leila Cohoon, explained the significance of the wreaths: "[They] are about family history and genealogy: It is a family tree in the form of human hair folk art." If you know this, the creations hanging in the modest museum gain special significance.

A family wreath is typically a horseshoe shape, allowing additional family members to add hair to it over time. Some of the wreaths are quite large, having diameters of two feet. Plamer explained, "It is believed that a hair wreath that has grown into a complete circle represents the end of a family line or name." All the wreaths are protected and displayed in glass-enclosed frames.

The jewelry comes in many forms, including bracelets, necklaces, earrings, brooches, and hatpins. An especially interesting variation on hair jewelry comes in a form called sepia. A scene or portrait that is meaningful to the artist is made with paints made from human hair, which is ground and pulverized, then mixed with paint and used to create colorful "remembrance" rings and necklaces. Hair as an art form dates back to the fifteenth century but has few practitioners now.

Leila Cohoon, a hairstylist, opened the museum in the 1970s. Since then, many thousands of visitors have marveled at the family histories represented here. Leila acquires the pieces through auctions, garage sales, direct hair sales, and donations. She has no favorites, saying, "My favorite piece is every piece. That hair is the only piece of that human being that is still here today and can be touched. I think that is very special."

There's famous hair here too, from Elvis Presley, Marilyn Monroe, Abraham Lincoln, Aaron Burr, and Daniel Webster. There is also a hair wreath donated by comedian Phyllis Diller, who is known as much for her remarkable string of bad hair days as for her ribald humor. But bad hair days were a moot point for some whose hair is on display. There are two wreaths made from the hair of two sisters who had to give up their crowning glory upon entering a convent.

The museum is also home to the Victorian Hairwork Society, a formal organization for people who have a passion for understanding and continuing this unique art form. The society's purpose is serious, but they are not without a sense of humor. Their first formal gathering, in 1998, was called the Hair Ball.

Leila Cohoon had the insight to recognize hair art's significance and the disciplined business acumen to create a museum for all to enjoy. But for Leila, who has spent her life involved with the betterment and presentation of a head of human hair, the collection and display is a labor of love. You may or may not find a visit here to be a hair-raising experience, but it is worth the insight you'll gain as to how humans have produced an art form based upon their own locks.

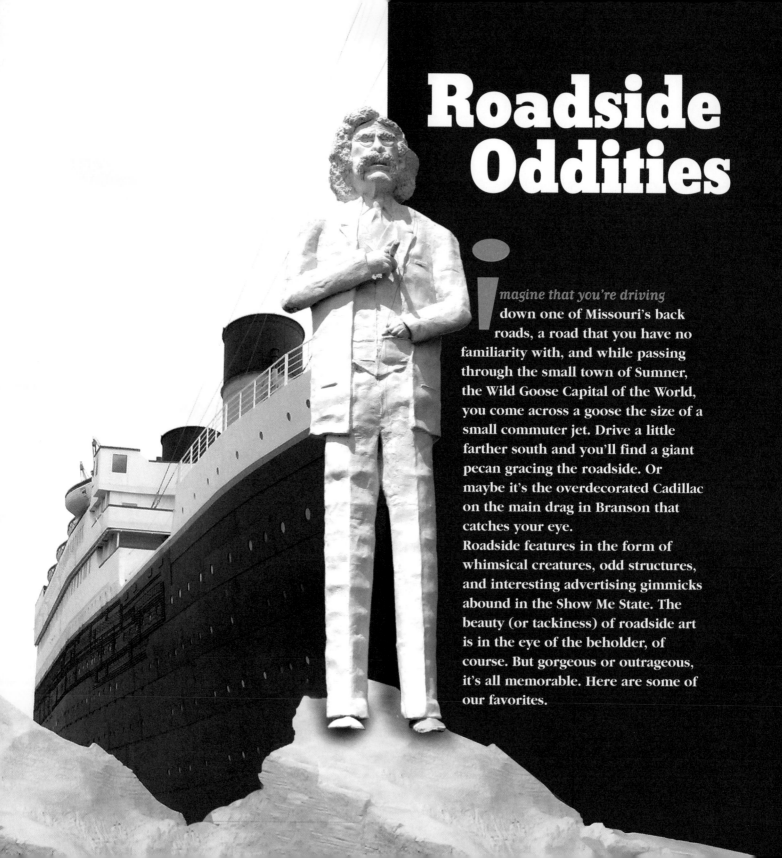

Roadside Oddities

imagine that you're driving down one of Missouri's back roads, a road that you have no familiarity with, and while passing through the small town of Sumner, the Wild Goose Capital of the World, you come across a goose the size of a small commuter jet. Drive a little farther south and you'll find a giant pecan gracing the roadside. Or maybe it's the overdecorated Cadillac on the main drag in Branson that catches your eye.

Roadside features in the form of whimsical creatures, odd structures, and interesting advertising gimmicks abound in the Show Me State. The beauty (or tackiness) of roadside art is in the eye of the beholder, of course. But gorgeous or outrageous, it's all memorable. Here are some of our favorites.

Missouri's Pole Signs

What would Missouri businesses do without the highway elevated pole sign? Or the creatures impaled on poles, or posed on rooftops, trailers, pedestals, and just about any aboveground location? Signs on the tops of poles are not unique to Missouri by any means, but the state has taken the concept to the next level in kind, altitude, and number.

The next time you are driving down Route 40, Route 44, or Route 70, take a look at the horizon and count the pole signs. Notice the creatures on display attempting to grab your eye. Signs competing against signs competing against still more signs! It's Sign Wars.

The poles are fascinating in their number and height, but equally if not more curious than the conventional signs are the objects mounted on top of these vertical icons. Cars on poles, horses on poles, cows on poles, boats on poles, airplanes on poles, bowling pins on poles . . . you get the idea.

About the only product not mounted on poles are poles themselves. Poles are Missouri's universal advertising platform, and they are in no shortage all across the state.

Puttin' on the Ritz in Frankenstein

Missouri has a unique connection to Frankenstein. The only city in the United States to own that name, Frankenstein is not large. But it has quite an impressive church, a very nice sports field just outside town, and was where the twenty-fifth anniversary of the Mel Brooks movie *Young Frankenstein* was celebrated.

The celebration brought film crews and media to a town rarely visited by such high-flying types. The highlight of the day's events was twenty-five sky divers dressed as Frankenstein and reportedly singing "Puttin' on the Ritz" while jumping. That must have been a truly monstrous sound.

Yeah, But They Don't Eat Much

We make no claim to being equine experts, but we're pretty sure that the metallic critters seen grazing in front of the Stadium West branch of the First National Bank in Columbia are of a breed that does not have to fear being sent to the glue factory . . . but then, there is always the metal scrap yard.

Penology, Vend-O-Matic Style

In 1886, Daviess County historian David Stark says a novel plan was presented to the Gallatin township city council—a new system of rotating jail cells that would enhance their existing two-cell stone jail. The plan was approved a year later, and the squirrel cage jail of Gallatin was constructed in 1888 for just over $11,000, or about as much as it took to feed the average prisoner of 2007 for about six months.

The cylindrical jail comprised eight pie-slice–shaped jail cells, each of which was designed to hold two prisoners. The jailer would use a wheel that was connected by gears to a rotating undercarriage that, when turned, would rotate each cell to a main door. It was here that each prisoner could be moved in and out of his cell, and where he was presented with meals. In the old days, the jailer was typically the sheriff's wife. She would prepare the meals, and in the case of the squirrel cage system, use the wheel to rotate each cell into position. When operating properly, the rotation did not require a lot of physical strength.

David Stark said, "It was the thinking of the jail's designers, city council, and the jailers that the rotating cells were much safer for both the jailer and the prisoner." Since it was constructed of brick, cement, and steel, it was believed that the opportunity for fire was remote. Stark also revealed that "because the roof was constructed of copper, it proved to be a weak link in the security, as several prisoners pried sheets of roofing apart in order to make their escape." And because the jail was a one-story facility, once on the roof it was an easy drop to ground level and a (usually temporary) freedom.

Leave it to a Missouri jurisdiction to develop a style of incarceration that was seventy-five years ahead of the fast-food industry. Whether you call it a criminal rotisserie, a wheel of misfortune, or a squirrel cage jail, it is one of only three left in the country.

W. H. Croaker

In its heyday, U.S. Route 66, the Main Street of America, inspired mile after mile of roadside attractions designed to catch the eye of tourists on their way to adventure. Sadly, Route 66 gave way to the larger, and less interesting, Interstate Highway System. And yet, although it was officially decommissioned in 1985, the classic byway refuses to fade away, still giving birth to the occasional roadside oddity. In Waynesville, one such curiosity had existed for eons before it was added to the highway's list of oddball attractions. Hidden alongside a stretch of asphalt that survives today as "Historic" Route 66, it took a demolition crew and a load of dynamite to unearth it.

As the Department of Transportation was adding lanes to the roadway in the mid-'90s, they blasted out part of Waynesville Hill, revealing a conspicuous stone outcropping in the process. When the highway was reopened, the locals adopted the old rock as their new mascot.

Of course, "Old Sedimentary" didn't make for a very good T-shirt. So first they had to turn the slab into something a little more tourist friendly. And since the outcropping seemed to resemble—at least if you squinted—a great big frog, they asked local tattoo artist Phil Nelson to paint it up and slap on some big, buggy eyes.

City officials named him W. H. Croaker (W. H. for Waynesville Hill) and immediately set about turning their greenback into some cash. For more than a decade now, Waynesville has been holding an annual Frog Fest, with Mr. Croaker as its figurehead.

Every May, visitors turn out to take pictures with the frog, eat frog legs, and—just let your imagination run with this one—participate in a frog-kissing contest.—*Wesley Treat*

This Is Too Precious

When you think of precious moments, do you think of holding your infant son or daughter for the first time? Or a special time with someone you love? Me too. But the Carthage-based Precious Moments Park and Chapel takes the precious concept several steps beyond what the average person might expect.

If you aren't familiar with Precious Moments, it is a culture unto itself, based upon porcelain figurines that millions of devotees collect, trade, and treasure for their unique look and inspirational messages. The figurines have huge, teardrop-shaped eyes and round faces that impart complete innocence. Created by illustrator Samuel J. Butcher, Precious Moments is about the love of man, life, and God's teachings based on a Christian frame of reference.

That culture has expanded to the park and chapel, also designed by Mr. Butcher. Every year tens of thousands of visitors tour the elaborate grounds and experience the inner wonder of the chapel.

Inspired by the Sistine Chapel, the Precious Moments Chapel is replete with murals depicting stories from both the Old and New Testaments, along with a large mural that represents a heavenly setting for children whose lives were taken too soon. In all, there are over five thousand square feet of murals, all hand-

painted by Mr. Butcher, including the elaborate ceiling. His tribute to Michelangelo, one would presume.

The grounds surrounding the chapel are bordered with many large statues of Precious Moment figures. Even on the way into the main parking lot there's a brightly painted display of a travel trailer with figurines standing nearby.

Whether you can relate to the Precious Moments experience or not, it is fun to watch visitors enjoy themselves unself-consciously. Many have traveled a great distance to be at the epicenter of the Precious Moments empire. As they exit their cars and walk into the main building, you can see their body language change as their anticipation for what awaits inside heightens. In a pretty rough world, that's sort of precious in itself.

Mark Twain: A Literary Giant

Mark Twain, the pen name of Samuel Langhorne Clemens, was indeed a giant of his day. A humorist, adventurer, and astute observer of life, in his literature Twain captured the hearts and imaginations of his time and ours. But was he really twenty-five feet tall? This likeness of Twain stands near the southbound lanes of Route 61, about three miles south of Hannibal.

St. Louis Baseball

The last ten years have been good for St. Louis baseball. In 1998, Mark McGuire broke the single-season record for home runs by hitting seventy of them. Since then, the Cardinals have taken seven Eastern Division titles, two National League pennants, and most recently, St. Louis won the 2006 World Series. The baseball sitting atop a building on Route 70 directly across from the Scottrade Center surely represents the city's passion for the game.

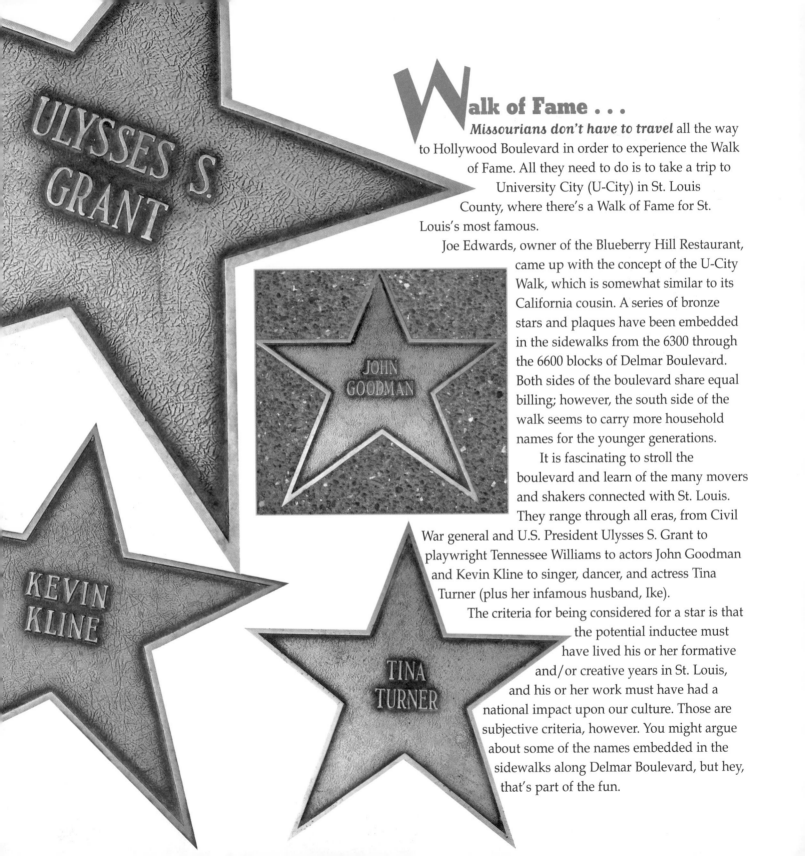

Walk of Fame . . .

Missourians don't have to travel all the way to Hollywood Boulevard in order to experience the Walk of Fame. All they need to do is to take a trip to University City (U-City) in St. Louis County, where there's a Walk of Fame for St. Louis's most famous.

Joe Edwards, owner of the Blueberry Hill Restaurant, came up with the concept of the U-City Walk, which is somewhat similar to its California cousin. A series of bronze stars and plaques have been embedded in the sidewalks from the 6300 through the 6600 blocks of Delmar Boulevard. Both sides of the boulevard share equal billing; however, the south side of the walk seems to carry more household names for the younger generations.

It is fascinating to stroll the boulevard and learn of the many movers and shakers connected with St. Louis. They range through all eras, from Civil War general and U.S. President Ulysses S. Grant to playwright Tennessee Williams to actors John Goodman and Kevin Kline to singer, dancer, and actress Tina Turner (plus her infamous husband, Ike).

The criteria for being considered for a star is that the potential inductee must have lived his or her formative and/or creative years in St. Louis, and his or her work must have had a national impact upon our culture. Those are subjective criteria, however. You might argue about some of the names embedded in the sidewalks along Delmar Boulevard, but hey, that's part of the fun.

World's Largest Goose

Sumner is the Wild Goose Capital of the World. Located in Chariton County in north-central Missouri, it is a quiet community, very aware of its unique importance. The area surrounding it is a paradise for avian creatures. Nearby, Swan Lake National Wildlife Refuge was established in 1937 as a resting and feeding venue for waterfowl. Sumner caters to bird-watching tourists and hunters, and every year hosts a Goose Festival during the third week of October.

Sumner has also become famous because of one very special goose. In 1976, the community decided to celebrate the bird that brings them their fame. Artist David Jackson of Kansas City was commissioned to design and build a giant tribute to the Eastern Prairie Canada goose, and Maxie was the end result.

Constructed of fiberglass overlaying a skeleton of steel, Maxie rises to forty feet above ground level, has a tip-to-tip wingspan of sixty-one feet, and weighs six thousand pounds. Convincingly painted to match the contours and colors of the species, Maxie is an impressive testament to the natural beauty of these creatures. To reduce the potential for wind damage, the goose is poised on a castering roller system allowing it to move like a weathervane into the wind.

This big bird sits proudly on display in the city park and makes for an excellent photographic venue; it will, conveniently, face any way you want for a picture. All you have to do is reach up to a wing tip and walk it around to face any point of the compass.

MAXIE
WORLD'S LARGEST GOOSE
SUMNER, MO.

The Big Pump

ETHYL   11 9/10 PLUS TAX

BRONZE   9 9/10 PLUS TAX

MOTOR   8 9/10 PLUS TAX

Gas Pump Matches Gas Prices

There are lots of ways to skin a cat and even more ways to compete for the good ole American greenback. Business owners are always brainstorming new strategies and methods of attracting new customers. Over sixty years ago, Kyle Phares, the owner of a gasoline station in Marysville, either created a tribute to his new electric gas pumps or was very motivated to draw customers to his business—we're not sure which.

His efforts resulted in a giant three-story replica of his smaller pride and joy. He hired Charles Foster to build a wooden-framed skeleton that was then covered by galvanized sheet metal. The structure was practical in that it also served as the station's office and bathrooms. It is no longer in Maryville, but it is available for viewing in the town of King City, just a few miles south of its original location. Part of the Tri-County Historical & Museum Society, the giant pump sits outside, proudly displayed for all to see any time of the day. It's located at the intersection of Grand Avenue and Highway 169.

Chief Osage Beach

This Indian chief in Osage Beach is big enough to have kicked the white European invaders back to their original domiciles all by himself.

Wichita Lineman?

Glen Campbell recorded his huge hit "The Wichita Lineman" back in the late 1960s. What does that have to do with *Weird Missouri*? Maybe it was the inspiration for the sculpted lineman on Route 67 south, near Fredericktown.

Thirsty?

Springfield is home to many interesting attractions, including the Dickerson Zoo, the Missouri Sports Hall of Fame, and . . . the Solo Cup. This cup serves as the company's visual reminder to all that they make paper products. Ya gotta admit, it IS a big cup.

Airway Drive-in Cheerleader

If you lived in northern St. Louis County during the 1950s, '60s, and '70s, the Airway Drive-in was probably where you spent a lot of your Saturday nights. A grade A drive-in designed by Lewis Wilson and opened in 1951, the Airway was known for its giant cheerleader neon sign and marquee, along with its neon spires bracketing the ticket booths. Its closing in the mid-'80s almost marked the end of a romantic era—but not quite. The community's desire to preserve the strutting baton-twirling cheerleader was a decision that would be popular with all. The surviving sign is a cultural icon, reflecting the fondness felt for the deposed facility, and our desire to keep a visceral connection to the past. Let's hope the Airway cheerleader continues to strut her stuff for many years to come.

Fork in the Road

If you run a company that deals with the food industry and market yourself as a creative "out of the box" thinker, then having a giant stainless-steel fork at the entrance to your building is right in character. The really big fork is actually quite handsome and an unmistakable way to let people know this building is indeed the Springfield headquarters of Noble & Associates. Care to dig in?

Branson's Bizarrities

Eye of the Beholder

You might struggle to see the beauty in the Caddie sitting adjacent to the War Memorial Museum in midtown Branson. But perhaps beauty was never the goal. Perhaps the artist accomplished his or her task in just attracting another Curious George of the moment. Art is supposed to make the observer think in different directions on a journey to a new dimension. Well, kudos to the Caddie artist, because attempting to catalogue the items that now define this car's exterior will take you on a journey to the twilight zone. That car is a hoot!

Branson's Mt. Rushmore

It's hard to say whether Branson's version of Mt. Rushmore is sacrilege or the sincerest form of flattery. Either way, this roadside creation can be seen attached to the front of the Hollywood Wax Museum on Highway 76. It is located right in the thick of things where, on a busy Saturday afternoon in July, you learn Branson's true purpose—which is to earnestly demonstrate the conditions that try men's souls.

A Sinking Feeling

One of the newest attractions in Branson is the R.M.S *Titanic* Museum. Almost as if raised from the depths, the new *Titanic* comes complete with four hundred artifacts from the sunken double-hulled ghost. Additionally, visitors will be able to stand on a replica captain's bridge, walk a re-creation of the grand staircase, check out the world's largest "complete" *Titanic* model, and attempt to send that much-needed SOS. It is prominently located on the slow crawl part of 76 Boulevard and Highway 165—you cannot possibly miss it.

World's Most Photographed Bathrooms

It was the ornate and sophisticated restrooms in the Shoji Tabuchi Theater that had piqued our curiosity. Having listened to descriptions of the men's room's magnificent mahogany pool table and the gallery-style seating, where men could watch other men knock one another's balls around, it was difficult to imagine how that process blended with the process of answering nature's call just a few feet away.

One element of the answer is found in the size of the facilities. The bathrooms are huge. The pool table is isolated from the business end of the room, leaving the action taking place within the privatized water closets unperceived by those playing pool. And there are flowers and large potted plants lending a fresh, aromatic atmosphere. Deep leather lounge chairs are available for seating near the washbasins, which are an independent pedestal-style and never run short of hand soap and clean towels.

The same conditions exist within the confines of the women's bathroom, less the pool table. However, the women have wonderful arrangements of orchids next to every washbasin and elaborate chandeliers lighting beautiful jeweled glass. All things considered, not a bad way to do your business.

These are the facilities provided to people attending the Shoji Tabuchi show. A classically trained violinist, Tabuchi was converted to country music after hearing Roy Acuff work his magic on the fiddle. From that point on, Tabuchi became a country western fiddler of exceptional talent. His journey to Branson took almost two decades, but once the Tabuchi Theater opened, his act quickly became one of Branson's most popular and sought-after tickets. That is, if you don't spend the whole show in the bathroom.

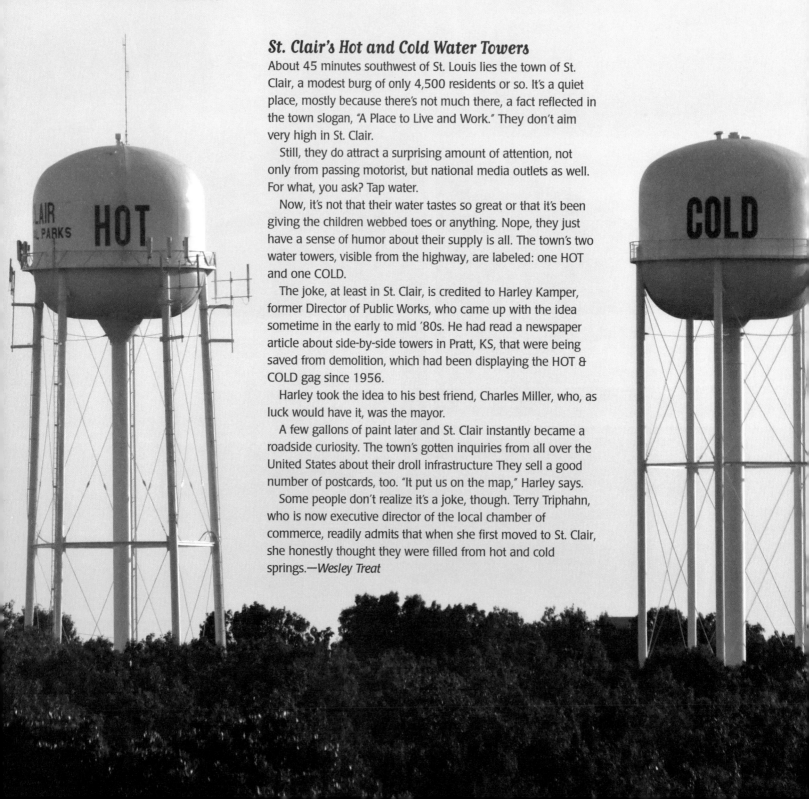

St. Clair's Hot and Cold Water Towers

About 45 minutes southwest of St. Louis lies the town of St. Clair, a modest burg of only 4,500 residents or so. It's a quiet place, mostly because there's not much there, a fact reflected in the town slogan, "A Place to Live and Work." They don't aim very high in St. Clair.

Still, they do attract a surprising amount of attention, not only from passing motorist, but national media outlets as well. For what, you ask? Tap water.

Now, it's not that their water tastes so great or that it's been giving the children webbed toes or anything. Nope, they just have a sense of humor about their supply is all. The town's two water towers, visible from the highway, are labeled: one HOT and one COLD.

The joke, at least in St. Clair, is credited to Harley Kamper, former Director of Public Works, who came up with the idea sometime in the early to mid '80s. He had read a newspaper article about side-by-side towers in Pratt, KS, that were being saved from demolition, which had been displaying the HOT & COLD gag since 1956.

Harley took the idea to his best friend, Charles Miller, who, as luck would have it, was the mayor.

A few gallons of paint later and St. Clair instantly became a roadside curiosity. The town's gotten inquiries from all over the United States about their droll infrastructure They sell a good number of postcards, too. "It put us on the map," Harley says.

Some people don't realize it's a joke, though. Terry Triphahn, who is now executive director of the local chamber of commerce, readily admits that when she first moved to St. Clair, she honestly thought they were filled from hot and cold springs.—*Wesley Treat*

Owning the World's Largest Pecan Does Not Make You a Nut

The pecan season is short in Missouri, but during two busy months in the fall the James Pecan Farm in Brunswick harvests and cracks over sixty thousand pounds of pecans from a stand of ten thousand pecan trees.

In the early 1980s, Bill James—or Farmer James as he likes to be called—realized his family's pecan farm needed a Madison Avenue touch if they wanted to grow their business as efficiently as their pecans. He thought big, and he and a friend created a convincing and huge replica of the Starking Hardy Giant Pecan: a large, thin-shelled variety discovered on the James family farm in 1955. The ponderous pecan has a diameter of seven feet, is twelve feet long, and weighs six tons.

The giant roadside pecan has been attracting thousands of locals and tourists to the James Pecan Farm and Nut Hut for over twenty-five years. And once out of their cars, visitors learn there's more to crack here than this giant nut. That's because Farmer James is a creative man who loves children. Spurred on by a spontaneous vision, he created Wham and Petey's Pop-Up Theater, located just a few short steps from the Nut Hut. Once seated in one of the three rows of bench seats, the audience is treated to a personalized performance that is also the result of Farmer James's creative streak.

Farmer James is also the author of *Wham and Petey: The Harvest,* and the theater's main attraction is a giant version of that book. At eight feet tall, it's the world's largest children's book. During the performance, Farmer James turns its pages as he lip-synchs to music that tells the story of *The Harvest.* And by now, it shouldn't surprise you to learn that Farmer James is also a musical composer and lyricist. He is lip-synching to his own recorded music.

A Doozy of a First Step at City Museum

The school bus mounted atop and extending halfway off the roof of City Museum in downtown St. Louis would have students walking off into thin air. When you first notice the bus, a typical reaction is, What the . . . ? Same with the giant steel praying mantis perched atop the old International Shoe building on Seventh Street, and the salvaged jet aircraft mounted high on top of an elaborate array of other recycled industrial materials, in which children are seemingly suspended in midair as they maneuver the spans between airplane and building. But then you remember that you are at City Museum, and things begin to seem normal.

Within the bounds of the museum, strange combinations of unlikely materials marry to create a vast freeform playscape. The creation of St. Louis artisan-entrepreneur Bob Cassilly, it serves as both a window into his mind and soul and an opening through which adult visitors can again become childlike, if just for a few hours.

Every aspect of the City Museum's many theme areas—MonstroCity, Enchanted Caves, World Aquarium, Art City, Circus Day, and the Tiny Train Town—has been thought out and executed with the precision of fine surgery. Viewed as a whole, City Museum is like a living entity with separate, yet connected, areas of wonder that become a huge creature of mass entertainment. Use a little bit of

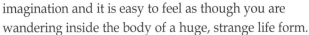

imagination and it is easy to feel as though you are wandering inside the body of a huge, strange life form.

Visitors are immediately confronted with not-so-subtle examples of Cassilly's creative genius. Floor-to-ceiling columns are wrapped in interlocking metal gears that Cassilly probably picked up for pennies on the dollar. The exterior of the public restrooms looks like a shiny armored bunker, but is actually made up of inverted cafeteria food warmers. Other areas are made of recycled plastics, metal, wood, cement, and many other materials.

While studying the creative elements alone is enough to keep any visitor occupied, their function also thrills those in attendance. Watching the experience of other people in this unique playscape is half the fun. For example, we saw one middle-aged father and his son tackle one of the first prominent features in the museum: an ascending spiral of wound-steel tubing. It was amazing to see how the father kept pace with his son as they crawled, twisted, and contorted their way around the spiral. He completed the chase, laughing like his son all the way.

With the many complex turns, twists, ascents, descents, tight crawl spaces, and fully-enclosed-yet-open-air walks, it is a wonder City Museum has never needed to call 911. Cassilly assured us that none of the museum's four million plus visitors in the last ten years have been injured. Such an impressive safety record further reveals how well engineered this dynamic tribute to unbridled fun truly is.

Many functional safety features, such as barriers to prevent falling, are also lovely sweeps of carefully positioned industrial materials. In Cassilly's world, form follows function follows form, and everywhere you look, the creative relationship between materials, space, and the end product is satisfying.

World's Largest Jewel Box

The Jewel Box, located in Forest Park, St. Louis, is a unique and dynamic glass frame structure with an art deco influence. Constructed in 1936 for just a tad more money than a top of the line modern German luxury car, it is the ultimate showcase greenhouse.

Recently renovated (at a cost roughly thirty times that of its original construction) with new glass, plants, and flowers, it stands 50 feet tall, 55 feet wide, and 144 feet long. It offers 7,500 square feet of light-drenched floor display space. In addition to its being a world-class floral conservatory, it is also a multipurpose structure that is available for weddings, receptions, and special events.

Route 66 Mural City

Cuba is the city of murals. But it wasn't always that way. A city-based organization, Viva Cuba, adopted a project that began with a mural commissioned by the local Peoples Bank. That started the concept of "muralizing" the town, and Viva Cuba picked up the ball and ran with it. The end result is the Mural Project.

The first mural, created in 2001, commemorated the hundredth anniversary of Peoples Bank. It depicted the first Model T Ford in town, owned by the bank's first cashier, who later became mayor of Cuba. Eleven murals have followed, which are scattered throughout the downtown area. The collection has been designated Route 66 Mural City by official proclamation of the Missouri house of representatives and the senate.

Subjects of the other murals cover elements of Cuba's rich history. One depicts an apple-picking scene. Another highlights the ten-year tenure of Mayor Al West Sr. Other murals show river action, re-create an old millworks building, and illustrate the prosperity and social process of the 1900s. There is a chain of nine murals on Buchanan Street that depicts scenes from the Civil War. These murals are our favorites; they make Buchanan Street a visual historical treat.

Two of the murals highlight Cuba's brush with fame. One features Amelia Earhart. It seems that on September 4, 1928, the fearless female aviatrix was on her way to Los Angeles when some manner of trouble forced

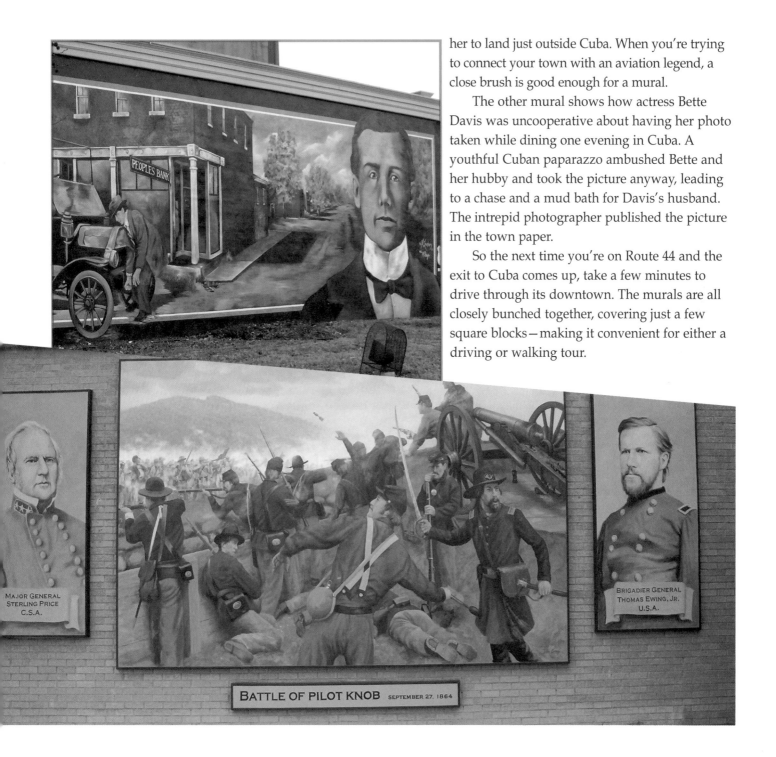

MAJOR GENERAL
STERLING PRICE
C.S.A.

BATTLE OF PILOT KNOB SEPTEMBER 27, 1864

BRIGADIER GENERAL
THOMAS EWING, JR.
U.S.A.

her to land just outside Cuba. When you're trying to connect your town with an aviation legend, a close brush is good enough for a mural.

The other mural shows how actress Bette Davis was uncooperative about having her photo taken while dining one evening in Cuba. A youthful Cuban paparazzo ambushed Bette and her hubby and took the picture anyway, leading to a chase and a mud bath for Davis's husband. The intrepid photographer published the picture in the town paper.

So the next time you're on Route 44 and the exit to Cuba comes up, take a few minutes to drive through its downtown. The murals are all closely bunched together, covering just a few square blocks—making it convenient for either a driving or walking tour.

Shuttlecocks, Giants, and Spiders: Oh My

The Henry Moore Sculpture Garden at the Nelson-Atkins Museum in Kansas City has sculptures tailor-made for the pages of *Weird Missouri.* For example, the landscape-dominating shuttlecocks, each eighteen feet tall and weighing fifty-five hundred pounds, that are the work of artists Claes Oldenburg and Coosje van Bruggen.

These are only part of the "big" artistic experience of the midtown museum district, however. On the front lawns of the nearby Kemper Museum sits the *Crying Giant,* a work of Tom Otterness, along with a spindly-looking spider, the creation of Louise Bourgeois.

Stiletto on Steroids

Just outside the main entrance of the Brown Shoe Company in Clayton sits an extraordinary piece of art. The Brown Shoe Company is usually identified with the millions of pairs of saddle shoes it made for Catholic school girls or the size 37 wingtips they made especially for Robert Wadlow, the Alton Giant.

But what sits in front of the headquarters building is a shoe so large, all eight feet eleven inches of Robert Wadlow would have fit comfortably in it while lying down. Made up of two thousand individually cast, solid aluminum, adult-size high heels, the fantastic statue of a high heel made of high heels is a unique eye grabber.

Artist Victoria Fuller's inspiration for the massive shoe was created from a thought process where each individual shoe was to represent a cell of the larger entity: Like part of a DNA recipe, the big picture is made up of multitudes of the smaller identical elements. Probably the most photographed shoe since the notorious collection of Imelda Marcos, the giant heel is almost as impervious to the elements as it is to opinions about its significance.

Glorious Glore Museum

While the human mind is still very much a conundrum for which we still seek answers, mental health has come a long way since 1874, when State Lunatic Asylum #2 in St. Joseph was initially dedicated. After the turn of the twentieth century, the name changed to the less abrasive State Hospital No. 2, and in 1952 the hospital accepted its final name change, to St. Joseph State Hospital. But no matter the name, St. Joseph's has always served as a psychiatric facility, and compared to when it first opened, we now live in an age of enlightenment.

Longtime state mental health employee George Glore has an appreciation for this change. He is the founder and driving force behind the Glore Psychiatric Museum, located adjacent to the state prison. He's gathered a comprehensive collection of the devices and techniques developed over the last hundred and thirty years in an effort to extract normal behavior from those incapable of providing such.

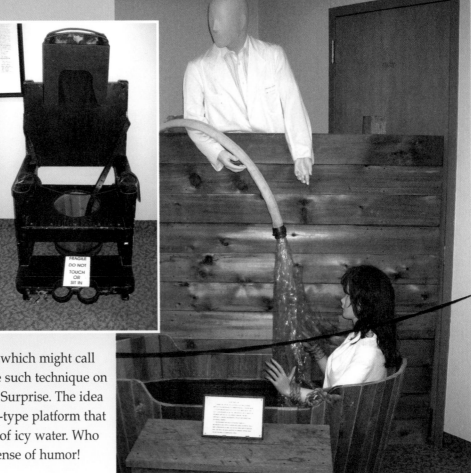

Treatment back in the days when State Lunatic Asylum #2 was founded was far more aggressive than today's prescription, which might call for just swallowing a pill or two. One such technique on display in the museum is the Bath of Surprise. The idea was to place the patient on a gallows-type platform that would suddenly drop him into a vat of icy water. Who said that psychiatrists don't have a sense of humor!

Another technique was the Tranquilizer Chair. Probably not a favorite of patients, who would sometimes endure up to six months of chair-bound "tranquilization" therapy. This chair was the brainchild of Benjamin Rush, signer of the American Declaration of Independence and the father of American psychiatry (also a big believer in bloodletting and the use of leeches).

Patients could also be treated on O'Halloran's Swing, another creation that called for being strapped into a chair, which would then rotate at speeds of up to one

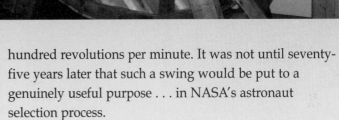

hundred revolutions per minute. It was not until seventy-five years later that such a swing would be put to a genuinely useful purpose . . . in NASA's astronaut selection process.

Other items on display include a wide variety of seemingly medieval torture toys and a huge collection of items swallowed by patients afflicted with the Swallowing Disease. One patient actually swallowed 1,446 items, which are proudly displayed in a rosette shape in a glass case. The most notable of the swallowed items is a Timex watch, evidently gulped down by a patient who was just trying to pass the time away. She was ultimately successful, and when she did pass the watch, it was still ticking! Brings new meaning to the old "Takes a licking, and keeps on ticking" commercial.

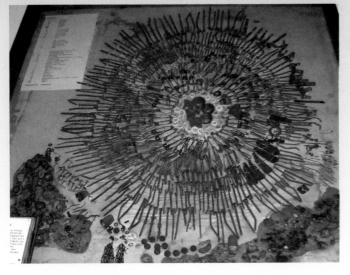

Roads Less Traveled

Many Missouri roads, for one reason or another, are not heavily traveled. For some it's because of rumored supernatural qualities that lead even skeptics to keep a wary eye out for the inexplicable. Zombie Road, for example, is known for so much bizarre activity that travelers may wonder how so much weirdness can happen in one place. Other mysterious roads are host to strange lights or ghostly voices, testing the fortitude of legend-tripping teens, or maybe just giving their girlfriends a reason to snuggle closer as the ghosts or goblins draw near.

Then there are the roads abandoned to progress, including a stretch of old Route 66 that runs through the state. On these byways you'll find the tattered trappings that go with less-traveled roads: mom-and-pop motels, abandoned drag strips, and ancient gas pumps. They reflect the change in American culture that came with the interstate and serve as a warning to enjoy similar weird Missouri roads while you still can.

Zombie Road: Where Urban Legends Ring True

Within the citified sprawl of St. Louis lies a remote area called Zombie Road. Urban legend tells a variety of eerie tales about this road, including its being host to ritualistic practices that spawn inhuman and demonic entities. Other tales tell of those who met a peculiar demise and still roam this desolate road in the afterlife.

Centuries of erosion have forged a transversal path through

the bluffs along the Meramec River, also known as the River of Death. It was named the latter by those who called the area their home centuries ago. Many have come through the naturally carved corridors in the bluffs to a crossable ford in the river below.

Some say this is called Zombie Road because the railroad workers who had once worked here rise from their graves at times and roam about. Some insist they have heard old-time music and have seen anomalous moving lights and other ghostly sightings from that forgotten era. Another tale tells of a

patient nicknamed Zombie who escaped from a nearby mental facility, never to be seen again. His blood-soaked gown was found lying upon the old road later named after him.

During Prohibition, a nearby town housed speakeasies and the summer homes of well-known gangsters. Allegedly, individuals dealt a bad hand by such public enemies resulted in their permanent placement within the ground or in the Meramec River, never to be seen again.

The railroad still proves that "Death hath no mercy" because many have met their final fate upon its tracks. Lifelong residents remember multitudes of tragic occurrences dating back to the 1950s. One of these occurred in the '70s when two teens were struck by an oncoming train. During the '90s a mother and her five-year-old child were crossing a bridge when an oncoming train met them. The mother's last action was to push her child off the bridge. The engineer was able to stop the train and save the child. Although the mother died, this is still one of the few happier endings to a Zombie Road story.

More recently, the area has become a refuge for those wanting privacy to practice the occult and other rituals. Who knows what true doorways to the darkness and unknown were opened here?

The area has also seen its share of suicides and murders. In the 1970s, a hunter stumbled across a car still running at the end of the road. Closer inspection revealed a hose going from the exhaust pipe to the inside of the car where the driver slumped over the steering wheel.

One can agree that there is no lack of legends or tragedies surrounding this area that can explain the bizarre and eerie encounters of those who visit. I was one who became truly intrigued and attracted by such lore and was determined to either prove or disprove the urban legends surrounding it.

Missouri Paranormal Research, the paranormal investigative team I belong to, investigated this area on several occasions. Our visits converted many true skeptics into true believers of the paranormal, including myself, on the first visit. I even remarked that "this is going to be like Winnie the Pooh looking for a ghost in the Hundred Acre Woods," prior to descending onto the old road.

Within an hour, several people observed a human-size

shadow figure as it descended upon them from a small bluff nearby. It then ran onto the road, stopped, and disappeared into the darkness of the night. Throughout the night others heard unexplainable voices, were touched by the unseen, and witnessed the unexplainable. This was one night our group concluded that some urban legends are real!
—*Gregory and Judith Myers,*
Missouri Paranormal Research, www.catchmyghost.com

Of Chevy Vegas and Asylums: Zombie Road

This has to do with the road once called Old Fawler Road off Ridge Road in Eureka. It's commonly referred to as Zombie Road, and was used from the 1800s through the 1960s. It's shut off now near the elementary school, and not labeled, but you can still see the curb. It's a worthwhile visit and a good hike.

The other entrance is by the miniature railroad line Pacific and Wabash, near the entrance to the Old State Road. It stretches along the Meramec for quite a ways and is enclosed in a deep wall of trees that is being encroached by development.

One story is that of a couple driving down the road in their Chevy Vega. The creek that ran nearby supposedly washed out the road and the car flipped. They both died. I myself have been there, and I've seen the totaled car.

There's also supposedly an abandoned cemetery and asylum along the road, but I haven't been there to see it. Although I'm planning to go soon, before a bulldozer takes hold of another forgotten location. You can reach Zombie Road by taking 44W to 109, 109 to Old State, and Old State to Ridge Road.—*Josh Cross*

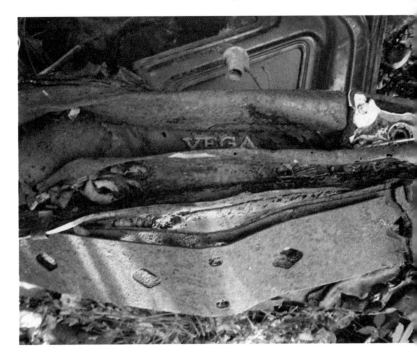

Upper Blackwell Road

I grew up just a short drive away from Blackwell and wanted to write to make sure you knew about a road there. This road has got to be considered one of the most terrifying, haunted roads in the entire country. I am a skeptic by nature and even I, after all the strange things I have encountered there, have a belief that something is off when it comes to Upper Blackwell Road.

There are a number of stories about Upper Blackwell Road that anyone who grows up in this area knows well.

Probably the most famous legend regarding the road involves its bridge, a dark and lonely span referred to as the Black Tram. The bridge is haunted by a mysterious ghost car that seems to protect the bridge, as it chases visitors off of it, then promptly disappears. It is said that the car appears when travelers drive across the bridge and flash their lights three times. I myself have never actually seen the ghost car, but I can say that the bridge is ominous in general, and there have been times when I've flashed my lights and the feelings of dread on that bridge have increased ten fold. I can say personally that there is something seriously twisted and evil about that bridge.

There are also the legends of the ghost couple that wander up and down Upper Blackwell Road. They are famous for waving their arms wildly as cars passed, summoning help. But when drivers pull over to see what the matter is, the couple promptly disappear. People say that they were a pair of young lovers who were hit by a car and killed on the road back in the '50s. I myself have never seen them, but a number of friends who I trust very much claim to, and I have no reason to doubt them.

The one legend of Upper Blackwell Road that most people agree on is the story of the disappearing signs. I know dozens of people who claim to have experienced this one. While driving down the road, signs will be alongside the road, but as you pass them, they just disappear. One second they'll be there, then you'll look in your rear view mirror after driving by and they will be gone. I have been pulled over here and asked the police about the signs, and even they say they've seen it and can offer no explanation.

There are a few stories regarding Upper Blackwell Road that have nothing to do with ghosts, but are just as scary. There is a restaurant located along the road that seems normal to the naked eye. But stories abound that the restaurant is actually the secret headquarters for a sect of Satanists that call the road home. I have heard that the evil of the road has attracted them, and they harness it for their nefarious rituals.

I once took a trip to the road and slowly drove past the restaurant a few times to see if I could discern any Satanic activity taking place inside. On my third trip past the restaurant, a black SUV roared out of the driveway and initiated what turned into a high-speed chase with me. He was right on my bumper, flashing his high beams. When I got a few miles away, he jammed on his brakes and turned off his headlights. I got

out of there. While I can't claim that they were Satanists in that truck for certain, I can vouch that someone wants to defend the secrets of whatever is going on in this place.

I would encourage all of your readers to check out Upper Blackwell Road. I know I'm biased from being local, but I truly believe it is one of the scariest places the United States has to offer.—*Alan Ford*

Nolan Road

Have you ever visited Nolan Road, off of Sycamore Church Road, in Branson? It's pretty freaky. A bunch of kids died there in an accident. Now, if you drive down there, you will find all sorts of handprints on your car when you get to the end. These are supposed to be the handprints of the kids who died there, pushing your car away to safety so you don't get hurt like they did. Very freaky, and worth checking out.—*Jerry Scugs*

Lebanon's Train Tunnel

Growing up in Lebanon, THE place to go to freak yourself out is the train tunnel. Many people have died here. In the 1800s, this was a lynching spot, where people would be hung. Of course, many of these people were innocent of any crime. Train accidents happened here as well, claiming more lives. When cars became the norm, accidents almost immediately started happening here. And any time a young person dies, their name gets spray painted on the wall here. Something about this place attracts death.

There is a rite of passage that many participate in growing up here. The cool thing about it is that it all depends on how much guts you have. You drive your car out to the old tunnel and roll down the windows. Then, you turn it off—all the lights, the radio, the engine, everything. Supposedly, if you sit long enough, you'll begin to hear whispers from the people who have died here. The longer you stay, the louder and clearer the whispers get.

I myself have tried it and have never made it very far. Just a slight breeze tends to get me to turn the car on and get the heck out of there. There's just something very foreboding and dark about the place, to the point where I can't stomach being there for very long.—*Kate Merris*

Spook Hollow

I have been a personal witness to one of the oldest and most well known ghost stories in Missouri. Located along Old Orchard Road, between Jackson and Cape Girardeau, is an area known as Spook Hollow.

For hundreds of years, people have seen a strange white mist appear in the area. Newspapers first began reporting this phenomenon all the way back to the 1880s. Obviously since that time, much development and change has come to the area, yet the strange fog still appears.

I have seen the mist on two occasions. It isn't like a fog that just sits. It swirls and moves on its own, in a way that makes it seem like it's almost alive. Everyone from this area knows about it, and most have seen it. The ghost of Spook Hollow is accepted as a part of life in these parts.
—*Mark Brunder*

Don't Mess with Spook Hollow

Spook Hollow is no joke. That white mist doesn't just appear and then go away: It terrorizes you. My friends and I once saw it and drove towards it. It did not like this. Instead of dissipating, it instead came right at us and surrounded our car. We pulled a U-turn and sped down the road. It sped up with us, and kept up for close to a mile! It was one of the scariest things I've ever experienced—don't mess with Spook Hollow!
—*Jessica McCann*

Bloody Bridge of Greene County

There used to be a bridge in Greene County that crossed the Pickering Creek. It had acquired a notorious local handle of Bloody Bridge. Next to it was a local watering hole that carried a similar moniker: The Bloody Bucket.

With such naming conventions, questions arise about where the blood spilled first. Did the bridge's dangerous nature produce bloody automobile accidents, and the tavern took on the name by reason of close proximity? Or was The Bloody Bucket one of those cowboy-type places with chicken wire in front of the stage to protect the band from flying beer bottles? If so, then maybe the bridge gained its name as a result of the bloody brawls in the bar.

But there is a third possibility. Knowing how it takes multiple accidents, often fatal, before the bureaucracies responsible for our roadway safety place warning signs or lights at dangerous locations, and knowing how some folks get after drinking too much in a watering hole, the reality is that they could have both been naturally bloody venues.

Either way, both the bridge and the tavern are no more. And if all that is contained in this story is true, good riddance to them both!

Show Me Your Kicks on Route 66

The 1940s and '50s were the heyday of U.S. Route 66, the Mother Road, famous in book and song. Starting in Chicago, the westbound journey on Route 66 would have you descend southwest through Illinois, continue southwest across Missouri, catch the very southeast corner of Kansas, on southwest through Oklahoma, cutting directly across the short chimney of Texas, straight across New Mexico and Arizona, and then on over to Los Angeles.

In its day, it was America's Road — a route for family fun lined with mom-and-pop motels and tourist attractions, the way west for hungry migrants during the Great Depression. Then along came President Dwight David Eisenhower and his National Defense Highway System. Recognizing the need for a modern, high-speed interstate system, Eisenhower signed legislation that would transform the face of America. It also spelled doom for Route 66. Towns and businesses along the old road were no longer easily accessible to the cars whizzing

by on interstate highways, signaling the beginning of the end for many of them. New businesses made sure they were located as close to an exit ramp as possible.

Not all has been lost, however. A mini culture has evolved to keep the spirit and history of the old Route 66 alive in the minds of those who traveled it in yesteryear and to the new generations curious about its magic. People come from all over the world to make a journey along the road: some in period automobiles, others on bus tours, and still others on motorcycles. In fact, an organization in Norway makes annual journeys to the United States with Wild West destinations and a Route 66 tour.

Route 66 is of such importance in America's cultural history that many stretches are listed on the National Register of Historic Places. It is definitely here to stay: a road less traveled, perhaps, but for those who do, nostalgia for a time when the family car trip was king. Here are a few locations unique to the *Weird Missouri* Route 66 experience, where it ran from Chain of Rocks Bridge through to Joplin.

Devil's Elbow

There is a tight bend in the Big Piney River, about five miles east of St. Roberts. Back when the river was used to float logs to the mills, this turn was a natural bottleneck, further aided by a large boulder in midstream that helped to lock the logs in place. The loggers felt that bend to be a devil of a problem, hence the name, Devil's Elbow.

The famous river bend is now home to an equally famous eatery. The Devil's Elbow Inn,

known for its BBQ and friendly social atmosphere, has been a popular part of the Route 66 experience since it first opened its doors in 1929.

The inn was included in a popular early '60s television series called *Route 66* and has also been a focal point of several documentaries about the Route 66 experience. There is much tradition associated with this inn under the trees. It's very biker friendly but doesn't have an intimidating or threatening environment. In fact, it is just the opposite.

There is also an interesting and optional tradition in which first-time female visitors may engage. The ceiling of the inn is replete with the brassieres of countless adventurous women who have voluntarily added their supporting garment to the collection. The tradition began in 1997; since then many women have generously donated to the cause.

Left, Devil's Elbow Inn; above, John's Modern Log Cabins

John's Not-So-Modern Log Cabins

John's Modern Log Cabins in Newberg, about nine miles west of Rolla, were at one time a place to rest your tired frame after traveling Route 66. Just off the side of the westbound lanes of the old Mother Road, the cabins offered the bare amenities to provide comfort and shelter. It was the workingman's place to spend the night.

Several tiny old log cabins are still there today, under a grouping of trees from which one can see a faint vestige of that legendary concrete motorway. They are sadly in a state of rapid decay, with roofs near collapse, and

windows and doors that stopped serving their purpose many years ago. The old cabins are barely recognizable from their glory days, when they stood witness to the shenanigans of the many rowdy characters who frequented the neighboring gin mill, Bill and Bess's Place.

Route 66 organizations have expressed a desire to restore the dilapidated buildings, and it's possible they will. All it takes is money. But given their condition, it would purely be a labor of love. Who can put a price on that?

Ironically, the very interstate that consigned these tiny cabins to a less than glorious demise is that same piece of concrete that can transport you to them. But you'd better hurry, as time seems to be working at double speed to send the tired structures to complete collapse. An easy way to find them is to look for the Vernelles Motel. The cabins are just a few hundred feet south.

Munger Moss Motel

At first blush, the name sounds like it could be the stuff hanging from live oak trees in the southern United States, but it's actually the name of a popular Route 66 place to rest travelers' weary bones: the famous Munger Moss Motel.

Located in Lebanon, Laclede County, just off Interstate 44 on the old Route 66, the motel has been at this site since 1946. Its style is vintage auto court. Its earliest rendition was a series of fourteen cabins that came with a carport alongside. Later expansion found those carports filled in to become revenue-generating sleeping rooms. It presently has a count of forty rooms that all have the feel of yesteryear. It's the kind of place where you might expect inexplicable orchestral music to spontaneously begin as Elvis Presley and Ann Margaret emerge from a room to tease one another with a pop music routine.

Current owners Bob and Ramona Lehman took possession of the motel in 1971 and have lovingly continued the Munger Moss experience. You will not get any reward points as you do from larger hotel chains, but you can experience the magic of the old days through multiple theme rooms that give you the sense of what the Route 66 life was like half a century ago.

Slip Slidin' Away

Route 66 isn't the only place where you can find whiffs of old roadside life. Located up on the southern bluff in Fenton, this attraction certainly had the most impressive water slides of its time. However, as this photo reveals, it really ain't what it used to be. It has been some time since the water sloshed and you could hear the joyful voices of children and adults as they careened down the slides' twists and turns. Closed down and vacant for long enough to have been attacked by hundreds of morons with spray paint cans, the water slides at Fenton are just another reminder of days gone by.

Devil's Hollow

In between the towns of Fulton and Hams Prairie is a desolate county road. Many people don't even realize that it exists. Those who do know it as Devil's Hollow.

When I was in high school, Devil's Hollow was the premiere weekend hangout for my stoner friends and I. No matter how we started out our Friday or Saturday nights, it seemed that at some point or another we'd take a trip down this road. We were drawn to it, and I for one still am.

Like many, my friends and I have seen the odd lights that bob up and down the road. These ghost lights are one of the more famous haunts of the Devil's Hollow. We saw them on about half a dozen occasions. One thing that we found was pretty curious. Whenever we mentioned the lights, or the possibility of seeing them, they'd never appear. It was only on the occasions that we never spoke about them that they'd show up—glowing pale yellow and moving along the road. While their appearance is definitely shocking, I would say that these lights do not have an evil presence. To me, they always seemed more playful than frightening.

There is one legend of the Devil's Hollow that I have never seen first hand evidence of, but that is worth including in my letter due to its popularity and frightening nature. I have tested it many times, but to no avail.

Supposedly, if you drive down the road with your car's lights off, then turn them back on while still moving, a car will be careening directly towards yours. This is the ghost car of the Devil's Hollow. No matter what you do, you can't avoid crashing into it—except that no impact comes. Instead, the car passes right through yours, leaving you terrified beyond belief. Some say that splashes of blood even appear on the outside of your car after the ghost car passes through it.

Again, I have not experienced that one first hand, but I think anyone would agree that a legend that terrifying is worth mentioning.

Overall, Devil's Hollow is one of the scariest roads in Missouri. I have seen much of its scary side first hand, and can vouch for this.—*Steve Cuff*

The Devil's in Dark Hollow

The devil worshipers of Dark Hollow, also known as Devil's Hollow, are a real phenomenon! The rumors of these people have been around for decades. One night, I was driving down the road when a cop aggressively pulled me over—when I say aggressive, I mean he was up on my bumper, lights flashing, sirens on, shouting at me over his car's loudspeaker. When I pulled over, the cop was at our window in a flash, with his flashlight in our face and his gun drawn. He was panicked. When he realized we were just kids, he breathed a huge sigh of relief, but told us to get out of there immediately for our own safety. We asked him what was wrong, and he wouldn't tell us. But he was willing to say, "There are people who hang out down here that are no joke. Kids like you come looking for ghosts, but there's people that are scarier than any of the ghosts." We apologized for bothering him on such a stressful night, and he sent us on our way. We turned around, and before we even got all the way out, he was speeding in the other direction, looking for who knows what. Needless to say, we haven't been back there since—that cop was genuinely spooked and his warning that night was more than enough to convince me to stay away.—*James Rivers*

South Main Street Haunts

St. Charles is a small town along the Missouri River that dates back more than two centuries. The footsteps of history have certainly left their mark here, which may be one reason why it's considered to be so haunted, especially along the brick streets and cobblestone walks of South Main Street. It's a quaint historic area with a number of old buildings. And it's not only the passage of time that has left spirits here: Some believe an old cemetery may have something to do with it, as well!

St. Charles is where Lewis and Clark outfitted their expedition before departing for the western frontier, and it even became the first capital of Missouri in 1821, until a permanent building was constructed in Jefferson City. Daniel Boone came to St. Charles from Kentucky in 1795, and his home, located near the town, is where the ghost of his wife, Rebecca, is said to linger near her grave site.

The town's history seems to lend itself to ghosts, and nowhere is this as evident as on the historic Main Street, which lies along the river. One large section of the area, which includes a quaint former inn called the Farmer's Home, is built directly on top of an old cemetery. Perhaps this is why South Main Street has a reputation as a very haunted place.

One site is a delightful restaurant called the Mother-in-Law House. Francis Kremer, the owner of a flourishing mill in the

city, had the house built in 1866. It earned its peculiar nickname because Mrs. Kremer was homesick for her mother. Her husband built the house with both sides exactly alike: One for the family and the other for his mother-in-law.

Today the restaurant hosts both hungry customers and an unearthly spirit. Owner Donna Hafer had long said that nothing ever seemed to go right on the northern side of the restaurant. Over the years, customers have spoken of strange events, including glasses, drinks, and utensils disappearing with no explanation, coffee cups that upend and dump in the laps of guests, and food that inexplicably changes temperature.

According to reports, the Boone's Lick Trail Inn is also said to have a resident ghost. The owners state that this spirit is actually very helpful, assisting them as they climb a certain flight of stairs, which are narrow and uneven. The previous

Left, Mary Sibley; below, South Main Street

owner had warned them about other activity, but so far a well-placed hand to steady them on the staircase has been the only sign of a presence. Some have suggested that this ghost may be the spirit of a former occupant who met his death on these stairs.

The David McNair House at 724 South Main is home to a "cooking ghost." Occupants have reported over the years that at the oddest times, the house suddenly fills with the smell of home-cooked soup, even though nothing at all is cooking there.

The ghost of a little girl has been reported in a number of different buildings along South

Main Street, including in 523 and 519. The stories say that she is the ghost of a child who died after being badly burned near a stove in the 1940s, but no one really knows for sure. A former employee of a shop at 523 used to talk to the little girl quite often. While working, she would sometimes see racks sway and spin by themselves. Whenever the staff member spoke up and asked them to stop, they always did. There was also a miniature sewing machine in the store that the little ghost girl liked to play with. The employees would put it away at night, and when they came in the next day they would find it out on the counter or in another part of the store.

Also in St. Charles is Lindenwood University, long said to be haunted by the ghost of its founder, Mary Easton Sibley. It was founded in 1853 and was the first university for women west of the Mississippi River. Mary's ghost is said to be responsible for the good luck

that has come to the school, because before her death she reportedly promised the students that she would always watch over them. Her body remains behind as well—she is buried with her family in a small cemetery on the campus.

The most famous haunted spot on campus is Sibley Hall. This was the former Sibley family home and later became the school's first residence hall. Back in the days when it was being used as a dormitory, many of the residents claimed to hear loud noises in the vacant rooms and could find no cause for the sounds. They also heard footsteps going up and down the stairs and the sounds of a piano being played in the empty hall where Mary Sibley's piano was stored. They'd also find furniture rearranged and would often report lights turning on and off in parts of the building that were always closed up and locked.—*Troy Taylor*

The Roads No Longer Traveled

The following stories aren't about roads less traveled, but of memories of road-related experiences that no longer exist. As such, they are roads traveled in Missouri minds of a certain age.

Hall Street Was a Drag

While Wentzville had Mid America Raceway for the pros, St. Louis had Hall Street for the rest of us. During the latter part of the 1960s, Hall Street was known to be a haunt for people who had a need to jam gears in the wee hours of the morning. The street had all the qualities needed for drag racing on the margins of legality. It was straight as an arrow for much longer than even the pro strips, in an isolated industrial area, and usually lightly policed. It was a place to take your muscle in the form of American horsepower, and to then line up and have at it. May the best shifter win!

That was then, this is now, and the cycle repeats itself yet again. Richard Wilkes, director of public relations for the Metropolitan St. Louis Police Department, told us that "Hall Street is still occasionally a place where racing takes place. However, it is now usually in the form of motorcycle races and stunting." He also says that the police are "more aware of the dangers of Hall Street racing, due to a couple of motorcycle fatalities."

Yes, Hall Street was a place to "haul the mail" and then, after the racing, make about twenty-five loops through Steak & Shake to proudly display your feathers.

Drive-in Memories

Some of the best memories of those who were teens in the '50s or '60s are of visits to drive-in movies. In northern St. Louis County there were two: the Four

Screen and the Airway, both located on the St. Charles Rock Road in St. Ann.

If you've never been to a drive-in, you've missed out on more than a movie or two. In the early 1960s, admission was just $5 per carload of people—and, man, were cars ever loaded! People even piled into the trunks, and cars went through the ticket gate so loaded down in the rear that it looked as if they were smuggling Krugerrands. For some reason, the ticket sellers turned a blind eye.

There was always the annoyance of someone arriving late and destroying your night vision when they swung their headlights through your field of view (usually with the high beams on). And the fun of watching teenagers goof on one another by running from car to car, or to try to get a look into the cars occupied by those who came to the drive-in to do everything but watch the movie. And of course, before movie soundtracks started playing over car radios there was always someone who would pull away

from his parking spot with the pedestal-mounted speaker still attached to his car's window.

For those of us lucky enough to live near one of America's nine hundred currently operating drive-ins, we can transport ourselves to the open-air movie experience of the 1960s. Missouri still has several functioning drive-ins. As of this writing, the Moberly Five Drive-in is open for business, as are the Phoenix Drive-in in Houston, and the Horseshoe Lake screen in St. Joseph. And for the Route 66 crowd, the old Route 66 Drive-in in Carthage is open for moviegoers young and old.

Gas from the Past

I was on my way to find the world's smallest tombstone, located in the cemetery on the east side of Butler, when I realized that it was time to pump a few gallons of Saudi Arabia's finest blend into the tank of my American four-wheel-drive rental car. I pulled into Carl's

Sinclair and started to pump the gas.

It didn't take long before a casual fellow strolled out to pump the gas for me, so I told him to fill 'er up. While pumping, he gave me splendid directions to the cemetery, and we started talking about America's situation with gasoline.

Soon he pointed out that the pump right behind the one that was filling my SUV was from the early 1970s, and that it would register a price per gallon no higher than $1.99. He then pointed to a much newer pump that would register no higher than $3 per gallon. After my tank was filled and I gave an explanation of my mission in Missouri, he kindly invited me inside to show me a collection of period oil cans. As he talked, he also calculated the total for my gasoline purchase.

"Let's see," he said, "that's $19.78." Hearing that number, my spirits soared, and then he followed up with, "Multiplied by two, that'll be $39.56." I laughed, and he joined in. He said, "It just isn't worth the trouble or expense to install new pumps that will register today's prices, so we just take the pump total and multiply by two."

The pump total multiplied by two makes perfect sense in the circumstance of Carl's Sinclair. I just hope that the rest of the gasoline-providing world does not follow suit.

Speed Has Its Limits

The state's first posted speed limit of 9 mph was established in 1903. They must have had some very accurate speedometers back in aught three, or it would take a pretty skilled driver to maintain such an odd speed limit. Unusual speed limits have popped up all over the world, but a recent weird limit of 17 mph can be found at an apartment complex in Chesterfield. Most cars idle at that speed!

Show Me the Ghosts

Remember the days of the old TV show *Spook Spectacular*? Every week kids looked forward to what were, even in the early 1960s, dated horror flicks. Bela Lugosi was just a naturally creepy looking guy, and to this day, he remains the archetypal Dracula. And then there were the *Werewolf* movies starring Lon Chaney Jr. and Boris Karloff, as the prototypal monstrous creation of Dr. Frankenstein.

It was all great stuff, providing wonderful childhood memories. However, in the end, we knew the stories weren't real. Spooks, ghosts, and demons all offer Hollywood endless opportunities to demonstrate its special effects, although most people believe that ghosts exist only in the realm of fantasy.

But there are people who believe otherwise. They have had terrifying experiences that convince them there really are strange entities out there, trapped in some ephemeral space between this world and the next. Normal people—people like you and me—have had their homes and lives invaded by something beyond their ability to explain, something that scared the daylights out of them.

Now, full disclosure: Your author is a skeptic. Maybe the idea of tortured souls struggling to rejoin the world of the living is just too terrible to contemplate. But personal paranormal defense mechanisms aside, no effort was spared in digging up for this chapter the best stories out there about ghosts, gates to and from hell, and trapped spirits seeking both revenge and release in our state. Read at your own risk.

Haunting the Diamonds

When travelers journey back in time by cruising nostalgic Old Route 66, little do they know of the dreams and determination that brought about the building that sits at the fork of Old Highway 100 and Highway AT in Villa Ridge. Nor are they aware of the playful and sometimes mischievous ghostly residents that forever reside there, refusing to pass on since their last good-byes on this earth.

What Spencer Groff started as a fruit stand morphed into a roadside mercantile operation that by 1927 became The Diamonds, which soon boasted being the World's Largest Roadside Restaurant. In 1947, the restaurant burned down— the latest in a series of unlucky events for Groff, who gave in and turned the business over to one of his longtime employees. It was the former employee who built the brick building that stands at the site today.

Route 66 brought much prosperity to The Diamonds, but the completion of the interstates in the 1960s drew cars away from Route 66. A new Diamonds was erected near the new interstate and opened in 1968. The old icon was sold and became the Tri-County Restaurant and Truck Stop.

It seems that something supernatural refused to hop onto the interstate along with the rest of the traffic and continues to reside inside this onetime icon. During the 1960s and '70s, employees and customers experienced being touched by unseen forces, hearing voices and whispers from people who were not there, and seeing anomalies they could not explain. During the 1980s and '90s, employees became afraid to go into the basement after they witnessed eerie shadow figures

and small objects moving on their own there.

The new millennium brought sightings of a translucent ghostly male wearing a plaid shirt and tan pants. Further experiences included unseen forces holding doors shut, turning appliances off and on, and moving objects on the tables while customers were dining. When children started to report seeing a ghostly man and a bloody woman, a call was made to Missouri Paranormal Research, a paranormal investigative and research group in the area.

The ghostly residents didn't take long to greet this paranormal team. While the investigators were dining, a full coffeepot levitated in midair before crashing to the floor. That night investigative meters acted erratically, temperatures fluctuated, and unexplainable voices were recorded. Tom, the team photographer, captured one of the ghostly residents on film, and his subject retaliated by manifesting next to someone using the urinal, causing the man to urinate on his own shoe.

During subsequent visits, this team documented a wealth of activity to fully support the alleged haunting. Such experiences included having both a lightbulb and a rusty butcher knife thrown at them while in the basement. As earlier, photographs and video captured ghostly apparitions, while audio equipment recorded unexplainable voices.

Tri-County Restaurant and Truck Stop finally closed its doors. It's now another faded memory along Old Route 66, standing vacant and waiting for a new proprietor to come along. We can only wonder whether or not a new owner will be welcomed by the ghostly inhabitants of this historic landmark.—*Gregory Myers, Missouri Paranormal Research, www.catchmyghost.com*

Sikeston CSI

At least forty years ago Sikeston was the site of a tragic school bus accident, or so the storytellers say. A bus filled with children was attempting to cross railroad tracks in the middle of town. The driver's badly judged attempt ended when a train broadsided the bus, killing many children.

Those children are apparently now trapped between worlds. Trapped, but not completely incommunicado. To interact with them, all you need to do is dust your car with talcum powder and park it on the train tracks . . . but only after making certain that no trains are coming! Within moments, child-size handprints will appear all over your car.

Forensic science is now routinely used to backtrack through time to pinpoint guilty criminal parties and clarify identities. It seems a perfect opportunity to take these children's handprints from the hereafter and try to cross-reference them with old medical and health records. Where is CSI Sikeston when you need it?

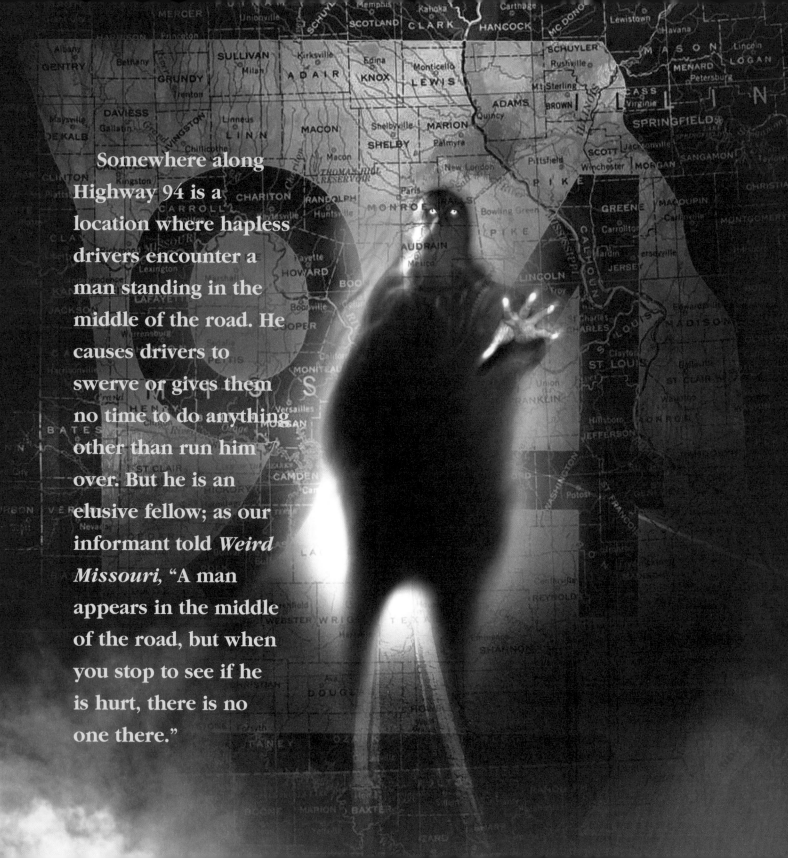

Somewhere along Highway 94 is a location where hapless drivers encounter a man standing in the middle of the road. He causes drivers to swerve or gives them no time to do anything other than run him over. But he is an elusive fellow; as our informant told *Weird Missouri,* "A man appears in the middle of the road, but when you stop to see if he is hurt, there is no one there."

Headless Horseman of Breakneck Hill

The name Breakneck Hill offers an obvious explanation as to why a horseman haunting this spot near the border between Christian and Stone counties could be of the headless variety. Not much is known about this particular horseman, and no one seems to know when or how he lost his topknot, or if he really does prefer brisk autumnal nights with full moons, or attacking lone travelers of this gravel-covered sloped road. He may prefer blue moons, as it seems he appears about as frequently as they do. But when he does grant some poor unfortunate an audience, it must surely be a memorable experience.

The road is canopied with trees from end to end along the Breakneck portion of the hill. Looking along its length from either end makes it easy for imaginations to run wild and envision the visible breath from the snorting nostrils of the doomed horseman's galloping steed. And it would be equally easy for the imagination to create flowing capes and windmilling arms as he swings his menacing sword overhead . . . at least, over where his head would normally be.

Legends, rumors, and scary stories aside, if you can picture in your mind's eye the quintessential road down which a headless horseman would gallop, Breakneck Hill would be it.

Orphaned Spirits at Pythian Castle

Buried behind the many fast-paced businesses that are sandwiched together along Glenstone Parkway in Springfield is an honest-to-goodness castle. Located on East Pythian Street, Pythian Castle's appearance is a far cry from the glassy modern architecture nearby. Its stone edifice has a sense of importance and permanence that its designers and stonemasons must have meant to convey.

A fraternal organization called the Knights of Pythias had the castle built in 1913 as a rather elaborate orphanage. It has since had other occupants, including the United States military, which owned it for five decades.

Justus H. Rathbone founded the Knights of Pythias shortly after the Civil War ended, modeling its tenets on a Pythagorean-based belief system that frames loyalty and trust as pivotal elements of a man's character. But pity the poor orphans who might not have been familiar with the philosophies of the organization that housed them! Two intimidating-looking statues of dogs flank the front steps. The dogs are whippets and meant to convey pride and dignity, but they could easily be mistaken for the hounds of hell.

The true hardships of orphanage life could explain the many lingering spiritual malcontents who haunt this Springfield landmark. Possibly the many voices that are frequently heard are the pleas of children lost in an afterworld of loneliness and pain. But we prefer to think the happenings throughout Pythian Castle are the actions of playful entities that in the afterlife are making up for what they may have missed while alive.

People have also bumped into an "invisible mass," which might be the frustrated soul of a person who in his most desperate hours took control over what he could and laid an immovable claim to that piece of the between-worlds. And the slamming doors could be ancient anguished energy that caroms around within the limited eternity defined by the castle walls.

You can form your own opinions by contacting the

castle and scheduling an investigation. Such activity is open to any individual or group. Several established paranormal groups have been involved in extensive investigations there, all spending time measuring, listening, recording, photo documenting, and speculating like the rest of us do about the weird goings-on within Pythian Castle.

A Is for Aileen

There's a home in Warrenton—a small town nestled just west of St. Louis—that looks just like any of the other well-kept homes in its middle-class subdivision, with their neat lawns and freshly painted facades. But this house hides something that makes it very different from the rest of the neighborhood.

A woman named Aileen died in the home in October 2002, after fighting a long battle with cancer. Aileen wasn't exactly a nice person in life, and her ex-husband, David, would find out a lot he didn't know about her after she died. He learned that she had affairs, embezzled money, and did not pay their taxes for the years that they were married. His family claims she was an evil person, and one of David's sisters said that Aileen told her she sold her soul to the devil prior to her death.

The home actually belongs to David. Just two days after Aileen's death, a strange event took place there. David was in the kitchen discussing with his family some of the dirty secrets he learned at Aileen's funeral when the light fixtures suddenly exploded all over them for no reason. It gave the family a bit of a start, but nobody was injured and they brushed off the event.

Shortly after that, David's grandmother moved into the house. From the moment she arrived, she complained that Aileen was pulling her hair, trying to trip her on the stairs, or otherwise harm her, but the family just laughed it off and paid no attention to what she was saying.

The activities in the home began to increase in February 2003, when David became engaged and his fiancée, Bonnie, moved in with him. Bonnie began to experience minor events: something tugging at her hair, items disappearing from one place, only to reappear in a different spot, and hearing conversations and someone walking in the house when she was the only one home.

On one occasion, Bonnie had a scratch on her back that appeared to be the letter A.

She kept her experiences to herself until the day of a family gathering, when David's sisters were laughing at their grandmother's claims that Aileen was trying to hurt her. They shared with Bonnie some of the stories the older woman had told them, and she was shocked. She told the sisters she was having some of the same experiences in the house.

In the following months, the activity accelerated into what David and Bonnie called malicious. Heavy vases were pushed off the tops of cabinets, just missing their heads by inches. Doors would slam open and shut, and light fixtures frequently exploded. The couple would see "shadow people" walking around the house at all hours of the day. On one occasion, Bonnie had a scratch on her back that appeared to be the letter A. The house's haunting hot spot seems to be the master bedroom, where Aileen had died. Bonnie claimed this is where most of the activity took place.

The electrical disturbances finally became so frequent that the couple hired an electrician to determine if there was something wrong with their wiring. To their concern and amazement, nothing was wrong. The electrician had no explanations for why they were having these problems.

The couple decided to paint the inside of their house, and hired David's sister's boyfriend to do the work. He was in the home for about two days but left without finishing the job. He claims that while in the house he heard voices and saw someone walking around when no one else—at least no one from this world—was there. His equipment kept disappearing, only to reappear in another spot. The same events happened to another man doing some work in the house. Both refused to set foot in the home again, as do many family members.

Call In the Investigators

Bonnie eventually contacted Kari Morrison, co-founder of WISP (Working to Investigate the Supernatural and Paranormal), for assistance with their haunting, and the WISP team has been investigating and collecting evidence in the home for two and a half years. In that time, they've found that paranormal activity peaks in May, June, and October, which they believe is tied to significant events in those months: Aileen found out she had cancer in May, her birthday was in June, and she passed away in October.

In just the first investigation, the WISP team documented doors opening and shutting on their own, foul odors emanating and disappearing in the master bedroom, and objects being moved. They also experienced a high electromagnetic field (EMF) and temperature spikes in the home, which can indicate paranormal activity.

The most disturbing event during the first investigation was scratches that appeared on the backs of David and two members of WISP after the group had brought up the subject of Aileen's lesser qualities. There were other investigators in the room at the time, but nobody saw anyone inflicting scratches upon themselves or anyone else.

WISP conducts all investigations under a controlled environment and sets up cameras around the house to keep track of where team members are during investigations. They've come up with no natural explanation for any of the events occurring in the house.

David and Bonnie continue to live in the house and report paranormal activity on a regular basis. The couple says the haunting in their home has opened their eyes and has made them, and many family members who once were skeptical, strong believers in the paranormal.

—*Kari Morrison, www.wispteam.net*

Ghost in a Jewel in a Pigsty

When looking at the architecture of any mid-nineteenth-century structure, whether it's Victorian, Georgian, or Renaissance-revival style, it's easy to imagine an ill-defined figure standing in an upstairs window looking out at a living, breathing world that it isn't technically part of anymore. To the observer, curtains in the windows seem to move even when hanging as still as death, and overcast days bring a gloom that intensifies the sense of foreboding. These buildings look the part of a haunted house.

Such is the case for Missouri's Governor's Mansion, in Jefferson City. Designed by architect George Ingham Barnett, the mansion was constructed in 1871 for $75,000. It sits on immaculately manicured grounds and presents great character and history to those who view it. During its initial construction, the mansion was actually once referred to as a "jewel in a pigsty" because of the primitive living conditions surrounding the area in which it was built. Today, the Governor's Mansion attracts 60,000 visitors each year, all of whom may enjoy guided tours of the rooms—but not the attic.

That the attic is not part of the tour is no surprise. There's no reason to visit here, as it's used just for storage. But the attic does have a history, and it's not one that involves matters of state or political intrigue, quiet hanky-panky, or even strange scientific experiments. The attic's history is paranormal. It is theorized that the hauntings there draw from the past lives of the Crittenden family.

Thomas Theodore Crittenden was the governor of Missouri from 1881 to 1885. He was a Civil War veteran, an attorney, and the man who put up a $10,000 award for the capture of Jesse James, an offer that would soon lead to the robber's death. By any definition, Crittenden was a strong personality and not accustomed to being weakened by severity of circumstance.

However, Crittenden was also the father of a little girl named Carrie, who was the love of his life, and he

was devastated when his precious daughter died of diphtheria in 1882.

At some point during the tenure of Governor Christopher Bond (mid-1970s, early 1980s), a construction worker spent the entire day in the attic doing repair work. At the end of the day, he made a comment that the governor's daughter was still upstairs in the attic playing and that she had spent the entire day there. He was told that the Bonds did not have a young daughter.

Was the little girl the spirit of Carrie Crittenden? Some say yes, others are unsure, but there is one construction worker who was concerned enough about this possibility that he did not return to complete the work in the attic.

The Man of the House

By Steven A. LaChance

Do you believe in ghosts? I used to be like most people—a true skeptic, a real disbeliever. Now I do believe, and I wish I didn't. Even now, four years later, I am still awakened in the night by the memory of the screaming man and the dark ghostly image that turned my world upside down and changed my beliefs forever.

I was a single father living in Union, and I desperately needed a place for myself and my three children to live. One evening I received a call from this landlady telling me about a house. She said it was a rather large old place that was in very good shape. She invited me to an open house that coming Sunday.

When Sunday rolled around, you can't imagine our surprise when my daughter and I pulled up in front of this large, old white house. We walked in and stood in a living room with all the original woodwork intact and a string of cherubs surrounding the top of the walls.

The first night in the house went by without much fanfare. As I look back on it now, I wonder if that may have been because the house wanted to draw us in a little closer before beginning its series of attacks and assaults upon me and my family.

The house had two floors, three bedrooms, and a large family kitchen with a mudroom that led to the back door. It was more house than we ever imagined for the price, and we immediately made up our minds that we had to have it. As I handed my application to the landlady she asked, "You understand the responsibility that comes with living in an old house such as this?"

"Oh, yes, I understand. It's beautiful," I quickly replied, not really understanding what I was agreeing to.

After about a week or so, the phone rang. It was the old landlady, who was excited to tell me that she had selected us to live in the old house. We signed all the necessary papers and moved in at the end of that week, which was Memorial Day weekend.

I was removing the last few items from the moving truck when a car slowed down, almost stopping in front of our new home. The passenger said from the window, "Hope you get along okay here," and then they drove away.

The first night in the house went by without much fanfare. As I look back on it now, I wonder if that may have been because the house wanted to draw us in a little closer before beginning its series of attacks and assaults upon me and my family.

The first incident happened in the living room. I was hanging a large picture of two angels. My daughter thought that this would complement the cherubs that surrounded the room. I hung the painting and turned to walk away. Then CRASH! I turned to see that the picture had fallen to the floor. I hung the picture once again and turned away. Crash—the picture was on the floor. As I hung it a third time and turned to walk away, I felt a rush of air and something hit the back of my ankles.

What the . . . ? I thought. I turned to see the picture lying at my feet. More determined than ever, I hung the picture again, then stated loudly, "Stay there dammit." I had to laugh, because I was alone. Who did I think I was talking to? The kids were playing on the front porch at the time. "Dad, come and see this." My daughter's voice rang through the front door. I stepped out onto the porch. "Sit down and watch this!" she said excitedly.

"Watch what?"

My daughter pointed to an old man walking down the sidewalk toward our house. But when he reached our property line, he quickly crossed the street and continued his walk on the opposite sidewalk.

"They don't like walking in front of our house, Dad! Isn't that weird?" my daughter observed. And right she was. I sat on that porch for a good hour, watching neighbors cross the street to avoid our house. A couple of times I motioned as if to say hello, and they just dropped their heads and continued on their way, quickening their pace. Maybe they are uncomfortable with new neighbors, I thought, trying to make sense out of the senseless.

He moved into the family room, pausing in the center of the floor. His form was still a mass of churning, turning blackness. He stood there for what seemed an eternity, but in actuality, it was only a few moments, and then he melted into thin air.

That Sunday the kids came home from church excited because we had set aside the whole day to work on our yard. This was a big deal for us because the only outside property they had ever been able to call theirs was the balcony of our old apartment. We mowed the grass and cleaned the leaves out from under the porch and in the front yard. At some point, I asked my youngest son to go inside and bring out the garden hose that was in the basement. A few moments passed; then I heard him screaming from inside the house. I ran in frantically to find him. He was standing in the middle of the kitchen floor shaking. "What's wrong? What happened?" I asked.

"Something chased me up the basement steps."

"What chased you?" I asked, already thinking the overactive imagination of a little boy was at play here.

"I don't know, Daddy, but it was big."

My two other children and I checked the basement, but found nothing except for the garden hose that my youngest had dropped in fear.

On the following Sunday, we were all sitting in the living room talking. The kids had their backs to the family room, which I am still thankful for. Because what happened next still haunts my dreams to this day. I was getting ready to take a trip the next morning to Indianapolis for work. We were discussing the plans that had been made for the children's stay at their grandma's. I noticed it first out of the corner of my eye: a quick glance of something moving, then standing at the kitchen doorway that led into the family room. But not something—someone. I looked toward it again. It was a dark figure of a man, even though there was full light in the room. He was solid in form, except he appeared to be made up of what looked like a moving, churning, dark gray-and-black smoke or mist. I looked down because I was sure I was seeing things. My eyes were playing tricks on me. I was sure that when I looked up again, it would be gone.

After a moment passed, I looked up again. He was still there. And he began to move. He moved into the family room, pausing in the center of the floor. His form was still a mass of churning, turning blackness. He stood there for what seemed an eternity, but in actuality, it was only a few moments, and then he melted into thin air.

I remember the thoughts that were racing through my head: I have two choices. We could run out of the house screaming into the night like those crazies you always see in the movies. Or we could get up quietly, leave the house, and figure all of this out.

My hand was shaking uncontrollably, and I said to myself, That's what we'll do. We will go quietly, orderly, as if nothing was wrong. I stood up shakily. And in my nicest, calmest Daddy voice, I said, "Let's go get a soda and see Grandma." My youngest was instantly excited at

the prospect of a soda before bed, and the older two looked at me as if I'd lost my mind. "Come on, guys, it will be fun."

Thank God my car keys were on the coffee table in front of us. We moved in an orderly way out the front door. As I turned to lock the door, the muffled, painful wail of a man came from inside the house. It was loud enough that it could be heard by the neighborhood dogs, which began to bark.

To hell with orderly! "Get in the car!" I screamed at my children. The drive to my mom's house is still a blur to this day. I do remember that as we were driving away, my youngest son was very scared and said, "Daddy, the basement monster is standing in the upstairs window." I looked back, and sure enough, the black form was there, standing in the window, watching us leave.

That night we stayed at my parents' house. Early the next day I gathered my things and left for my business trip, leaving the kids at my mom's. I had a whole week of rationalizations by the time I returned home. Where else were we to go? I had put everything I had saved and then some into the move. We had to go back to the big old house. Besides, after a week of talking myself out of the events of that night, I was ready to return.

We went back that Friday, and the weekend passed without incident and very little sleep. My parents convinced me that maybe it wouldn't be such a bad idea to call the strange old landlady and ask her some straightforward questions about the house. It was the most awkward phone call of my life and the strangest. Once I was able to reach her, I asked in my most normal of voices and my most careful choice of words if she had known of any of the previous tenants' mentioning perhaps, a ghost?

Well, of course, at first she said that she could not remember. Then she mentioned that there was this one tenant: a girl who claimed that her dead father came to visit her, but the old woman always thought she was crazy. The girl had left some of her stuff behind in the shed, but she couldn't get her to come pick it up. And there was another guy who had lived there and had left in the middle of the night without his things. But, no, she had never heard of anyone talking about the house being haunted. The phone call wasn't of much help, and it didn't calm my fears. Much.

The rest of the weekend came and went. I actually had convinced myself that it was just a one-time ordeal because nothing was happening now—that was until that Monday night.

I was on the phone with my mom. The kids were off playing in my bedroom, which was also located on the first floor. While talking to my mother, I heard the doors rattle. Not the outside doors, but the inside doors of the house. I listened. They rattled again. I yelled at the kids to quit playing games. I told my mom that everything was okay—just the kids playing tricks. The doors rattled again, this time harder. So I scolded the children, this time a little louder, asking them to behave and stop playing tricks. At this point, my daughter's scared voice cut me off.

"Daddy, I'm in here reading, and the boys are asleep."

Just as soon as I heard my daughter, the temperature in the house instantly dropped thirty degrees. With it,

this electrical-charged feeling ran through my body. Along with its energy came a horrible stench. And then the screaming started, softly at first, but building in volume. I screamed through the phone at my mother to come help, because we were getting out.

The whole house at this time began to shake and come alive. From above, I could hear something large coming down the stairs. Boom. Boom! BOOM! The screaming of a man, over and over. The screaming of my daughter, "Daddy, what's happening!" And the thought that one of my two bedroom doors connected to the stairs. BOOM! BOOM! It was coming down those stairs! I had to get to my children! The whole house was alive with noise.

The floor beneath me was shaking as I hung up the phone. I felt something behind me, and I knew I didn't want to turn around to see it. By the time I made it to my bedroom door, I was screaming myself. I threw myself against the door, but it wouldn't budge. I threw myself against it again and again. It finally flew open. My daughter was in shock by this point. I instructed my middle son to grab his brother and run out the front door and head for the car amid the continuing screams and bangs of the house.

Whatever it was, it was on our trail, and I knew I couldn't let it reach us. We reached the front door and ran out onto the porch. I slammed the front door behind us. We got to the car and could still hear the angry noises coming from the house. I drove away and parked at the top of the street, where I could look down into the house and wait for my parents to arrive. While there, my children and I could see something through the windows. There was a blackness moving through the house from room to room, methodically. It seemed to be searching— searching for us! That was our last night in the house. My children never returned.

I went back to get a few of our things when needed, but never alone. One day while I was down in the dim basement, my brother snapped a picture of me. I can't really say why; perhaps after all I'd told him about the house and its spooky basement, he just wanted to kid me about it for years to come. Nobody was joking around, however, when we developed the photo and saw the cloudy image of a man hanging right behind me in a darkened corner of the cellar. Though shadowy, the figure was clear enough that we could make out some details about it. The man seemed to be from a different time, with thick muttonchop sideburns and a ribbon bow tie. His face was a very angry one.

About a month after moving, my brother sent me an e-mail with a link to a Web site that he desperately wanted me to see. He said he had been doing some poking around online, looking into local history, when he found something incredible. "Put 'John T. Crowe, Union, Missouri' into your search engine," he instructed. I did. The face of a man came onto my screen. It was the same face that showed up in the picture my brother had taken in the cellar that afternoon. The man was apparently quite well known as a Civil War captain—a hero, in fact. He was also a very well-respected town citizen in his day and had once owned the house and surrounding land that my kids and I had fled from in the night. But nothing about why his spirit might still be in the house.

About a year ago, someone I know saw a police car race up to that house one night and watched a family running out of its front door in their nightclothes. After that, the old lady turned the place into a dog kennel. I guess she ran out of people who could live in that old white house. I still drive past it every once in a while when I get up enough nerve; as I look up at the upstairs window, I can still imagine him there— watching, waiting, angry.

High School Ghost on Tape?

One night the security cameras at Fort Zumwalt West High School in O'Fallon caught the image of something, maybe a ghost. But it was moving up the walls of our high school. The night janitor came running out of a stairwell scared stiff by the ghostly image. The image is on the security camera tape and kids could go to the security office and watch the tape.—*John Reese*

City Museum Ghosts

A supposedly haunted place is the City Museum in downtown St. Louis. Used in the 1930s as part of the International Shoe Company, it originally had huge chutes where the shoes would tumble down that are now used as slides. Supposedly, during the Great Depression little kids died there from the cold.

My girlfriend worked there for two years and says they have three or four ghosts: one older male and three kids. She told me of an experience she had where she was driving the mini train there. Little kids would see their breath as they passed through a tunnel, and they would ask who the little girl was that played with them. She also said that on one of the off-limits floors there is a room filled with hats and a poltergeist-like entity moved the hats around and stuff.—*Josh, a.k.a. The Ghost Hunter*

A Spirited Collection of Books

Robert Snyder Jr., son and namesake of the wealthy businessman who built Ha Ha Tonka Castle in Camdenton (see the "Abandoned" chapter) had a fascination with texts about Missouri's folklore and local history. He'd eventually own over one thousand books, which he kept in the castle's library. After his death, the collection was donated to the University of Kansas City, which would become the University of Missouri at Kansas City. The library may also be home to Robert Snyder Jr.'s spirit. It is pure speculation, but some believe the man's passion for his book collection may have brought his curious spirit to the U.M.K.C. campus. It could explain why people have reported the sense of being watched while in the library housing his collection. Is the junior Mr. Snyder standing guard over his books? If so, his presence is nonthreatening and produces little more than the rustling noise of pages being turned in the aisles holding his collection. Possibly his spiritual benevolence is a result of his living with the "laughing spirit" of Ha Ha Tonka all those years at the castle.

The Sad Tale of the Lemp Family Mansion

The Lemp Mansion is located on Demenil Street, in the brewery section of South St. Louis. It is in exquisite condition and has a regular flow of people who tour, dine, and even sleep overnight in bed-and breakfast–style accommodations.

In 2003, a couple seeking a romantic "haunting" getaway got their money's worth at the Lemp Mansion.

The woman told *Weird Missouri*, "We heard strange noises and saw things that were not there. Or were they? We took photos around the house, and when they came back, there was the shadow of a woman in the tub in our suite, an odd misty shape in the gazebo, and a face in the hall light. [We heard] voices screaming, doors being kicked [in], things being knocked over. It made my husband a believer."

But what had transpired in the past that would provide a modern ghost-hunting couple with such prolific paranormal action in a B and B operating in the first part of the twenty-first century?

The Lemp family built their mansion close to their business, and a labyrinth of natural tunnels exists underneath its inviting facade. Tunnels are generally known to be optimal surroundings for spirits to congregate within and perhaps even to make the lives of those living above more interesting.

Another element is the downfall of the Lemp family itself. While the family initially gained much wealth and local influence as a result of its beer-making success, following generations did a good job of destroying what their ancestors had built. The founder of the Lemp empire, Johann Adam Lemp, died twenty-two years after starting the company, leaving it in the capable hands of his son, William. Success might have continued, but one of William Lemp's sons died prematurely, at age twenty-eight. His devastated father soon followed this son into death, by a self-inflicted revolver wound to the head. In doing so, he started a tragic family trend.

William's death left the company in the hands of the family lightweight, William Lemp II, who promptly led the firm into financial ruin. Along the way, he destroyed his loving wife's life and produced an illegitimate son who likely had Down syndrome and was the butt of cruel nicknames in the family. It's rumored that this boy spent his entire life cloistered away in the mansion's attic to avoid causing embarrassment to his relatives, and he reportedly makes ghostly appearances on the third floor of the mansion.

When Prohibition drove the final nail into the coffin of the already depleted Lemp fortune, William II ended his destructive life in 1922, using a revolver to shoot himself through the heart.

William II's siblings didn't fare much better. Two committed suicide: Elsa in 1920 and Charles in the early 1940s (before he did himself in, Charles killed his Doberman Pinscher in the mansion's basement). In 1970, Edwin—the reclusive and last offspring of the Lemp family—died of natural causes in the mansion.

Given the sad history of the house, it is no surprise that visitors have heard the sound of a howling dog in the basement. Also on the roster of ghostly experiences are shadowy figures, objects moving by themselves, footfalls from upstairs (Charles killed himself on the second floor), and slamming doors. There are even reports of a ghostly Peeping Tom in a downstairs ladies' room. Ghosts aren't known for appearing when you want them to, but experience shows you might have better luck seeing one at the Lemp Mansion than elsewhere.

St. Charles: Haunted City

One of the most haunted cities in Missouri, possibly even the entire United States, is St. Charles. Its Main Street is home to multiple entities that inspire different tales about why they are being stranded between the worlds of the living and the dead.

Situated along the western banks of the Missouri River, St. Charles has had much drama in its past. It's

always been active with the hustle and bustle of river life, where men and women plied their trades and established their futures two hundred years ago.

Weird Missouri knows one St. Charles ghost story that comes from an unimpeachable source who told us that she and her husband have encountered this entity on more than one occasion at Rumples, an Irish-influenced eatery and bar. This spirit likes to brush up against people, remove silverware from tables, and in general just make everyone a little bit uncomfortable.

However, no one who works at Rumples seems to be the least bit concerned about the ghost's presence, and in fact they are eager to share their experiences. Rumples Pub is located at 221 North Main Street. Today it's where the only obvious spirits around are those served at the bar.

Stairway to Heaven

Under edict of Andrew Jackson's forced relocation plan, spanning the year 1838–1839, the Cherokee Indian Tribe (along with the Creek, Choctaw, Seminole, and Chicasaw tribes) was forced to leave their fertile lands in the Tennessee Valley and move west of the Mississippi River to what was virtually a dust bowl in the Oklahoma Territory.

Of the fifteen thousand Cherokee who began the pilgrimage, only eleven thousand survived the eight-hundred-mile test of will. This is now known as the Trail of Tears.

The land route that eventually traversed the Show Me State began in Charleston, Tennessee, ran northwest through what is now Nashville, on up through Kentucky, across the very southern portion of Illinois, then entered Missouri at Cape Girardeau, where it looped over to Springfield and down through the northwestern tip of Arkansas, finally ending near Tahlequah, Oklahoma It was, under the best of circumstances, an extremely challenging journey.

This harsh route of relocation created a population of Native American spirits who still roam its path. Or so it was communicated to Larry Baggett of Jerome. Mr. Baggett's property sits on a hill just west of Jerome, in Phelps County, and is the site of a great deal of unique and artistic statuary, stone arches, steps, and walls. It was Mr. Baggett's stone wall that became the problem for spirits attempting to complete their westward journey across Missouri.

Sometime after his wife's death, Mr. Baggett began to be awakened during the night by knocks at the door. Every time he answered the knock, he found no one there. He was later told by an elderly Indian that the knock on the door was a Cherokee spirit wanting to tell Mr. Baggett that one of his stone walls was blocking the

path of the spiritual Trail of Tears. He took the story to heart and built a set of steps over the existing wall. Then, lo and behold, the knocking stopped.

It is a story that serves to remind us that our past is not unsullied. Mr. Baggett's property, with its distinctive stone archway and meandering walls, is hard to miss. It is located on the north side of Highway T after one takes the Jerome exit off Route 44.

Tales from the Grave

Some people find cemeteries depressing, but *Weird Missouri* is fascinated by them and the many ways people in this state have honored and memorialized their dead. From the world's smallest tombstone to the over-the-top monuments found along Millionaire's Row in St. Louis's Bellefontaine Cemetery, we've got grave sites that raise immediate questions about those buried under them or entombed within.

Dramatic stories involving cemeteries are rife here. In Paris, a man buried three wives, side by side and in quick succession, and then seemingly disappeared. Some visiting Peace Church Cemetery have reported seeing what might be the ghost of a mass murderer. And we've got enough glowing graves in Missouri to call us the Glow Me state.

But Missouri cemeteries are not all about death. One couple recently chose to take their vows in a cemetery in the city of Pacific, effectively making their beginning among so many ends.

Have a Seat

Mount Olivet Cemetery, located on a hilltop on the south side of Hannibal, is the resting place for the real-life version of Tom Sawyer's nemesis Injun Joe as well as several other lesser-known but notable people. All share in having unique if not weird memorial monuments. When visiting the Chriscinske grave site, there is a not-so-subtle invitation to take a load off and visit a while.

World's Smallest Tombstone

Butler is home to the world's smallest tombstone. The tiny memorial, about the size of a three-by-five card, is a frequently visited grave site in Oak Hill Cemetery, thanks to a mention in *Ripley's Believe It or Not!* Perhaps due to constant questions as to its location, the cemetery has been kind enough to place a sign pointing the way to the diminutive marker; otherwise, visitors might wind up looking for it long enough to make it into *Ripley's* under the category of longest search for smallest tombstone!

A Mount Olive Mummy

The remains of Joseph Marconnot are sometimes referred to as the Mount Olive Mummy, or King Tut, or even as just "the odd guy behind the stainless-steel door." But it was not always that way.

Marconnot was a man of modest means who got it in his head that he wanted to be remembered and admired after his death. His plan for being remembered involved the construction of an elaborate tomb with a transparent glass door as its permanent closure. He wanted to be dressed to the nines in a tuxedo and placed on display for all to admire.

While his wishes were indeed complied with, there were those who were skeptical of the security and sanctity of his grave site at the Mount Olive Cemetery in Carondelet. Many worried that vandals would deface or break into the vulnerable tomb. Thus, the glass door was replaced with stainless steel.

Mr. Marconnot is no longer visible to the public, which is probably for the best because, hey, decomposition happens and that tux is probably not looking very sharp anymore.

It Glows!

Maybe it's just bad lighting or radioactivity or some kind of gas that makes things in these Missouri cemeteries glow. Or . . . maybe it's a more supernatural source. We'll let you decide for yourselves.

Glowing and Floating at Carpenter Cemetery

We heard about Carpenter Cemetery from a very nice hotel desk clerk who had familiarity with the place from her high school days. After she told us her animated story, she followed by saying in heartfelt terms that she would never go back! The experience scared the bejeebers out of her.

Carpenter Cemetery is located on Route 61 just south of Morley. It's easy to find, with a small sign denoting the cemetery's presence. A narrow dirt road leads back to nicely cared-for grounds, with the road dead-ending at railroad tracks that run at right angles to the road. Obviously, you need to go there at night, specifically midnight. It seems that if you shine your headlights across the cemetery and then turn them off, the tombstones will begin to glow. Most eerie is the added oddity of the names inscribed on those glowing tombstones. They slowly disappear. Or so the story goes.

There is also another version of this tale that says by shining headlights across the cemetery at midnight you'll bring forth a floating blue baby who meanders around the cemetery's boundaries, possibly looking for an avenue of escape.

Sizzling Tombstone

In Jefferson City, there is a haunted cemetery with a few tombstones that glow green: My brother has a videotape of this. And if you spit on the tombstone, your saliva begins to sizzle. It is very strange and creepy. We don't know the mystery behind it yet, but if you give me some time I could come up with the whereabouts of this cemetery and you could check it out!—*Kenneth Pyland*

Leeton's Glowing Gravestone

In between Warrensburg and Clinton on Highway 13 is a town called Leeton. There is a cemetery there that has a glowing gravestone. I don't know what causes the stone to glow, but it's quite eerie.—*Lindsay Harmon*

Roy Rogers and Dale Evans with Trigger, who was mounted following his death in 1965 and now is exhibited inside the Roy Rogers–Dale Evans Museum.

Horsing Around

On Route 6 about twenty miles west of Kirksville is a cemetery that stands out because of the multitude of American flags that line its inner driveway. But as you admire the flags, something else might catch your "weird" eye.

That something is the grave site of Arthur Jackson, who died in 2001 at the age of eighty-four. Jackson has an additional memorial to keep him company: a small black-and-white horse, about the size of a miniature horse, which stands eternal vigil over the grave. We assume Jackson was an equine lover.

Some horses, however, rate their own Missouri graves. One is Dan, a horse owned by Frank James of the James Gang fame. When Dan died, Frank buried him in a field far away from the house he lived in on the James Farm, in Kearney.

Frank's postoutlaw lifestyle included giving guided tours of the James farm, which included a stop at Dan's grave site. As Frank aged, however, he was less enthusiastic about including Dan on the tours because of the grave's distance from the house. The solution? He moved the headstone near the house and called that the location of the burial plot. Who'd have thought that Frank James would ever pull the wool over anyone's eyes?

Another equine grave can be seen at Huer's Stables in Cape Girardeau. Rambler was also known as Huer's Valentine, having been born on February 14, and his Cupid connection must have made him quite the

stud, as he sired several champions in his life. His tombstone reveals that he lived from 1960 to 1977.

And in Branson you can find the very public resting place of one of America's most famous equines. Remember Roy Rogers's golden palomino, Trigger? Trigger's taxidermied remains are on display in the Roy Rogers—Dale Evans Museum, forever posed in the rearing-up position that kept so many of Roy's enemies at bay. Also on display is Buttermilk, the horse ridden by Roy's wife, Dale Evans.

Bone Hill Cemetery

Take a sheer cliff and stampede some buffalo toward it and you have a buffalo jump, a method used by some American Indian tribes to kill buffalo en masse. When there were no sheer cliffs to be found, a steep hillside would also prove effective: stampede the buffalo down the hill, let them stumble into a big broken pile, and then finish them off. Efficient, but it made for a lot of work, including leaving the bones to bleach out in the sun.

In Levasy, it's rumored that the discovery of some of the leftover bones is how Bone Hill Cemetery got its name. The cemetery, also known as Ebenezer Church Cemetery, is located atop a hill that is certainly steep enough to have been used to create a pile of buffalo.

Today, Bone Hill Cemetery is nicely tended, with privacy gates, manicured grass, and striking views from atop the hillside. People still come to pay their respects to the souls resting there . . . even though it appears that some might have trouble settling down.

The story goes that during the Civil War an unnamed family sold a large section of property for gold, then buried it near a stone fence that today is on cemetery property. Then the family, possibly motivated by the ugliness of border warfare, moved away, saying they would return in seven years. They left the gold in what they felt was a safe hiding place.

But seven years passed, and the family didn't return. Instead, a mysterious light appeared near the stone wall. Some think this is the spirit of family members returning to protect the location of the buried gold, and the light supposedly returns on a seven-year cycle. It hasn't been seen recently, leading some to theorize that the spirits finally made off with the gold. More scientific types think it may be gases that seep from the seams of the limestone-and-slate-composite hillside.

An Ending for Some, a Beginning for Others

Cemeteries serve a pretty conventional purpose. People, unfortunately, inevitably die. Their remains must be interred, their resting places marked, and the ritualistic and emotional needs of the surviving loved ones accommodated. And that is how most of us use cemeteries.

Unless you are Scott Amsler and Miranda Patterson, residents of Collinsville, Illinois. They decided to tie the knot in a most unconventional manner. Scott and Miranda chose the City Cemetery in Pacific as the venue for their marriage vows, and on September 8, 2007, they began their wedded years together within the confines of a piece of real estate that is usually a terminus.

Highly publicized prior to the event, the wedding itself was low-key with a small throng of well-wishers and relatives in attendance. The bridal party was conveyed to and from the cemetery in hearses, which the bridegroom happens to restore. The *Weird Missouri* team wishes the newlyweds the very best that life can offer.

The Dead Wives' Club

We make no claims to having any abilities as detectives, but when it comes to the curious deaths of one man's young wives during the middle of the nineteenth century it doesn't take Columbo to see a pattern that goes way beyond coincidence.

Founders Cemetery, in Paris, Monroe County, is a small and humble resting place for just over two hundred souls, including three women who were married to the same man: Daniel W. Dulany. His first wife was just nineteen when she married Dulany in 1841, and she died the following year. He married his next wife in 1845, and she also died within a year of taking her vows. Dulany interrupted his wife hunt for a couple of years, marrying again in 1851. She died in 1853.

Today, Dulany's ill-fated wives rest under a three-gabled tombstone, with weathered but vigilant carved angels overlooking their souls. Did these three early pioneer women share a taste in men with deadly charm?

Although they were young, all three could have died of natural causes; it wasn't uncommon for the times. Dulany might have just been one unlucky guy. But three marriages in a row where the longest-lived bride survived less than two years? We're thinking pattern.

Just who was this Dulany guy, and where is he laid to rest? It certainly isn't in Founders Cemetery!

A Grave Coincidence

My wife and I began looking at old houses once our children left home. The house we bought, which was built in Lexington in 1866, had a very interesting history. Apparently, the man who had built the house, a sergeant in the Civil War, had shot and killed himself there. I also learned that his granddaughter, Maxine Harlow, was married in the house in 1933, and that she had tragically lost both her husband and her young daughter—just two hours apart—in a food-poisoning incident. They both died in the house.

This interested me because my grandmother, Mildred Clark, lost her husband in an electrocution accident at work, and two years later her daughter (my mother) died at the young age of 20 while washing dishes at home. So both Maxine and Mildred had suffered the tragic loss of a husband and a daughter.

I went to the cemetery to find the graves, as I wanted to get dates that I might use to research both of the stories related to my new home. The sergeant's marker did not have a date. However, when I arrived at the marker for the father and daughter, I had to stop and catch my breath. It couldn't be!

I took a photo of the marker in Lexington, and then went to the cemetery in Kansas City where my mother is buried and took a photo of the marker there. It was really weird to put the photos side by side. The markers at both cemeteries read FATHER EDWIN, DAUGHTER SANDRA.

Mildred and Maxine were born just ten days apart in 1910. My grandmother Mildred passed away in 2001 at the age of 91. Maxine, whom I was hoping to meet, passed away in 2005 at the age of 95.—*Warren Calvert*

The Last Cuckoo

Ezra Milford Jones died on June 6, 1932, and if what we think we know about the afterlife's system of rewards and punishment holds true, he was heading for hard times. Mr. Jones was a mobster—a little-known wannabe among the infamous crooks of that era. Jones was a member of St. Louis's own "Cuckoo Gang."

Jones met his lackluster end in a nightclub. While he was probably the last of the Cuckoo Gang, his cause of death was no different from that of the majority of the other gang members: "lead poisoning." In keeping with his marginal notoriety as a gangster, Jones's death was treated as a minor news event.

Documents show that Jones was buried in Valhalla Cemetery, on St. Charles Rock Road, on Monday, June 20, 1932, at three fifteen p.m. He was buried not as a Valhalla-bound Norse warrior, but as a lowly hoodlum in a wooden coffin, sealed in a steel vault. He spent a lot of his life on earth housed behind steel, so eternity makes sense also. If for some inexplicable reason you wanted to visit the Jones grave site, he is buried in lot number 119, section 16. However, the final revelation about how disrespected Jones was is that his grave has no marker.

Short-Lived in Hannibal

Mount Olivet Cemetery in Hannibal is home to not only Mark Twain's infamous Injun Joe but also to a man about whom very little is known. Except that his life was cut short.

From a distance, the tombstone of William P. Harrison looks to be a tree that had been topped at about twenty feet, with its lower limbs clipped short. It looks real enough to be mistaken for part of the aging tree population in the area.

Sure, there are bigger and more expensive monuments out there, but they don't convey the message that Mr. Harrison's does. Sadly, there's a companion grave that is home to the remains of little Mary Harrison, who died at age four. Poetic as it is, the younger Harrison is represented by a miniature tree trunk, a stump that reflects the size and age of a child who died decades too soon.

Harrison's Tree is located in the back side of the cemetery, sitting about center in its grave field.

The Rich and the Dead: Bellefontaine

Many of Missouri's elite make their final resting place in Bellefontaine Cemetery. Names like Anheuser, Busch, Tate, Lemp, Brown, and Wainwright forever rest within the beautiful confines of this old St. Louis cemetery. These wealthy businessmen and their families attempted to remain as large in death as they were in life. The over-the-top element of Bellefontaine may merely reflect the atmosphere of the times, or it may reveal that ego prevails regardless of the time frame. And just as in real life they formed a financially elite clique, so too in death they remain close to one another.

Millionaire's Row largely comprises the cemetery streets of Prospect, Birch, and Woodbine and is home to many ostentatious displays of postlife opulence.

Brewer and financier Ellis Wainwright is housed for eternity in a structure designed by Louis Sullivan, the same architect who designed the Wainwright Building in downtown St. Louis. The Wainwright Building, one of the first skyscrapers, is handsome and balanced in its design

and quite pleasing to the eye. The tomb is more an expression of Sullivan's accommodating his client's serious case of postlife "look at me." It worked, as Wainwright's tomb is often called the Taj Mahal of St. Louis.

St. Louis is synonymous with Busch Beer, so the grave site of Adolfus Busch memorializes not just him but his company's influence. The tomb resembles a Gothic castle or cathedral. Impressive in its stature, it again reveals the competitive mindset existing within the rich families of the St. Louis area of that era.

Regardless of the motivation for such displays, the cumulative effect of visiting Bellefontaine is impressive.

Its 330 acres are immaculately manicured and pastoral, complementing the huge population of monolithic obelisks and monuments that stand guard over the dead.

If you're ever lacking something to do and want to marvel at the wide range of afterlife memorials that exist in the Show Me state, check out Bellefontaine Cemetery. It's full of odd, unique, and expensive carved-stone memorials that promote awe within the mind and heart of the visitor. Here is just a sampling of some of the more interesting ones.

Luyties's Beauty

Wealthy businessman Herman C. G. Luyties founded the Sanitol Chemical Laboratory Company in 1898. Sanitol became a giant in its niche, and St. Louis was at one time the world leader in the manufacture of tooth powder (which predates paste).

Along the way, Herman met many interesting and powerful people, but none held as much sway over his ability to think straight as a young woman who caught his eye and forever his heart. On a trip to Italy, he became infatuated with a supremely attractive model. Unlike any business decision he might have made, he foolhardily proposed marriage to the beauty who had so impressively compromised his judgment. To Luyties's great dismay, she declined his proposal.

Not broke but heartbroken, Luyties commissioned a sculptor to create a giant likeness of his heart's desire. The end result was a marble diorama of the voluptuous one who got away. Apparently, it stood in his home until his death in 1921. This tribute to a woman's beauty now stands eternal vigil at his grave site at Block 289/299, Lot 5790.

High-End Totem Pole

Native Americans of the Pacific Northwest used totem poles for a variety of reasons: to relate a family story, to record elements of their culture, or for ornamental purposes. But there is a unique grave marker in the form of a totem pole that leaves much to the visitor's imagination. William and Eliza Page are the two people who lie beneath the towering monolith.

While Native American totem poles were constructed of available standing timber—usually red cedar to resist insect infestation—the Pages chose a medium of considerably greater expense and durability: red granite. But much like the Native Americans, the Pages took advantage of indigenous materials, since Missouri has lots of the stone.

The message on their grave site, WAITING . . . FOR THE TRUMPET SHALL SOUND, AND THE DEAD SHALL BE RAISED, suggests that they were both confident in their eventual rebirth into a better life and place. The towering pole may simply be a way to get noticed by the trumpeters.

Just Like D.C.!

We have no idea what the obelisk count is in Bellefontaine, but it has to be in the many hundreds. They are of various heights, styles, and stones. If cleverly photographed, the monument that identifies the grave site of Charles S. Hills could easily be passed off as the Washington Monument. The giant granite obelisk stands forty feet tall and weighs a hundred tons.

Bare-Knuckle Champion

Back in the day when men were men, professional boxing matches were fought with bare knuckles. Bare-knuckle fighting has probably been a sport as long as the human species has been cognizant enough to give it an audience. A few nineteenth-century bare-knuckle pugilists are still household names, like John L. Sullivan and Gentleman Jim Corbett. Then there's a lesser known champion named Tom Allen. Allen is buried in Block 9, Lot 27-706. His claim to fame is recorded indelibly on his tombstone: He was the FIRST INTERNATIONAL BARE-KNUCKLE HEAVY-WEIGHT BOXING CHAMPION OF THE WORLD.

Unmarked Madam

A lonely grave site sits overlooking Cypress Lake. It contains the remains of a person who performed a valued, if somewhat notorious, service for the country during the Civil War.

Eliza Haycroft was a well-known madam in St. Louis. She and her ensemble of ladies of the night satisfied the needs of countless Civil War soldiers and other clientele in the city. Her services were a matter of common knowledge and her business was allowed to exist in relative peace. The people making the decisions that allowed it to exist—and to thrive—were of course

powerful persons of the male sex, even perhaps clients. However, in typical hypocritical style, when Madam Haycroft died, there was much angst about how she should or could be buried.

Bellefontaine Cemetery was her choice, but the self-righteous of that time did not want her buried in what was then a new and prestigious burial ground. Ultimately, they allowed her to be buried on a very pretty hillside in the cemetery, but there was a caveat. For her to rest in Bellefontaine she had to lie without a grave marker.

So it was then, and so it is today. Eliza Haycroft forever sleeps, unmarked, in Block 20, Lot 2076.

Sociopathic Ghost at Peace

Billy Cook had issues. His mother died early on, and his father simply left Billy and his seven siblings to live like animals in an abandoned mine shaft. Once discovered by the authorities and dispersed into foster homes, all of the children seemed to adapt, except for Billy. His emotional wounds would never heal, and he was in and out of reform schools and jail. He then devolved into the worst kind of human being.

His maniacal rage finally exploded at a level of cold-blooded violence that had yet to be seen in 1950s America. He carjacked a family of five, forced them to drive from state to state for over three days, then got paranoid and executed them. He later dumped their bodies in a mine shaft near Joplin. But it was not enough, so he hijacked another car and killed its innocent driver before transporting himself to Mexico.

By then, there were all-points bulletins with his picture sitting on the desks of every law-enforcement organization in the southwestern United States and Mexico. A Mexican sheriff arrested him, and he was returned to California to stand trial for murder. He was expeditiously convicted and executed in the gas chamber at San Quentin.

His body was returned to the Joplin area, but nobody wanted to remember him or even acknowledge that he had existed. A burial at Peace Church Cemetery finally took place, with his remains being placed into an unmarked grave outside the legal confines of the cemetery.

It is his tortured soul that many believe to be the shadowy figure that haunts Peace Church Cemetery. And most disturbing: In addition to the visual presence, there is frequently a ghostly voice that can be heard, telling the visitor in no uncertain terms to "GET OUT."

Rivers of the Dead

Having lived in St. Louis for the first 28 years of my life I am reminded of a story that happened in Missouri in 1993, when all the major rivers that run through the state, the Missouri River, the Meramac, and the Mighty Mississippi, flooded to catastrophic levels. The deep, raging waters destroyed dozens of homes and businesses, and washed a few people away to their deaths. The creepiest thing that happened, though, was that an old cemetery in an outlying St. Louis county area had completely flooded and stayed submerged under many feet of water for weeks. The water soaked and seeped into the ground so much that it loosened the earth, sending all the airtight, unvaulted caskets below shooting up through the earth and out of the ground. Seven hundred and ninety-three caskets floated around flooded subdivisions like boats, and the water was actually high enough that the coffins crashed through first-story level windows of a few homes. It wasn't until after the water had receded that the real horror of it all was exposed.

As area residents went back to their waterlogged, mud-caked homes to salvage personal belongings or whatever was left, they opened their doors to find caskets lying about their living rooms and kitchens. Like a scene right out of *Poltergeist*, it was discovered that some caskets had even burst open and spilled out corpses, and a good many bodies were found strewn about inside on beds and countertops. Outside was just as horrific— bodies were everywhere, in fields and parking lots, on top of cars and tangled in chain-link fences. A guy I know told me that his uncle found the decayed head of an old lady hanging from the swing set in his backyard. Her long grey hair had tangled around the swing chain and her body had ripped away with the flowing water, leaving the skull and hair behind.—*Stephen, Marina del Rey, CA*

The Missouri Giantess

In 1913, a Missouri resident of immense—both metaphorical and literal—proportions passed away. Not surprisingly for someone her size, her shadow still looms large over the state today.

Ella K. Ewing lived just outside Gorin, in a peaceful, spacious rural area. This makes sense, as Ewing must have needed a lot of room in her life. After all, the famous performer stood a colossal eight feet four and a half inches and weighed in at a whopping two hundred and seventy-seven pounds. Her physical size was rivaled only by the size of her fame. In her day, she made appearances across many countries and continents, meeting thousands upon thousands of people who paid good money to meet a woman of her size.

Ella began growing quickly after birth due to a pituitary-gland disorder. By the age of twelve, she stood at five feet seven inches tall. A mere two years later, she was six feet three. By her midteens, she towered above her own father. Childhood friends recall in newspaper articles that despite her size, Ella had the normal attitudes and countenance of a young girl.

Due to enduring mockery and stares throughout childhood, Ella didn't enjoy appearing in public during her youth. At a certain point, however, Ella's needs became difficult for her parents to accommodate, although they tried. They were rebuilding furniture annually, and their daughter's increasing size made it hard for her to live in their modest working-class home. Ella and her parents decided that she could live more happily and support the family by making public appearances. In this capacity, she thrived. She toured with both Buffalo Bill and P. T. Barnum. Thousands of

people came from far and wide for a chance to see the nationally renowned Missouri Giantess. For extra money, they could even shake her hand.

Ella's home life was quite different from her famous public persona. She sought comfort, peace, and quiet, and to the credit of her Missouri neighbors, she got it. Ella lived on a large amount of acreage she purchased, in a home she had custom-built with large doors and windows. She was active in the community church and was beloved by locals, who would often meet her at the train station and welcome her home after her long tours around North America and Europe. She also used her fortune to build her parents a new home. The girl who was once scared to be laughed at by the public used their curiosity about her condition to finance a comfortable life for herself and a better life for her family.

Ella had marriage proposed to her by dozens of suitors. However, she remained wary of their intentions, noting that these men came forward to profess their love only after Ella had gained a small fortune touring on the road.

Upon her death from pneumonia at the age of forty-one, nine hundred people came to the funeral to offer their good wishes—and none were gawkers. They all considered themselves friends of the gentle lady. However, Ella's death matched her life despite this. Even her funeral, where ten pallbearers helped carry her remains, had an element of spectacle to it. A 1973 article from *The Sentinel* describes that:

> The Embalming Burial Case Company of Burlington, Iowa, was said to have put its entire force to work all one night and half the next day to make her casket, designed with a fancy octagon end and covered with white plush. The casket was so long that the seat in the horse-drawn hearse had to be removed to allow the rear doors to close.

Ella with her parents

Ella's grave at Gorin's Harmony Grove Baptist Church is still visited by many who are curious about the life of this gargantuan woman. Her plot extends farther than those it shares a row with.

Ella's life, and death, left huge imprints on the nation and on the community of Northeast Missouri. She is still remembered today, most notably at the Downing House Museum in Memphis, Missouri. There, people still visit to look at a plaster model of Ella, as well as to gawk at her size twenty-four shoes.

Satchel Paige: An Island Unto Himself

When Leroy "Satchel" Paige said, "I ain't never had a job, I just always played baseball," he was being somewhat disingenuous. Paige earned the nickname during his teens, while working as a bag boy. He'd carry so many satchels that his fellow baggage handlers just anointed him with the now famous handle.

Satchel Paige was the Negro League's greatest pitcher and the oldest to play in the major leagues. His real age isn't known, but his estimated birth date of July 7, 1906, would have made him forty-two when he started in the major leagues. Such a thing would never happen now.

Known for his confident and sometimes grandstanding style, Satchel Paige packed the Negro League bleachers for over twenty seasons. The secret to his success was a keen analytical eye when it came to sizing up his bat-wielding opponents. It's fascinating to speculate about how he would have done had his entire career been in the major leagues. And even though his time in the majors was relatively short, the strength of his career in total earned him a place in the Baseball Hall of Fame.

Paige left a legacy of quotes that places him just behind Yogi Berra and Dizzy Dean as one of baseball's most quotable characters. His observations and language so defined him, his tombstone is in part advice to the world shared from the grave. A sample: DON'T LOOK BACK, SOMETHING MIGHT BE GAINING ON YOU.

Paige is buried on what we are going to call the Mound. His grave site in Kansas City's Forest Hill Cemetery is located almost dead center in the cemetery on a plot called Paige Island. Just as in the arena of baseball where he was clearly the star on any team, in death Satchel Paige still remains center stage.

PAIGE

HE BEGAN WORK CARRYING SUITCASES AT MOBILE UNION STATION AND DEVISED A SLING HARNESS FOR HUSTLING SEVERAL BAGS AT ONCE. THE OTHER RED CAPS SAID HE LOOKED LIKE A "WALKING SATCHEL TREE" THUS LEROY BECAME SATCHEL. AND SATCHEL BECAME A LEGEND.

HOW TO STAY YOUNG

1 AVOID FRIED MEATS WHICH ANGRY UP THE BLOOD.
2 IF YOUR STOMACH DISPUTES YOU, LIE DOWN AND PACIFY IT WITH COOL THOUGHTS.
3 KEEP THE JUICES FLOWING BY JANGLING AROUND GENTLY AS YOU MOVE.
4 GO VERY LIGHT ON THE VICES, SUCH AS CARRYING ON IN SOCIETY. THE SOCIAL RAMBLE AIN'T RESTFUL.
5 AVOID RUNNING AT ALL TIMES.
6 DON'T LOOK BACK. SOMETHING MIGHT BE GAINING ON YOU.

Younger's Not Getting Any Older

Cole Younger was just another wild man of the Wild West. He robbed, pillaged, and generally created years of unwanted and unnecessary mayhem. He finally got as good as he gave after the botched Northfield Minnesota Robbery, when he was shot up during a gunfight with a posse that was chasing him. He did time in a federal penitentiary but was freed just after the beginning of the twentieth century. He lived out his life as a "lecturer" and an actor in the Cole Younger and Frank James Wild West Show, and died in 1916.

Located in Lee's Summit, his primary tombstone is one of the better-looking grave markers associated with that era's collection of bad men. If you had no knowledge of Younger's dark past, his grave would lead you to believe that he was a special man who did special things. His secondary marker labels him as a "Captain" in Quantrill's Raiders, the significance of which can be summed up as "six-gun-wielding nightmare."

Cole Younger's grave and his handsome tombstone are in Lee's Summit Historical Cemetery. While there, you can admire the markers of the rest of his troubled family: James, Robert, and his mom Bursheba. She mercifully died in 1870 and did not have to witness the twisted lives her sons pursued.

The Real Injun Joe

In Mark Twain's The Adventures of Tom Sawyer, the character Injun Joe is unquestionably a bad actor: angry, mean, and ultimately self-destructive. He's controversial and brings up several issues, including that of an author using a real person to develop a negative fictional character.

Twain never said that Injun Joe was based on a real character. But there was a half-Indian resident of Hannibal named Joe Douglass, now buried in the Mount Olivet Cemetery. Is it mere coincidence that the man buried in the same town in which the Tom Sawyer adventure took place is also a man who very much resembled Injun Joe? Joe Douglass had facial scarring associated with a severe case of smallpox. To make matters worse, he had been scalped at some point and wore a horsehair wig. He was probably a rough-looking individual, and would have been a good starting point for Twain's imagination in the creation of a bad man. But Joe Douglass's tombstone states in no uncertain terms that HE HAD ALWAYS LIVED AN HONORABLE LIFE.

Given what a bad man the character Injun Joe was, it's understandable that Mr. Douglass would want to distance himself from such a comparison, and after being on this earth for 102 years we'd like to think that he had the last laugh.

R Stands for Guts in Kansas City

Rufus R. Jones was an imposing physical specimen. He stood six feet five inches tall and weighed 275 pounds. His impressive dimensions served him well all through his life, but especially during his twenty-two-year career as a professional wrestler.

Known for his hard head (literally) and his amazing physical strength, Rufus was a headliner for the World Wrestling Federation back in the 1970s and '80s. His extreme style of wrestling was to simply run people over. If that did not finish them off, he'd pick up one or even two opponents at the same time and body slam them into submission. Also known for his many multicolored costumes, his ferocious ring demeanor belied his easygoing personality.

Rufus was also famous for how he introduced himself. He would say, "My name is Rufus R. Jones, and the R stands for guts!" We're not sure what he meant with that statement, but it is memorable and maybe that was his only motivation. Those WWF types are astoundingly clever promoters.

Jones died on November 13, 1993, of a heart attack while on a hunting trip—no doubt a trip that was intended to bag some wild game to be included as part of his restaurant's menu. He owned a popular eatery in Kansas City, the Ringside Bar and Grill, on Twenty-third and Vine streets. His style of eating and cooking was old school, and with items like hogs' heads and spaghetti and meatballs with corn as part of the conglomeration, one had to be a little adventurous to eat at the Ringside. When it came to eating, Rufus would say, "If eating hog jowls and black-eyed peas gives you good luck, then eating steak should make you even luckier."

Rufus's luck may have ended at age sixty, but his larger-than-life legacy is forever preserved in the pages of *Weird Missouri.* Buried in Forest Hill Calvary Cemetery, he rests both as Rufus R. Jones and with his original name, Carey Lee Lloyd. His grave is in the northeast corner of Block 101A.

Legend Enough for Two Tombstones

Jesse James is the infamous outlaw about whom countless books, movies, and songs have been written. Notorious for almost two decades of bad behavior across the Midwest, this preacher's son gone wild rode freely with his gang, robbing trains, banks, stagecoaches, and anything else that might be a source of money or valuables. In the process, they dispatched to the hereafter many unfortunates who got in their way. James himself is credited with killing seventeen people.

What goes around does come around, at least sometimes. It came around for Jesse on April 3, 1882. While Jesse was attempting to straighten a wall hanging in the living room of his St. Joseph home, the Ford brothers, who were trusted James Gang members, entered the room and drew their sixguns. Bob Ford fired first and struck James in the back of the head, killing him instantly.

James has a tombstone next to his boyhood home in Kearney that carries the epitaph, MURDERED BY A TRAITOR AND COWARD WHOSE NAME IS NOT WORTHY TO APPEAR HERE. He also has a presence in Mount Olivet Cemetery in Kearney, where he and his mother, Zerelda, lie side by side. On that tombstone, it simply says that he was ASSASSINATED. When it comes to a criminal like Jesse James, perhaps "bushwhacked" would have been a better choice of words.

Will the Real Jesse James Please Stand Up?

On April 3, 1882, as the history books tell us, Jesse James's renegade lifestyle finally caught up with him. Seeking a $10,000 reward for James's capture, Robert Ford entered Jesse's home and mortally wounded him. At the age of 34, Jesse James was confirmed dead and laid to rest in Kearney, Missouri.

He was also confirmed dead at age 95 and buried in Blevins, Texas, then again at 103 and buried in Granbury, Texas.

Despite his course of theft and murder, he seems to be a pretty popular guy. It's not every man who can say three entirely different towns want his body.

According to the folks in Granbury, James was not actually killed in

1882. Instead, he faked his death and relocated to North Texas. There, he worked as a railroad contractor under the name J. W. Gates, though he was more widely known as J. Frank Dalton. Near the end of his life, Dalton revealed his true identity as Jesse James to Granbury's sheriff at the time, Oran Baker. According to Baker, Dalton spent his final days recounting for the sheriff the adventures he had shared with his brother Frank and the rest of the James Gang.

On the day of Dalton's passing, Sheriff Baker conducted an examination of the body. He observed several scars that appeared to be from bullet wounds, a mark around Dalton's neck like that left by an unsuccessful hanging, burns on his feet, and the tip missing from one of his index fingers, all of which Baker said were consistent with incidents known to have occurred in James's life. Granbury is so convinced Dalton was telling the truth, they've placed signs in their cemetery leading the way to his grave site, where his headstone bears the name Jesse Woodson James. Below that it reads, SUPPOSEDLY KILLED IN 1882.

Meanwhile, farther south in Liberty Hill, Betty Dorsett Duke has been picking a fight to have her great-grandfather, James Lafayette Courtney, recognized as the true Jesse James. According to Duke, her parents always told her as a child that Courtney was the notorious outlaw, but she never much believed it.

Recently, however, she began to notice similarities between photographs of James and those she had of Courtney and compared images of Courtney's mother with those of James's mother, she was certain they were one and the same.

Duke believes the man buried in Missouri is actually Wood Hite, a member of the James Gang and Jesse James's cousin. She argues that Jesse James and Robert Ford, the man who supposedly killed James, conspired together to murder Hite and bury him in James's place.

The people of Granbury, on the other hand, believe the substitute is Charlie Bigelow, who was also a member of the James Gang. It's been said that Bigelow looked enough like James to pass the body off as his, so James could go on to lead a much quieter life.

So how does a person know who's really sealed away in each town's casket? Well, the same way you find out which chocolate is filled with the raspberry creme—you cracks 'em open and you sees what you gets.

In 1996, folks in Missouri did just that. After digging up Kearne's Jesse James, experts performed a DNA test using samples taken from two descendants of James's sister. The results indicated that, with very little chance of error, everybody else was hopped up on goofballs.

Betty Duke, however, didn't buy it. She claimed that no DNA had actually been extracted from Kearney's disinterred body, but that the DNA used for comparison instead came from a tooth retrieved from the James Farm museum, a tooth that had never been documented to be Jesse's. Besides, since Hite is the man buried in Kearney, and since he happened to be Jesse's cousin, any DNA taken from the body would have shown a match anyway. Incidentally, much of her family is in complete disagreement with her over the whole affair, wondering why she would want to be associated with such a dreadful criminal to begin with.

Then it was Granbury's turn. Bud Hardcastle, a used-car salesman and avid Jesse James enthusiast, who probably wishes reporters would stop identifying him as a used-car salesman, volunteered to represent three of James's supposed grandsons in a search for resolution.

After years of legal wrangling, Hardcastle was finally granted an exhumation in February 2000. Unfortunately, when Hardcastle's team opened the coffin, they discovered a corpse with a missing arm, which certainly wasn't consistent with the body of J. Frank Dalton or with any known history of Jesse James. No, they had simply dug up the wrong man.

Apparently, Dalton's earlier grave markers had been stolen enough times that the exact location of his body had been slightly misplaced.

So in the end, we're right back where we started. As for James's final resting place, we have one probable, one unknown, and a maybe.—*Wesley Treat*

Boone's Bones Lie in Marthasville, or Do They?

The lyrics to the theme song of the 1960s television show *Daniel Boone* have Daniel being an extraordinarily manly man by being "the rippin'est, roarin'est, fightin'est man the frontier ever knew." Those Hollywood people sure know how to build up the reputation of a frontiersman. On television, Daniel was played by actor Fess Parker, who had also played Davy Crockett in the television show with the same name. Crockett must have been a man's man too, because that show's theme song has him killing a bear (pronounced *bar*) at the tender age of three.

Television made Crockett and Boone household names across America, with theme songs swirling through minds young and old.

Born just east of Reading, Pennsylvania, Boone moved to the Carolina territories in his teens. His savvy as a hunter and scout made him a natural to blaze trails west into regions that white men had yet to set foot upon. He was once quoted as saying, "I can't say I have ever been lost, but I was once bewildered for three days." That humble swagger instilled confidence in others about his ability to cut trails where needed. His most vital adult years were spent establishing a trail leading west, and his knowledge, skill, and daring won him the contract to create a settlers' trail through the Cumberland Gap. His defiance of the British rules not to explore the regions of Kentucky opened the door westward and established him as the ultimate frontiersman. Kentucky was his home until the beginning of the nineteenth century.

Toward the last quarter of his life, Boone decided to follow his son Nathan northward to new unexplored lands. As the dawn of the next century approached, Boone relocated his family from Kentucky to the Femme Osage Valley area of Missouri. Upon arrival, he went about building an impressive four-story Georgian-style home that remains today as a pristine museum providing a precise view of how Boone and his clan lived.

Located in Defiance, St. Charles County, the Daniel Boone home remains much as it was during his waning years. Its two-and-one-half-foot-thick stone walls, smoked glass (so the Indians could not easily see inside), and period furnishings, make touring the home feel like stepping through a window in time.

But even giants die, and it was after Boone's death in 1820 that things got weird, competitive, and outright creepy. Daniel was laid to rest next to his wife, Rebecca, on a quiet hillside near Marthasville. Or was he? As happens so many times, stories come with caveats, and Boone's is no exception. It appears that there may be a mix-up. Twenty-five years after his burial, his bones were legally extracted from the Missouri grave site and reburied in Frankfort, Kentucky. For over a century, the arguments followed from the Missouri side that the bones that were exhumed were actually those of a man who needed a grave and Boone graciously gave his burial plot away. Thus, the contention was that Kentucky had buried the bones of someone other than Boone.

Of course, Kentucky turned its nose up at such a contention. But the question about bones may have been put to rest in the 1980s when a forensic anthropologist analyzed a plaster skull made from the head of the man in the Frankfort grave. The examination concluded that the supposed skull of Boone was actually that of a black man.

Kentucky's loss was Missouri's gain. The argument over Boone's bones will no doubt continue.

A Little Man with a Really Big Shoe

The name W. H. "Major" Ray might not mean much to you, but you probably have some recognition of Ray's more famous stage name—Buster Brown.

Buster Brown began as a comic-strip character, drawn by artist R. F. Outcault, but his likeness was licensed to many companies, including the Brown Shoe Co. Buster Brown shoes were born at the 1904 World's Fair in St. Louis and easily became the most famous product associated with the name. Between 1904 and 1930, the shoe company staged thousands of live appearances featuring Buster Brown and his dog—using children and little people to play the title role.

W. H. Ray was the little person who made the first of these appearances and today he is still fondly remembered for his portrayal of Buster Brown. He lived, and is buried, in Hornersville, making him a true hero of the Show Me State.

Ray, standing only thirty-six inches tall, was famous before ever donning the Buster Brown persona. He and his thirty-seven-inch-tall wife, Jeannie, toured the United States with the Sells Brothers Circus and were famous for being the "world's smallest couple." This was how they came to the attention of the organizer of the World's Fair. Ray was a big hit at the fair, and this led to his touring the country, making appearances as the diminutive Buster Brown.

Ray's grave in Hornersville is etched with a likeness of him in his Buster Brown getup. It shows his curly locks flowing forth from beneath his hat, his ruffled tie, and his boy shorts with hiked-high socks. Next to him is his dog, Tige, wearing sunglasses. His grave is a local landmark and a source of pride for town folk, who all seem to know about the little man's grave.

William S. Burroughs

It is fair to say that William S. Burroughs has one of the largest and most rabid cult followings in the history of American writing. An early member of the Beat generation, the author of *Naked Lunch* is remembered for his outlandish behavior, run-ins for both drugs and murder, and most of all, for his writing.

Burroughs passed away in 1997 and is buried at his family's plot in the Bellefontaine Cemetery in St. Louis. Actually, two William S. Burroughses, the writer and his grandfather, are buried there. For many years, the writer had no stone marking his actual grave. Now he has a small rectangular marker above his burial site listing only his name and the phrase AMERICAN WRITER. His grandfather takes prominence, with his name being listed on a grand obelisk that stands nearby.

Many legends surround the contents of Burroughs's coffin. Alongside the remains of the writer himself are a number of items that speak to the life Burroughs led. The poet John Giorno was with Burroughs when he passed away, and helped organize the items that went with his friend to the grave. Among them, according to him, were one of the author's favorite guns, a pen to symbolize his writing, and both marijuana and heroin. On top of this, the friends of the deceased made sure he was dressed to the nines.

There are few writers who have had as much of an impact on the American literary scene as William S. Burroughs. While the man's grave stands quietly alongside the graves of his family members, what's inside that grave stands as a reminder of the life he lived.

The Old Drum Memorial

One of the most famous memorial sites in all of Missouri doesn't even belong to a human being. It belongs to Old Drum, a hound dog, and it stands as a testament to how far man sometimes goes to honor his best friend.

In 1869, Old Drum lived with his master, Charles Burden, on his farm outside Kingsville. While Burden had many hunting dogs, Old Drum was easily his favorite.

Burden's brother-in-law, Leonidas Hornsby, owned the property adjoining the Burden farm. While Hornsby had nothing against Old Drum in particular, he did seem to have a chip on his shoulder regarding the canine species in general. He was constantly fuming that local wolves and stray dogs were wreaking havoc on the animals he tended to. Hornsby had made it known that he was going to begin aggressively exterminating any strange canines he saw on his property. Simply put, he would shoot them.

Old Drum, sadly, one day wandered over the Hornsby property line. Hornsby realized that the dog might not be feral, so he had his nephew load up a shotgun with corn pellets and fire it at the dog. Instead of sparing the dog, as Hornsby intended, it simply led Old Drum to slowly suffer on the way to his demise. People in the area heard the injured dog howling through the night, before abruptly going silent.

After initial denials, Hornsby finally admitted that he had ordered the shooting of Old Drum. Burden decided that was unacceptable and took his own brother-in-law to court. A huge series of hearings erupted around the death of the dog, and every single lawyer in the trial later went on to political success—one became the governor of Missouri, and three others were later elected United States Congressmen. After four separate trials and appeals, Burden was finally validated when justice sided with him; he was awarded fifty dollars. As part of the final trial, the lawyer George G. Vest made the oft-quoted speech, "Eulogy of the Dog," which is cited as the origin for the phrase "Dog is man's best friend."

After the sensational case, Burden set out to build an appropriate memorial for his late pal Old Drum. Two actually stand today. One was erected along the creek where Old Drum's body was found. Money and material were donated from over sixty-seven countries for the building of this memorial, including stones from the Great Wall of China and the White Cliffs of Dover. While it has been vandalized, portions still stand. The more famous Old Drum Memorial is in Warrensburg. A bust of Old Drum stands atop a large stone platform, upon which A TRIBUTE TO THE DOG is engraved.

Warriors' Monument

In 1804, William Clark and Meriwether Lewis met the Nez Percé Native American tribe while making their way across the North American continent. The tribe befriended the explorers and their band, giving them food, shelter, and supplies at a time when the adventurers were starving to death.

In 1831, Clark and the Nez Percé met again. This time, four representatives of the tribe made their way to St. Louis to seek out Clark's counsel. They came looking for information on Christianity and the Bible. Before they could get a chance to learn about these Western conventions, city life took its toll on the natives. They were exposed to new diseases in St. Louis and quickly succumbed to them. Two members of the tribe, Black Eagle and Speaking Eagle, died in St. Louis. The other two, No-Horns-On-His-Head and Rabbit-Skin-Leggins, died on the journey back to their people, and their bodies were never recovered. Black Eagle and Speaking Eagle were baptized and buried in Christian cemeteries, although their bodies were moved a number of times due to health concerns regarding the cemeteries in general. Eventually, they were placed in an unmarked mass grave in St. Louis's Calvary Cemetery.

In the year 2000, representatives of the Nez Percé tribe built an eight-foot-tall monument to the memories of these four warriors. It stands in Calvary Cemetery, where the bodies of two of the four warriors are buried. The memorial is in the shape of a large feather, and its base is carved with an account of the warriors' tale and a dedication to them.

An A-Maze-In' Grave

Joe Barzantny was building mazes before he knew how to talk. He would take childhood objects and arrange them in specific patterns. As he approached school age, this tendency continued. Drawing mazes came easy to Joe, as did math. He could sit down and within an hour, have a complex, hand-drawn maze that even adults found hard to complete.

By the time he was nine years old, Joe had published his first book of mazes. Many more followed, and eventually many of Joe's mazes were compiled in the book *A-Maze-In' St. Louis!* Joe was featured on many television programs for his natural abilities and became a local celebrity.

Unfortunately, Joe's life took a tragic turn as he grew older. He had been diagnosed with attention deficit disorder as a child, and by his late teens his conditions had morphed into bipolar disorder and schizophrenia. In 1992, at the young age of twenty-one, Joe Barzantny took his own life.

Joe's grave is in St. Louis's famous Bellefontaine Cemetery. Etched upon its surface is a complex, mind-boggling maze drawn by Joe himself. HE FOUND HIS WAY OUT OF THE MAZE, the inscription below the image reads, AND NOW HE'S HOME IN A MAZE ING GRACE. The back of the stone is inscribed with the simple words JOE— THE WIZARD OF MAZE.

The Clayton Times

May 13-19
1981
Number 63

F

Als
issue:

T
TC L
TO

of
librar
an

F
A ha
acc
tipsy
b

Trailblazing Maze Maker

Abandoned in Missouri

Abandonment is a concept that invites and promotes melancholy. Human abandonment is of course an unforgivable event, but *Weird Missouri* avoids the unforgivable and instead focuses on the unavoidable, produced by the passage of time. Time marches on, and we all struggle to adjust to the changes witnessed in the forward motion—what we like to call progress. Progress almost always produces abandonment. Obsolescence, wear and tear, newer, zoomier, faster, shinier—all create fodder for the pages of this chapter. Had it not been for the ravages of time and the very real need to sustain a safe and efficient infrastructure, abandoned tunnels (Missouri has a bunch) could not be a topic in this book. Nor could old missile silos (actually, we don't miss the missile silos), or airports from yesteryear (we DO miss the old airports). Abandonment is a function of time and man's need to improve on his circumstance.

This chapter is like a series of windows into Missouri's past that should help the reader appreciate the efforts and styles of those days. There are stories of once grand spas, crumbling mining operations, pathways to the nether regions, and much, much more. And as you read, remember that in some unknown future time, THESE will be the good old days, and what is new today will be abandoned.

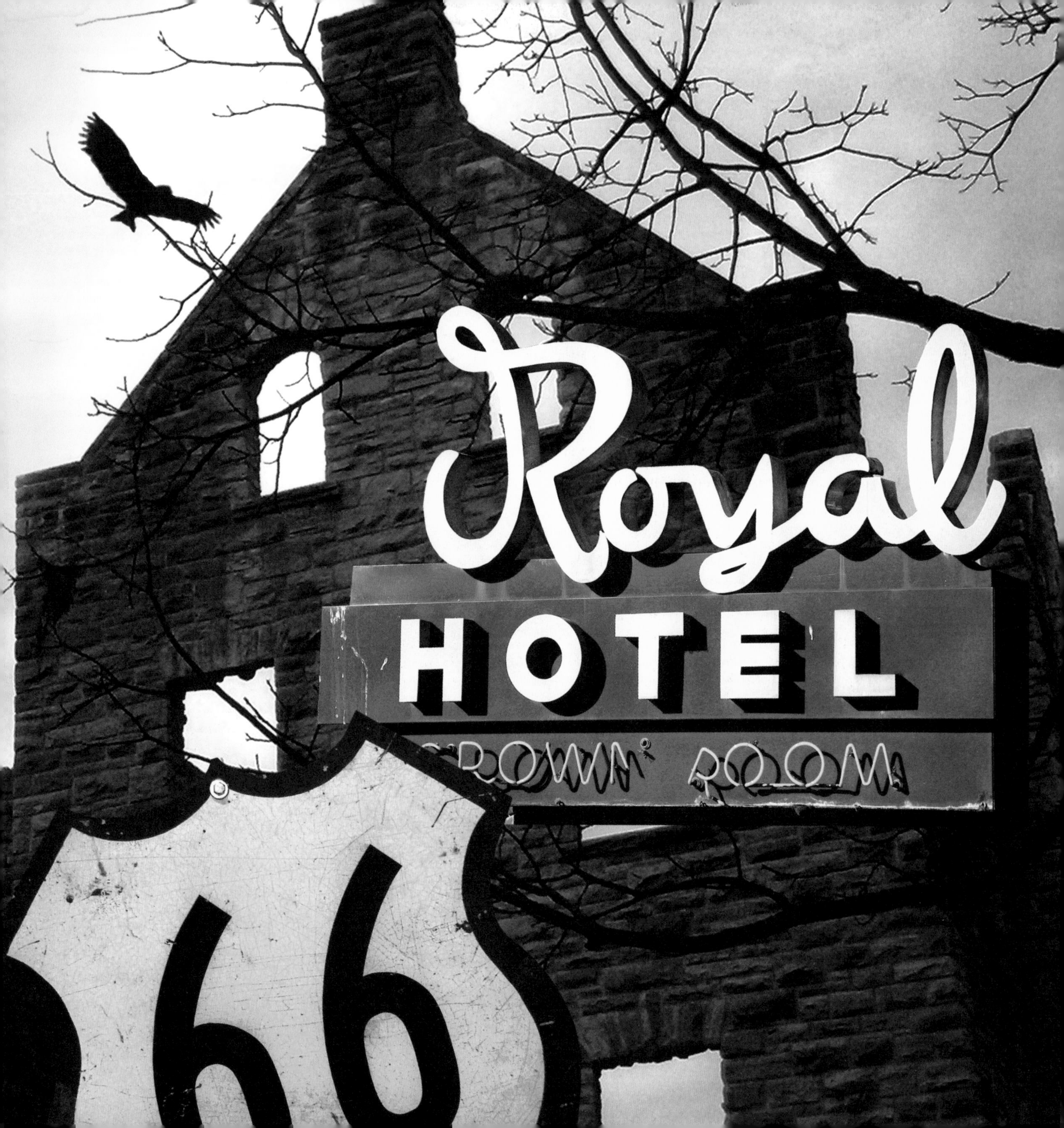
Royal
HOTEL
CROWN ROOM
66

Valles Mines Railroad Tunnel

When the St. Joseph Mining Company needed to create a railroad infrastructure to serve the Valles Mines in Jefferson County, thousands of former slaves answered the call for workers. They completed the arduous task of laying railroad track and tunnels through the rugged countryside surrounding the mines, enabling efficient transport of the lead ore pulled from the more than one hundred mines then in operation.

Now abandoned, with the railroad tracks long ago removed, the Valles Mines tunnel remains a vivid reminder of yesterday's greatness obtained through raw determination, creativity, and the use of a desperate workforce. The tunnel is an impressive example of mid-nineteenth-century civil engineering and reflects the efforts of the workers who made it possible.

We have read various accounts of a ghost in the tunnel called Tunnel Bill, and we spoke at length about him with Steve Frazier, the curator of Valles Mines Lost History Museum. The one constant in the accounts of Tunnel Bill is that he was an employee of the St. Joseph Mining Company who was allowed to hang around the old train tunnel beyond its decommission date. Later, by some unknown means, Bill died at the tunnel, and he is reportedly now very protective of it. Some say he chases away unwanted trespassers, but others say he welcomes respectful explorers and bears them no ill will. Still others deny his existence.

You can find out for yourself by making arrangements with the Lost History Museum to visit the tunnel. There is a minimal fee for accessing the property, and a four-wheel-drive vehicle is highly recommended. Getting to the tunnel involves driving along the aptly named Mud Road.

Satan's Tunnel

Hawk Point is about an hour west of St. Louis, just north of Warrenton. It is home to what sounds as if it's the portal to hell: Satan's Tunnel. It may or may not be the gateway to and from the Dark One's home-stead, but some devilish people have visited the place. Satan's Tunnel is an abandoned underpass that has obviously been the location for countless parties and trysts. It is one of those isolated venues with flat concrete surfaces that scream out, "Graffiti me!"

The train tracks that once ran across the top of the underpass have long been removed, but their stories remain. At some time in the past, a man was struck by a passing train and thrown fifty feet down to the pavement below. Legend has it that his ghost can be seen walking through the dark abyss.

Another story involves a hanging that took place in the underpass. It's said that, at dusk, the phantom of the hanged person can be seen dangling from trees at various locations near the tunnel. Then there's the tale of a hobo who had taken residence in the cavelike structure, only to be found deceased, with an expression of fear frozen on his face. And there are stories of rag-headed, dancing Satan worshipers. (Are there any other kind?)

The road leading up to Satan's Tunnel is public, but the pavement leading to the tunnel and the tunnel itself are located on private property, so visits would be ill advised from a legal standpoint. But perhaps it's through the temptation to trespass that the tunnel got its name. Maybe it's a variation on comedian-actor Flip Wilson's tag line, "The devil made me do it."

The Twin Towers of Belton

Not much is known about the twin towers adjacent to the old Richards-Gebaur Air Force Base. There are tales of devil dogs howling at the moon, odd odors (which seem to be standard with devil dogs), cloaked shapes, and flames from ritual fires. And there are stories of cold spots from those who have found the intestinal fortitude to venture inside the towers.

Brian Lile of the Missouri Ghost Hunters Society confirms that physical evidence of ritual activity has been found within the confines of the twin towers. He also believes that paranormal energies exist there.

The most puzzling aspect of the towers is trying to understand why they are called towers in the first place; they are squat old silos that have a height-to-width ratio that makes it more appropriate to call them drums. Yes, they're sizable drums, but to place them in the tower category seems very generous, though maybe calling them that sounds spookier. You can check them out yourself by taking the MO 150 West exit off Route 71, then turning southwest on Andrews and left on Kensington Avenue. They are in a field off to the left.

Ruins of Ha Ha Tonka

Ha Ha Tonka is an Osage Indian phrase that translates to "laughing spirit," but if we were told that it meant "improbable home way up high," we would believe it. That's because Ha Ha Tonka Castle sits atop a tall bluff in Ha Ha Tonka State Park, about five miles southwest of Camdenton. Businessman Robert McClure Snyder had it built as an escape from the hustle and bustle of early twentieth-century life in Kansas City. And it's an escape for sure: Its isolation ensures that not many people would have the energy to seek it out.

From the bluff, the castle looks down on Ha Ha Tonka Spring and Lake of the Ozarks. It's an idyllic setting, but one that surely provided many challenges to those who constructed the building—one of which was transporting stone a few thousand feet from where it was quarried to the castle. This was accomplished by creating a rail system for a train of mule-drawn carts. Many trips were made to carry the stone for the eighty-foot-tall water tower, the carriage house, and the castle itself. A team of expert stonemasons from Scotland labored to finalize the vision of architect Adrian Van Brunt.

Tragedy brought construction to a halt. Snyder owned one of the early gas-powered automobiles and was one of the state's first victims of a fatal automobile accident. His death greatly slowed the work on the estate. Construction resumed under the direction of his sons, but it took another sixteen years before a fully enclosed building was complete. Even then, the castle fell well short of its elaborate original plans.

After the death of Robert Snyder Jr. in 1937, the castle was leased out as a hotel for a few years, until it caught fire. The wooden part of the structure was totaled, and the entire estate sat in decay for almost four decades.

In 1978, the Missouri State Parks Department acquired over three thousand of the original five thousand acres owned by the Snyder family. The castle, the derelict carriage house, and remains of the water tower (it was torched in 1976) stand as historical ruins that paint a vivid picture of an opulent past.

In addition to the Ha Ha Tonka Castle, the park also has sixteen miles of nature trails and eight caves, two of which may be toured on a seasonal basis. There are also scenic outlooks that are worth every torturous moment of bucking the traffic to travel to the Lake of the Ozarks area. After all, it was Robert McClure Snyder's intent to create a haven away from the commotion of city life.

The Tragedy of Times Beach

This story hits close to home for this *Weird Missouri* author. When I was a young child living on the Meramec River, the county road that serviced our modest property was cut with the blade of a grader. The grader would travel in one direction, turn 180 degrees, and return to cut in the other direction. The end result was a primitive dirt road with pronounced ditches on both sides and a central crown that could have been used as a skateboard ramp. (I had to wait ten years for the first skateboard to come along.)

It also meant lots of dust. Cars would blast down the road, leaving a rooster tail of dust that would filter into every nook and cranny of the houses along the way. The county's solution to this problem was oil. Oil sprayed from the back of a small tanker truck would hold the dust in check for a few weeks. The oil was applied to the road several times a year. I can remember the smell of oil mixed with river bottom soil baking in the hot August sun as if it were yesterday.

The town of Times Beach received the same treatment for its roads. However, during the early 1970s the oil used there was laced with dioxin, a poison that I can only hope was not contained in the oils of the early 1950s.

Times Beach was a residential community doomed from its earliest beginnings to experience troubles. It was a silt city built on a floodplain adjacent to the turbulent Meramec River. Because of frequent flooding, dirt roads were the rule until the early 1980s, when they were paved. But by then, the damage had been done. Topping the contaminated dirt roads with pavement merely captured a poison that caused cancers, miscarriages, and birth defects.

Dioxin was later labeled as the most toxic substance synthesized by humankind. Thus, the EPA condemned Times Beach; its population was forced to relocate, and all of its structures were taken down as part of the detox process. The site of this sad Missouri story is now Route 66 State Park. Must be a fun place to picnic.

A Visit to Toxic Times Beach

About ten years ago, when my husband and I lived in Missouri, we took my parents to see Times Beach. If you don't remember the name, it is the town that the U.S. government bought from its citizens after dioxin was mistakenly spread on the dirt roads of the town to keep the dust down. It is no longer on any maps.

We took I-44 south out of St. Louis to Exit 266, Lewis Road. We went north on Lewis Road until we came to some big warning signs and a guard tower. We acted like lost tourists when we saw the guard tower had guards inside. There were a few buildings left inside the high fence, which were visible from I-44, but the government was in the process of leveling them.

To this day, my parents still make comments about Times Beach being one of the most unusual sites we took them to see.—*Martha J. Mahlburg*

Excelsior Springs: The Town That Time Forgot

While visiting Kansas City, I saw that *USA Today* had published an article entitled "Ten Great Places to Take a Dip in Healing Waters." One of the places mentioned was Excelsior Springs, about 28 miles northeast of Kansas City. Having grown up near Saratoga Springs, New York, I thought that I'd like to see the Missouri mineral waters and partake in the pleasures that attracted Harry Truman and FDR to the area.

I rented a car and asked the clerk at the car rental desk whether there was anything interesting in Excelsior Springs besides the mineral springs. He laughed a little and said, rather definitively, "The unemployment line. But, hey, don't drive too fast on Route 69; you might miss the cutoff for the town. The James boys did and look what happened to them!"

So past the Wal-Mart, the Sinclair Dinosaur (that's right, they still sell gas with the Sinclair logo in Missouri), and well beyond the "Kum & Go" gas station/rest stop and the Barbee Memorial Presbyterian Church, there's a sign that says EXCELSIOR SPRINGS, THE HALL OF WATERS. I followed the arrow pointing to a cutoff exit road that, in helix formation, spiraled my car into the main road to town. I followed all the signs to the Hall of Waters, and wound up between two abandoned behemoths of red-brick buildings with broken windows and doors perched precipitously on upper floors leading outside to what once were fire escapes. Windows not already broken sported various obscenities. One building had a sign on it that said ROYAL HOTEL CROWN ROOM and the sign on the other read MINERAL WATER BATHS AT THE HOTEL OAKS.

The next road sign for the Hall of Waters pointed down a little alley on South Street, which was closed and the street was dug up, so I continued straight on to the next turnoff, which looked like a main street. After turning right, I noticed a sign for the Chamber of Commerce.

There were plenty of parking spots, as the street was somewhat abandoned, unusual for a Saturday afternoon. My rental car was, by far, the newest vehicle on the street as most cars were from the 1970s. Someone sped by in an old '71 Skylark, a model I had once owned, in the same condition I owned it—with rusted-through holes and dents.

A group of older teenagers congregated

nearby. The most distinguishing feature on these kids was that they all wore flak jackets made from camouflage material, right from a Vietnam-era Army-Navy store. And there was an old man walking by, having a decent conversation with himself about "his dawg." Only, he didn't have a dog with him, nor did he look like he lost one, either.

As I opened the door to the Chamber, I could smell must and mildew permeating the air. Two women greeted me, happy to see someone who didn't look like a local (I was wearing my *Weird N.J.* sweatshirt). The whole Chamber was a museum to the bygone era of Excelsior Springs, beginning with the

late 1800s, when a local stumbled across the healing iron manganese springs, right up to the 1970s, when the town and its source of income were virtually abandoned by tourism.

Glass-enclosed exhibits lined the walls, including an exhibit of the first bottling plant for the waters. Samples of bottles used for Soterian Ginger Ale were lined up against the wall. This beverage, made from local waters, won first place at the World's Columbia Exposition in Chicago in 1893. However, the formula, produced by the Soterian brothers, went to the grave with their deaths, and the once-popular drink was never produced again. A subsequent Pepsi plant, using local waters, came and went. The ladies told me, in unison, that everyone swore by the iron manganese waters that went into their local Pepsi, and no other Pepsi tasted like it.

There were pictures of movie stars who had vacationed in town (Brenda Joyce, from the silent screen, was born in Excelsior Springs), and of course, Harry Truman, who learned of his presidential victory while staying at The Elms Hotel, on the other side of town. The James Boys—Frank and Jesse—knocked off the Clay County Bank many times before losing their lives in a shootout "up the road a piece." Working artifacts from the early 20th century were displayed, including a Helene Curtis curling machine, which, I was told, still worked. Wires attached each curler to what looked like a mini-electric transformer, like you see near railroad tracks.

I asked about the abandoned hotels. The ladies showed me old postcards of these once beautiful treasures, with rooftop dancing and gardens, marble interiors and no lack of patrons on any night of the year. They were abandoned in the late '60s or early '70s (neither lady could remember the exact date).

Excelsior Springs started going downhill in 1961 or thereabouts, when the FDA decreed there was no proof the waters had any medicinal value. People slowly stopped coming and most of the water sources were capped. Both of the now-abandoned hotel interiors were filled with asbestos, and, after the town foreclosed on them because of unpaid taxes, there was no money to tear them down safely. So there they stand—along with a lot of other abandoned buildings. The town has been trying to reinvent itself, but arsonists claimed many of the buildings and the local

river, a tributary from the Missouri River, has flooded frequently. The V.A. Hospital, once bustling with doctors, nurses and patients, was converted into a Job Corps office 30 years ago.

I bought a guidebook from the 1930s (reprinted in 1980 on the same paper stock) that glorified the heydays of Excelsior Springs. Then the ladies told me to go up the block to City Hall. "What's in City Hall?" I asked.

"That's the Hall of Waters. Oh, yes, and the local Spa."

Following their lead, I went around the corner and found the Hall of Waters, also the municipal court and a host of other city offices. The art deco lobby led to an art deco bar, where two women served water from Excelsior Springs and elsewhere around the globe. The bar sign read SODA IRON MANGANESE AND CALCIUM WATERS . . . HOT AND COLD SALINE MINERAL WATERS. These ladies poured samples of all these waters, and sold bottled waters, from Russia, France and Missouri.

I asked about the spa and one woman said, "Let me take you there." She led me through a steamy hall and past the town records department. "Here's our bubble tub," she said as she proudly pointed to an old, cast iron tub filled with bubbling waters made

from some mechanism which resembled what a Foley artist would use in special effects for a movie set. There was a shelf next to the old tub on which a variety of yellow rubber duckies sat. The lady said, "You can pick your own ducky to have in the water."

The next booth was the steam bath. There were two types: one where you could sit down, with two

doors that closed in front of you, and the other, which looked more like an iron lung than a steam bath.

The next area was the massage parlor, where you could also have your toes manicured and your rear washed in a 1930s-style sitz bath. The shower was something from scary movies, with spouts washing all sides and pores.

I was handed a price list. In this bizarro world, the town hall hawked beauty treatments instead of having the local cops give speeding tickets—a unique way to build municipal coffers.

The lady then took me to a lower level, where there was an old huge abandoned swimming pool. She pointed to the ceiling. "See there? That's where the river came in during the flood of 1993. The pool's been closed since. We have no money to restore."

Seeing that I was totally amazed that such a place could be abandoned, she took me to the bowels of the Hall of Waters, past filing cabinets of municipal records. "Here's where we built a special private pool for FDR. He gave us the money in the 1930s and 1940s to build the Hall of Waters, and we built this for him." There, abandoned for many years, behind musty closed doors, was an exact miniature replica of the big pool, filled with years of dust.

On my way out of town, I stopped at the only living, breathing, operating hotel: the Elms Hotel. I asked the lady behind the desk about the abandoned hotels just up the road and she said, "Oh, those burned down five times each." Back in my car, I traveled past more people muttering to themselves and groups of kids in oversized Army jackets.

On the way out of town, I began muttering to myself too. "I've got to come back here. Excelsior Springs, Missouri, is absolutely WEIRD."

—Adriana Delia Collins

Excelsior Springs Has Its Say

Adriana Collins posted the previous article on the Web, and it seems to have tapped a deep well of offended civic pride in Excelsior Springs. There are many loyal supporters in the town, as the following comments show. It all goes to show that beauty—along with the appeal of old towns—is in the eye of the beholder.

Don't Put Our Town Down!

I just recently read your story about Excelsior Springs and found it to be rather insulting! Our town may be little, and we may have some weirdos in our downtown area, but if you are going to write a story about Excelsior, make sure you don't just write the bad things.

I can let you know the kids that you saw dressed in army wear and camouflage are not typical. Why would you write an article on a small town, that you visited once, and criticize our people and buildings? The article was rather interesting, but you've seriously put down MY TOWN. I am only 20 years old and for me to think you put it down is bad. I just wanted to let you know, that our town is like any other town!—*Jnb6884*

Excelsior Springs Is Springing Back to Life

I just read Adriana Delia Collins' article about the town that I grew up in, Excelsior Springs, MO. It was really interesting to read such an in-depth visit of the places that I was so familiar with as a kid.

I felt bad that as she went to visit, the town was abandoned so much. I do not know when her visit was, but the town has begun to grow again. There are shops now downtown where the chamber used to be. The roads have been fixed and there are more tourists now than there were several years back.

I would love to tell her more about the city that I ran the streets of everyday if she wanted to hear. Sounds like she ran across some patients from the hospital while she was there and I don't know if they gave a very good representation of the people living there. I want her to know that the city is still full of life and people who care about restoring its history.

There is also an in-depth look at the history of the town on the website. Its address is www.exspgschamber.com.

Thank you for your time and thank you for visiting Excelsior. I am now 22 and living in Kansas and I miss it there so much. It was nice to read your article and I hope that you will come back for a nicer visit with more to do. Maybe I could be your tour guide.—*Courtney Cole*

Blame It on the Job Corps Kids . . . and the Big Man

I have lived in Excelsior Springs for my entire life. I am 42. When I was a child in the mid to late '70s I thought I lived in the best little town around. In the late '70s, we were voted the All American City. The old Oaks Hotel was functional and very nostalgic. The Royal Hotel was somewhat outdated but had a little bit of a 1920s feel. The Oaks did catch on fire and was closed. The Royal was converted into an apartment complex for older folks and was eventually closed due to fire. Across the street from the Royal was the Marietta drug store. My grandmother would go in there to get sundries and prescriptions filled while I got a soda or sundae from the fountain bar. My uncle worked at that Hall of Waters from the time he was 17. He is handicapped and has a hard time seeing but he worked the maintenance and bottled water for around 35 years or more. I can remember the Pepsi plant and they had the best Strawberry pop EVER! My uncle recently told me that it was made with real strawberry flavoring and the mineral water. It is such a shame that Pepsi stopped making it; it was like having dessert in a bottle. Downtown was booming. We had a JC Penney's store, a Ben Franklin and a Mattingly's five and dime. There were little soda shops and burger stands. No one locked their doors at night and no one took their keys out of their car when they went into the store.

When the city sold the old VA Hospital to the Job Corps, that is when everything went down hill. The 7-11 downtown had to move out because they were being robbed blind. The gas stations and small grocers also had to go out for the same reason. Both theaters closed too. You could no longer leave your windows down on your car, someone might spit through the window or take your car. We all used to walk down to the

Elms to meet our parents after the football game, but the Elms decided we could no longer gather there due to the same reason. This is a farming community where everyone pretty much knows everyone else. All of my friends and I would hang out in the old hitch lot (named for where they used to hitch up horses in town) or a field party with a bonfire. The police decided that we could no longer gather there anymore, so slowly but surely, no one went downtown anymore. When Wal-Mart came to town, it pretty much ran all of the mom and pop stores out of town. They couldn't compete.

FYI, the street that was torn up had a ribbon cutting ceremony and they have added trees and old fashioned street lamps. We still have no budget to fix the pool, and most of us don't want to.

I am proud to say that I live in Excelsior. It was a good place to grow up and a good place to raise my children. It isn't the big booming municipality that it was when the water was good, but I look forward to growing old here with the rest of my family and friends.—*Edie Bisby*

P.S. Yes, I too have sampled the water as my Uncle Rick was the custodian, bottler and the building Superintendent. The calcium water is awesome. I have used the Sulfa water when I have been sick and I have tried the Manganese but didn't like it. I don't know anyone that it has made sick or crazy. Lastly, the kids you saw roaming around in the weird clothes . . . undoubtedly Job Corps kids. Give us a break . . . this isn't the big city and the big man has put most of the home owned businesses out of town. Take a look at any little town in middle America and you will see something very similar.

Hall of Waters Runs Dry

We stay at the Elms in Excelsior Springs a few days each year. In 2005, the Hall of Waters water bar was open, and also, the spa in the same building. Today, we went, 7-16-07 and sad to report the water bar with the ladies who work there and know the history is closed! The spa is there and the bathtubs, but also closed! Too bad they could not get that pool fixed; the old postcards I bought last time I was [there] made it look great, and it had mineral waters they said! I wonder what happened so the Hall of Waters and Spa had to close?—*Mari Green*

Urban Springnewal

You need to come back to Excelsior Springs. I stumbled across your article when browsing the web, and I just thought I'd let you know that the town has begun growing and our downtown area is being improved. The Royal Hotel is being renovated, changing it from a once abandoned building to apartments for older and retired folks. Many people have begun buying up the downtown buildings and turning them back into offices and such. We also have had new restaurants come into the area. If you come back, you should stop and eat lunch downtown at Ray's Lunch Box. It's no first class meal, but it's a friendly atmosphere and the guy who owns the shop has tons of information about Excelsior. I mean, he grew up here for goodness' sakes! And just to give you a heads up, the old man is still wandering around talking about his dog.—*A Proud Excelsior Springs Townie*

Weldon Spring: Spa of Destruction?

Weldon Spring sounds like it should be a scenic mountain resort, with a babbling brook and quaint cabins where vacationers can enjoy weekend retreats away from the chaos of city life. However, the background of this historic government facility is anything but pastoral, and its story encompasses all varieties of events: good, bad, and finally back to good (kind of).

With the United States becoming involved in World War II, the Department of the Army acquired over 17,000 acres of land in St. Charles County and created Weldon Spring, an ordnance works that operated from 1942 to January 1944. Located a mile south of the Route 94 exit of Route 40, Weldon Spring produced dynamite: technically, trinitrotoluene (TNT), and dinitrotoluene (DNT). During the plant's operational peak, it produced one million pounds of explosives per day.

This was the first good news, as explosives played an important part in America's victory enemies in World War II. The bad news came after the war. The plant sat dormant until 1956, when 217 acres were transferred to the U.S. Atomic Energy Commission. From 1957 to 1966, the plant processed uranium ore and a small amount of radioactive thorium (if there really is such a thing as a small amount of thorium). This would eventually create 160,000 cubic yards of radioactive waste.

In 1984, the army repaired many of the buildings; decontaminated floors, walls, and ceilings; and attempted to reduce the contamination that could leave the confines of the site. A year later the Department of Energy took control of the area, and in October 1985 the Environmental Protection Agency placed Weldon Spring on its "Priorities" list. Then what was essentially a small city was disassembled, decontaminated, and buried in a very large pit.

But not just any pit: The Weldon Spring pit is high-tech, lined with acres of an engineered plastic about fifty mils thick. Almost 1.5 million cubic yards of waste was placed into it and covered by countless tons of dirt, followed by large stones. The end result is a mound of rock that rises over sixty feet above ground level and covers an area of

forty-five acres. It is genuinely striking in its appearance and a contradiction in that its beauty masks a radioactive lethality. The final bit of good news: This $1 billion containment will retain its integrity for one thousand years. Or so they claim.

Weldon Spring's history is proudly displayed in a handsome museum situated at the entrance to the facility, right in front of the containment mound. Bring your cameras and binoculars, because you can actually walk from the museum to the mound, and then climb an impressive stairway to the top of the containment to see a panoramic view of much of St. Charles and St. Louis counties. On a good day, you can even see the top portion of the Arch on the St. Louis waterfront.

Getting Grouchy at Oscar One

Knob Noster, in Pettis County, is home to Whiteman Air Force Base, which in turn is home to the 509th Bomb Wing. It's famous as the operational base for the bat-winged B-2 Spirit bomber, the one "invisible" to radar.

The era of nuclear standoff spanning from the mid-1940s through the early 1990s, also known as the cold war, promoted prolific development of

ballistic delivery systems. At one time, Whiteman Air Force Base was home to the 351st Strategic Missile Wing. Oscar One was the Launch Control Facility (LCF) for 10 of the 150 Minutemen II nuclear-tipped intercontinental ballistic missiles (ICBMs) of the 351st Missile Wing. The 351st comprised fifteen launch sectors, with ten ICBMs per sector, and one Oscar One–style LCF per sector.

We had the privilege of a solo tour given by Tech Sergeant Shannon Banks. Banks, who is also a weapons loader on the B-2 Spirit, explained how the launch control facilities were completely autonomous entities capable of withstanding a direct hit from a twenty-five-kiloton nuclear warhead.

Oscar One gets its name from the Muppets character Oscar the Grouch. As the only LCF that existed on the property of an AFB, it was the venue for VIP tours. These tours frequently disrupted the routine of the underground missileers, and it made them grouchy.

Each LCF is a cylindrical steel-walled vessel mounted on massive shock absorbers. Forty-five feet beneath ground level, it was a self-contained living environment with a 750-gallon freshwater supply and an air filtration system, all backed up with power from an independent diesel generator. Surrounded by over 150 tons of highly reinforced concrete, with access available only through massive bank-vault–style doors, an LCF was the most secure such facility in the world.

In July 1991, the U.S.S.R. signed the Strategic Arms Reduction Treaty (START) just five months prior to the Soviet Union's demise. START brought a finish to the 351st Missile Wing.

All of the wing's 150 missile silos were emptied of their ICBMs, made available for ground and satellite inspection, and finally imploded to fill each structure with its own debris. Oscar One is the sole surviving element of the elaborate system that was part of the line drawn in the cold war sand. We feel safer already.

It may seem that what we are revealing here is classified information. In reality, Oscar One is completely open to the public. But if you want to tour it, get in line, because the wait can be months.

Airport Graveyards

For the last thirty years, there has been a disturbing national trend in which general aviation airports fail economically, are taken by eminent domain, or are sold for profit to land developers. The result is that a compelling representation of American forward thinking, sense of adventure, and outright tenacity is rapidly dying off. Small rural airports are the homes to one of the greatest forms of freedom: flight. And while America is not solely responsible for mankind's conquering the skies, our history is rich with examples of brave people who made significant contributions to the collective better understanding and development of amazing flying machines.

Missouri has an impressive aviation résumé, and St. Louis has been home to many aviation firsts. Balloons and blimps drew tens of thousands of curious onlookers to aerodromes and aviation competitions; United States Airmail opened its second contract route in Missouri, flying the mail from St. Louis to Chicago. Soon after airmail service began, the International Air Races were held in St. Louis. The Pulitzer Prize Race was an attempt to cement the area's value as an aviation mainland in the minds of local businessmen. The event drew throngs of onlookers and was very much a success.

As aviation gained both commercial and private popularity, airports sprang up all across Missouri. Many rural properties were home to small airplanes that gave their owners the freedom that only aviation can provide.

But as time passed and generations died out, things changed. Many privately owned airports disappeared as their owners died off and the heirs were more interested in selling the land to developers. Many privately owned but public-use airports have suffered the same fate. Other public-use airports deemed "deficient" have been consolidated into a modern landscape of tarmac and concrete.

Missouri still has approximately five hundred aviation facilities of all categories, including privately owned, public use, and larger jetports that support commercial and business aircraft. But even with Missouri's active aeronautical present, nothing looks more forlorn than a decommissioned airport awaiting the fate of becoming another shopping mall or subdivision.

INDEX Page numbers in **bold** refer to photos and illustrations.

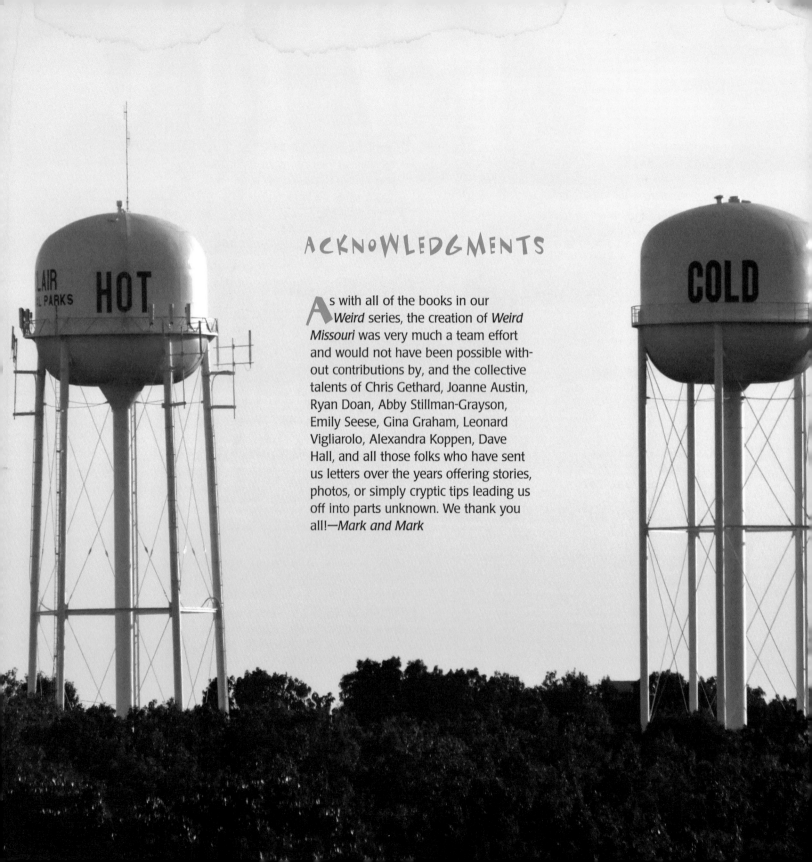

ACKNOWLEDGMENTS

As with all of the books in our *Weird* series, the creation of *Weird Missouri* was very much a team effort and would not have been possible without contributions by, and the collective talents of Chris Gethard, Joanne Austin, Ryan Doan, Abby Stillman-Grayson, Emily Seese, Gina Graham, Leonard Vigliarolo, Alexandra Koppen, Dave Hall, and all those folks who have sent us letters over the years offering stories, photos, or simply cryptic tips leading us off into parts unknown. We thank you all!—*Mark and Mark*

PICTURE CREDITS

All photos by the author or public domain except as indicated below.

SHOW US YOUR WEIRD!

Do you know of a weird site found somewhere in the United States, or can you tell us about a strange experience you had? If so, we'd like to hear about it! We believe that every town has at least one great tale to tell, and we're listening. It could be a cursed road, haunted abandoned site, odd local character, or bizarre historic event. In most cases these tales are told only in the towns in which in they originated. But why keep them to yourself when you could share them with all of America? So come on and fill us in on all the weirdness that's lurking in your backyard!

You can email us at: Editor@WeirdUS.com,
or write us at:
Weird U.S., P.O. Box 1346, Bloomfield, NJ 07003.

www.weirdus.com